S0-DLN-372

THE BLUE GUITAR

THE BLUE GUITAR

Political Representation and Community

Nancy L. Schwartz

The University of Chicago Press
Chicago and London

NANCY L. SCHWARTZ is associate professor of government at Wesleyan University.

The University of Chicago Press, Chicago 60637
The University of Chicago Press, Ltd., London

© 1988 by The University of Chicago
All rights reserved. Published 1988
Printed in the United States of America
97 96 95 94 93 92 91 90 89 88   5 4 3 2 1

Portions of Chapter 4 are drawn from Nancy L. Schwartz, "Communitarian Citizenship: Marx & Weber on the City," *Polity* 17, no. 3 (Spring 1985): 530–48. Reprinted with permission.

Library of Congress Cataloging-in-Publication Data

Schwartz, Nancy Lou.
   The blue guitar : political representation and community / Nancy L. Schwartz.
     p.   cm.
   Includes index.
   ISBN 0-226-74237-7
   1. Representative government and representation.
2. Representative government and representation—United States.
3. Political participation. 4. Political participation—United States. 5. Community. I. Title.
JF1051.S37   1988
321.8—dc19   87-34043
                                                 CIP

To the memory of
my father Bernard Mordecai
and grandmother Fannie

The Man with the Blue Guitar
Wallace Stevens
(1937)

I

The man bent over his guitar,
A shearsman of sorts. The day was green.

They said, "You have a blue guitar,
You do not play things as they are."

The man replied, "Things as they are
Are changed upon the blue guitar."

And they said then, "But play, you must,
A tune beyond us, yet ourselves,

A tune upon the blue guitar
Of things exactly as they are."

II

I cannot bring a world quite round,
Although I patch it as I can.

From Wallace Stevens, "The Man with the Blue Guitar," in *The Collected Poems of Wallace Stevens* (New York: Alfred A. Knopf, 1954). Reprinted with permission.

Contents

	Acknowledgments	xi
1	Introduction	1
2	The Transmission Belt Theory of Representation	23
3	Transmission Belt Theory in Practice	39
4	Sources of a Communitarian Theory of Citizenship	57
5	The Neglect of Representation in Classical Communitarian Theory	73
6	Towards a Theory of Political Constituency	89
7	Sources of a Communitarian Theory of Representation	105
8	Constitutive Representation	123
	Notes	147
	Index	177

Acknowledgments

My greatest thanks go to J. Donald Moon for his theoretical acumen and encouragement. At Wesleyan I also thank David Titus for his reading of the manuscript, Russell Murphy for suggestions on the American scene, Richard Boyd for comments on a chapter, Jane Tozer for typing and word processing, and Robert Wood for strategic and logistical support. I have been fortunate in having exceptional teachers. Foremost is Wilson Carey McWilliams whose knowledge of political theory is a rare gift. At Oberlin I also learned about American, comparative, and international politics from Thomas Flinn, John D. Lewis, and George A. Lanyi. Later Sheldon S. Wolin and Robert A. Dahl were of gracious help to one influenced by their writings. Far-flung friends and colleagues not mentioned above who aided this project include Ellen Comisso, Henry Plotkin, David Mayhew, Isaac Kramnick, Robert Pepperman Taylor, Dennis Hale, Timothy Paterson, Ellen Winner, Janet Saleh Dickson, Rey Koslowski, Gerald Pomper, Joshua Miller, J. Peter Euben, Sanford Thatcher, and Ron Fortgang. A fellowship grant from the National Endowment for the Humanities and Wesleyan University's generous sabbatical and leave policy made the research and writing possible. Errors in assumptions and argumentation here remain mine. I thank Jane and Jay Gould for their support over the years, and Joanne and Henry Wolf who inspired the imagery. I am indebted to Sidney J. Blatt, M. Catharine Newbury, and Nancy and Carey McWilliams. And I thank Joseph Carens for being my floor manager during this time.

ONE

Introduction

A Problem in the Political Theory of Representation:
The Question of Internal Boundaries

Political representation is an activity and an institution which connects the people, however defined, to the government. Representation "makes present that which is not literally present";[1] in political life, it makes the people present in the actions of the governing power of the state. Legislative representation is a medieval and modern notion; while there were some political practices that approximated its meaning, we do not find the concept among the ancients.[2]

Among the early Americans, there was "the widespread belief that the concept of representation was the only great discovery in theoretical politics made since antiquity."[3] John Adams, for example, considered it one of the "three discoveries in the constitution of free government since the time of Lycurgus: 'representation, instead of collections of people.'"[4] The politically active colonists made it key; their grievances against Britain continually converged on the power and legitimacy of this institution. It figured prominently in their crafting of the new government, first in the Articles of Confederation and then in the Federal Constitution. "No political conception was more important to Americans in the entire Revolutionary era than representation."[5]

In what sense is political representation a modern concept; why did the ancient Greeks lack the idea? The reasons are both quantitative and qualitative, and the qualitative differences are not mere reflections of changes in scale and technology. For a start, it is true that the number of citizens in the ancient Greek polities was small, so that in theory all the citizens could be present directly in politics, not through simultaneous attendance at the assembly but through continual involvement in governing.[6] These societies were also small in territory and relatively simple in their divisions of labor, at least compared to our times. Yet they had ample class, status, and family divisions which were in some respects more refined than in modern society, so that we cannot say that even within the citizen body there was homogeneity of social interest.[7] The qualitative differences are, first, that an individual citizen was not seen as an autonomous person apart from his political role; second, that citizens were seen as entitled to deliberate for a large body of noncitizens without their consent. The relations believed to comprise human freedom, participation in "ruling and being ruled," occurred within politics and within the citizen class; the citizens exercised domination or mastery over those beneath them.[8] What held this arrangement more or less together was the culture's shared belief in a pagan religion that sanctified customs of mastery in the social sphere as natural, and an emergent discovery of patterns in human conventions that were believed, for a time, to ensure natural justice.[9] The Greek religion in its polytheism also allowed for a certain diversity of arrangements among households and among city-states.[10] There was no one sovereign God.

Political representation is modern in its connection with the idea of sovereignty. The Greeks scarcely had this idea and, because of the conditions just described, they did not need it. Sovereignty, the notion of a full and unitary power over an entire society, arose as a political problem in Western Europe in the late medieval period and received its first full formulation in the early modern period. It has its roots in Roman imperial administration and law; was greatly influenced by the monotheism of Christianity which believed there had to be one ultimate source of authority; and assumed specifically human proportions as the church and state competed and kings worked to consolidate their earthly powers. The origins of political representation occur in the medieval practice of the monarch summoning the great men of the realm to give their assent to certain taxes he wished to levy.[11] Modern political representation starts as a device of political rule from the center, in the territorial ruler's search for human sovereignty.[12]

English and continental kings drew upon concepts developed in late Roman law under the emperors. These included the doctrine that there is and must be one supreme will in the community, that law is an expression of this will, and that human law is deliberately enacted (even if it is not until later that law is considered to be completely made by humans rather than found by them in the order of the universe). Monarchs also modified a maxim of Roman private law into a public one: a law or rule that affects all must be approved by all.[13] The adoption of each of these doctrines served to make the central power more powerful by rendering it more legitimate. The lords did not particularly want to play this role of shoring up the king's power, although they soon saw the possibilities in the situation and began to use the national forum for their own ends.[14]

In this early period (twelfth to fifteenth centuries), the practice of representation involved strong local ties, but the word *representative* connoted the national connection. The knights and burgesses summoned to the court were generally of local residence, paid expenses by those localities, and understood to act as attorneys for those localities.[15] Localities, furthermore, were often corporations, collectivities having a legal personality under the common law.[16] Thus a local constituency as a whole could be said to delegate the power of attorney to someone to act for it. Yet this person was then called just that—procurator or attorney, never the representative, nor even the representer, until the seventeenth century.[17] The word *representative* was reserved for what that person did when he was in the capital city, and that had less to do with local agency and more to do with national governance and, at a deeper level, with national symbolism. Hanna Pitkin has discovered the subtleties in the early etymology; I will be arguing that they have tremendous consequences for how we should think about representation. Rather than seeing representation primarily as a device for democratizing and limiting the state, we must first understand representation as a way to constitute national sovereignty. This goal is not as unproblematic as it now sounds: there have been eminent legal theorists, such as F. W. Maitland in England and Otto von Gierke in Germany, who deeply opposed the concept of sovereignty. But they are in a minority; the discourse of sovereignty prevailed.[18]

The search for sovereignty intensified in the aftermath of the English civil war. Thomas Hobbes presented the first great modern theory of state sovereignty, and his theory of representation is an integral part of his philosophy.[19] Like sovereignty theorists before him, Hobbes argued that for a state to be stable and strong there has to be one supreme and independent power in the society with the qualities of perpetuity and absoluteness.[20] Unlike earlier theorists, Hobbes put that sovereignty on a modern basis—the individual person, the concept of a person as an individual will. For Hobbes, men who are fearful of their deaths, prideful of their places, calculating of their chances, yet still desirous of great honor, can decide to form a sovereign state by entering into a social contract.[21] The social contract is an artificial, even hypothetical, construct.[22] Even before the contract, they all follow a language that is largely conventional, arbitrary in its sounds although depending on right definitions, and made socially objective by common usage. Individuals can then decide to cede the right which is theirs in a state of nature over to a power which will "keep them all in awe." This power is the sovereign leviathan whose purpose is to protect their security. The state is an artificial creation of their wills. It is also their representative.

Hobbes is the first to bring the two aspects of representation as agency and as symbol together in a theoretical system. The sovereign is, first, the attorney for the people; they have authorized him to act. They remain the "authors" of his actions, they "own" the actions, and he is their attorney or their formal "actor" with the right or authority to perform the actions of another.[23] They have given him unlimited authorization, at least with regard to the means he is to use, given the ends of "procuring their maintenance."[24] Secondly, the sovereign is their national unity, and this unity is, again, artificial, not natural. "A multitude of men are made *one* person when they are by one man, or one person, represented; so that it be done with the consent of every one of that multitude in particular. For it is the *unity* of the representer, not the *unity* of the represented, that maketh the person *one*."[25]

The imagery of Hobbes's prose suggests vastness—vastness of the territory, vastness of the sovereign's power, vastness of people's desires and insecurities, and of the gap between them and the sovereign, vastness of their terror and awe. Yet the logic of his argument seems to require at least this limit: that the state not be a world state, that it be a national state. This is so, not because he posits any geographical or historical preconditions to his social contract, but for two other reasons: one having to do with the possibility of the sovereign having enforcement power, and the other having to do with the notion of consent. The first is practical: the state must be able to possess effective enforcement power to make its will effective within its territory. This condition could possibly be met on a world scale under later technology. The second is theoretical: the doctrine of social contract requires the notion of consent, and consent in turn implies that one could have not consented. Consent, of course, can take many forms, from explicit acts such as signing an oath or choosing a representative to less overt acts such as inhabiting the territory or using the language, to "the most tacit whisper of implied consent."[26] All these cases imply, however, the existence of a state with boundaries, by which membership is defined, so that people can be said to have consented or come in, as it were. The boundaries are both physical—territorial borders—and spiritual—principles governing the polity. Thus, even in Hobbes, the state requires external boundaries.[27]

In the centuries after Hobbes, the locus of sovereignty was changed but the concept remained and was hotly contested. The early Americans might even have liked to avoid the concept, such were their experiences of colonial autonomy, but they could not; it was too pervasive.[28] Blackstone, in his *Commentaries on the Laws of England,* wrote in the 1770s that "there is and must be in all [forms of government] a supreme, irresistible, absolute, uncontrolled authority, in which the *jura summi imperii,* or the rights of sovereignty, reside."[29] By the seventeenth century in England, sovereignty lodged in the composite entity with medieval roots, the "King-in-Parliament."[30] The King or Queen-in-Parliament was supreme; its members both made the law and were the highest court to judge the law. The Americans then adopted the Whig interpretation of parliamentary sovereignty or legislative supremacy, took the king out of it, and divided the legislature into two houses elected on different principles.[31] This made the people who elected the dual legislatures "double agents" and paved the way for the next move of sovereignty. Radical reformers in England began to suggest that ultimate sovereignty did not lie within Parliament but rather in the electors outside who had chosen the members of Parliament. The American founders took this a step further, and much sooner than in England: they declared that ultimate sovereignty lay not even in particular bodies of electors but in the "people-at-large."[32]

This doctrine of popular sovereignty, or more precisely, of the sovereignty of the people as individuals of a nation, was developed in order to defeat the doctrine of the autonomy of the states. It was not intended as a democratic doctrine, even though later attempts were made to use it that way, with consequences we are still exploring today. But throughout its history, it has raised a definite problem for representative theory and practice: if the entity that is sovereign is the people-at-large, why not elect the representatives at-large? Why have local districts at all instead of larger ones or even one big district?

This is what James Madison, for example, wanted: much larger electoral districts for the national House of Representatives, and multimember districts for the state senates. Commenting on Jefferson's draft of a constitution for Virginia, Madison in 1788 suggested that the way to have representatives give "an attention to the interest of the whole Society [was] by making them the choice of the whole Society."[33] Distrusting the localism and what he considered to be the privatism of representatives from small and established districts, Madison sought a system that would attract eminent men of talent, education, and national ambition to the Congress; rather than have it be bogged down in particularistic loyalties and corruptions, a natural aristocracy would protect the national interest from the depredations of the very rich and the very poor. Madison assumes that individual interests are the main motivation in politics, that factions resulting from the pursuit of interests can endanger the republic, and that representation over extended areas can decrease the danger of interest groups.[34] His is a complex and original argument whose dynamics are not our concern here; what is important for us at this stage of our discussion is Madison's devaluation of the corporate character of localities, historic character of the counties, and political character of the states. In this, at least, he was in accord with the nationalism expressed earlier by John Adams, who called for an American national sovereignty at the Continental Congress in 1776. "The confederacy is to make us one individual only; it is to form us, like separate parcels of metal, into one common mass. We shall no longer retain our separate individuality [as colonies] but become a single individual as to all questions submitted to the Confederacy."[35] And, in a statement that Hobbes in his nominalism would have approved: "The individuality of a colony is a mere sound."[36]

We all know that the colonies did retain their individuality in the Federal Constitution in the form of two senators per state. But this can be seen as an historic compromise negotiated between the large and small states over representation in the two houses of Congress, a bargain that does not necessarily (although it may) give us any answer to the question: What about the legitimacy of political districts for areas that never were politically sovereign? Thus, there is an unresolved problem in the political theory of representation which arises from the primary connection of political representation to the concept of sovereignty. The problem is whether there should be any political districts for single representatives within the state: what might be called the problem of "internal boundaries."

Preface to a Solution to the Problem:
The Question of Citizenship

We have remarked that ancient Greek political thought lacked a concept of representation. Let us explore the Greek image of political life briefly, to see if it suggests another angle on the question we have raised. Classical thought had a distinctive way of talking about the relation of the individual to the state—the ideal of citizenship—and another way of manifesting this connection—direct participation. These concepts depart from the idea of persons enhancing state sovereignty in two significant ways: the citizen is different from a person, and the goal is autonomy, not sovereignty.

Citizenship was a status and an activity in which certain persons, while acknowledging their pre-political beginnings, took account of their public association together in fundamental ways. Politics was about the development and recognition of character as much as it was about the protection of interests. In Hannah Arendt's interpretation, private life was the realm of necessity and inequality, public life the realm of freedom and equality.[37] Thus Aristotle argued that the moral and intellectual virtues could be fully realized only in political life: only through direct interaction with one's peers in political friendship and political deliberation could a person express the highest human qualities.[38] Political participation was essential to form and express a human character. In Sheldon Wolin's interpretation, it was essential to creating a human character, politics itself being a "created" field.[39] Whether politics is discovered or created, citizenship was an activity understood to change the character of its members.

The citizen was thus an individual who was supposed to be fundamentally changed by membership in the polity. Using terms I shall be developing later, citizenship involved political association as much as it involved individual control. Citizens were made present in the actions of the state through an assumption of political responsibility that led them to identify part of their selves with the state. As Pitkin has written, "The Citizen image . . . concerns the transformation of narrowly defined self-interest into a larger awareness of one's ties to others, one's real stake in institutions and ideals. This is a transformation not so much from self-interest to self-sacrifice, nor even from narrowly defined short-range to prudent long-range self-interest, but rather in the understanding of what the self *is*, of the limits to the self."[40]

Participation in political decision was the way a citizen and the city-state could achieve freedom understood as autonomy. Autonomy, from the Greek *nomos,* law, and *auto,* self, means self-rule. It shares with sovereignty the idea of being a law unto oneself, of acting according to a rule that one has chosen for oneself. It differs from sovereignty, however, in that it presupposes plurality and requires self-limitation. There is never only one autonomous citizen, nor one autonomous city-state. The one can only be autonomous in the context of the many, who are similarly self-ruled. Self-rule, therefore, involves self-limitation, so that the others whom one values as peers and friends may continue to share in the common life.

Self-rule necessarily involves self-limitation because it is based on what might be called the classical view of human nature (although by classical I mean to suggest austerity and beauty as well as ancient lineage, since this view now spans Plato to Freud). This position assumes that there is an ahistorical structure to the soul, that the human passions are infinite and unruly, that reason can come to teach the passions, and that there is an ultimate harmony in which reason itself is transformed by love. The forms reason takes will vary with each historical era. Political reason can help limit the passions in two ways. First, it can discipline them, simply by confining their expression within bounds. Second, it can transform their objects from natural and social ones to cultural and political ones. Thus, political education might transform the untamed desire to touch bodies and acquire possessions into the desire to create art, cities, and philosophy. Now these are not simple transformations, nor are they unproblematic morally, for at certain junctures they require a violence which violates the ideal of autonomy. Be that as it may, this classical view asserts that as an adult a citizen could find a common law by which he could live in harmony with others, a law of self-limitation which is also a mode of self-expression.

The power and attractiveness of this ideal has led certain modern political theorists to assert that direct participation is the ideal and indirect representation is a paltry second best, albeit the best practicable arrangement given the size of the modern polity. This book will argue otherwise: that political representation is qualitatively superior to direct democracy.

Madison had argued in *Federalist 10* that political representation is superior to direct democracy because it mitigates the violence of faction. But Madison's representation is representation of individuals as they are now in civil society, of *persons* not of citizens, and therefore to overcome individual self-interest, Madison advocates at-large districts.

On the other hand, Carol Pateman, drawing on her reading of Rousseau, J. S. Mill, and G. D. H. Cole, argues that participatory democracy in both the government and society is necessary in order to educate the people to freedom. But even though she speaks of people as *citizens,* I do not think she takes account of the significant difference between person and citizens in the modern age. She writes that "Rousseau also believes that through this educational process [of participation] the individual will eventually come to feel little or no conflict between the demands of the public and private spheres."[41] In this she softens the hard brilliance of Rousseau's theoretical system and ignores the challenge he poses to the moderns—that citizenship in some way depends upon slavery, that for one part of the polity to be free requires that another part be in bondage.[42]

Two features, then, mark our situation as qualitatively different from the Greeks. First, free personhood is a separate status from free citizenship; second, and related, the political sphere cannot *de facto* dominate the social sphere without its consent. Whereas for the Greeks one could not be a fully human person, or even an owner of all kinds of property, without being a citizen, for us one can be a formally free person with civil rights without being a citizen. Liberal society accords the individual a status with rights before an objective law, even if ultimately this status is created and guaranteed by the state. The consequences of this formally free legal status lead to the second qualitative distinction from ancient times. Persons who are not active citizens cannot be dominated as natural entities, even if that mastery is intended to be in their best interest. In a healthy polity, the number of noncitizens is small, and aliens have the long-run possibility of becoming citizens. Whereas the Greek polity could assume natural and social mastery over a large and permanent group of noncitizens, the modern polity has to obtain, or contain the possibility of obtaining, the political consent of its subjects. *Domination* of individuals as *things* is replaced by *sovereignty* over individuals as *persons*.

If, however, the goal becomes *autonomy,* rule among persons as *citizens,* then one has to ask what happens to the nonpolitical aspects of life which previously were simply dominated or cajoled into consent. One has to ask this especially in bourgeois society where the division of labor has grown vastly in scope and importance, even if the import of the family has declined. If legitimate domination can no longer be exercised on others, then at times it has to be exercised on oneself, within the soul of each citizen who is also a person.[43] Personhood and Citizenship: we can no longer simply say which is the presupposition of the other; the totality has become a complex structure, a field of interacting forces. What we can say, however, is that the person and the citizen are two distinct statuses, whose independent value and reciprocal significance should be preserved. A theory that absorbs the person completely into the citizen in the modern age runs the risk of totalitarianism; a theory that conflates the citizen back into the person can degenerate into interest-group liberalism.

This book argues that political representation is qualitatively superior to direct democracy because only representation can capture the complexities of what it means to be both a person and a citizen in the modern age. What we shall be solving for is a political representation of *persons as citizens,* and for representation to approach these ends, I will argue, it has to be structured in certain ways. Most generally, political representation has to be based on "internal boundaries." Representatives have to come from single-member local geographic districts in order to provide the arena for direct interaction as well as the symbolic distance from personal life which is characteristic of citizenship. Citizenship will be seen as an essential moment in the logic of representation, even as representation also constitutes national sovereignty.

Influences and Approach

This book occurs within a certain tradition of discourse in political theory. Two current schools of interpretation have influenced the categories of the argument; these schools might better be called avenues of interpretation, given the idiosyncratic nature of works in political theory. They converge in what I would call an American classicism, political theory for America that draws on categories from ancient political experience. The main line of interpretation was opened by Hannah Arendt (1958) and Sheldon Wolin (1960) who independently reinterpreted Greek experience in new terms. This path continues along secular lines in writers such as Hanna Fenichel Pitkin (1984), and also takes a fork into religious paths which add the Christian tradition to the classical canon (Wilson Carey McWilliams, 1973).[44] Then there is a more recent line of interpretation of the Atlantic tradition of civic republicanism by J. G. A. Pocock (1975), which interprets American experience in terms stemming from Machiavelli.[45] While there are many differences between these theories, they share the interpretation that classical political thought created a qualitative difference between life as lived in the political realm and life as lived in the nonpolitical realm, and that citizenship, the name for the public life, remains a valuable ideal in the modern age.

Why the intellectual choice to use ancient terms in a situation that is so vastly different? We shall return to this question, but for now I note that it is a choice made self-consciously by these theorists. Nor is it a choice that precludes introducing new terms. First let us briefly survey the significant terms, and some of the question I think they raise.

Arendt claimed to be describing the categories of ancient Greece, but she did it from the perspective of twentieth-century politics, which had accepted the status of the formally free individual and welcomed the masses into politics in ways she considered dangerous. What passes as a description of Greek life has to be seen as a meditation on the divisions within the soul of the modern citizen. She proposed a sharp contrast between the "public" and the "private" life, two distinct arenas within the "active life" which also contrasted with the "contemplative life."[46] Whereas ancient and medieval theorists looked to contemplative reason, science, and philosophy to guide practical reason in the active life, the moderns have despaired of finding guidance there, and Arendt accepts this part of the modern situation.[47] The active life must now generate its own rules and shared meanings if there is to be any common life. What she does not accept is what she sees as the modern hierarchy of activities within the active life, in which "work" and "labor" are valued more than "action," valued both for their inherent significance as well as their causal efficacy. She deemed the private sphere to be base, consisting of the lowly activities of work and labor, categories she proposed and then described as repetitious and necessitous.[48] The public sphere of action was higher, more noble, because it was the arena where human speech was developed and qualitatively new things were said and done and perceived.[49] Her category of action is very broad, importing some qualities that had previously belonged to the contemplative sphere; thus action includes an aesthetic appreciation of new deeds as well as their performance.

Now there are a lot of questions that can be asked about this model. From the standpoint of Lockean liberal theory: Why does human thought and speech derive from the public sphere and not from the natural reason inherent in all people as children of God? From the standpoint of Marxian theory: How can one say that labor is merely repetitious, that it does not lead to anything qualitatively new? And from the feminist standpoint: How can she assert that reproduction produces nothing new? Yet Arendt, by highlighting the unique liberty of the citizen—who ideally had the complete freedom to take actions, make promises and break them, and grant forgiveness, in ways not so readily available to people bound to others in the other spheres—stressed an aspect of human life that even her critics then sought to integrate into their valued spheres: self-consciousness, human self-reflection about the possibilities of political autonomy as well as a deeply felt need to achieve public recognition from others of who one inexchangeably was. This is her idea of the citizen.

Accepting for the moment her overall categories, two questions relevant to this study arise. First, what do citizens actually do in that public sphere? And second, how do they do it? What they do, in Arendt's aristocratic vision, is perform heroic actions and speeches. But, some have asked, what do they act and talk about?[50] War and preparations for war—it was a central part of Greek life and the life of the citizen.[51] Governing and judging—the deliberation about rules of policy and equity.[52] Justice—finding new rules to relate the political to the nonpolitical spheres.[53] These are perhaps the missing elements in Arendt's system, giving content to its otherwise contentless form. Second, how do they do it? Direct participation in the ancient assemblies and in Arendt's idealization of modern workers' councils and ward republics. But this is undesirable, given the modern conditions of free formal individuality and the modern technologies of war. For full-time participation does not allow for the development of private individuals and, the greater the number of small states, the greater the danger of local wars that can escalate into a nuclear exchange.

One must come to a critical assessment of the significance of war for the Greek citizen, in order to see whether, if war loses its prime place, only justice and the seeking of other collective goods remain as fit activities for the citizen. The significance of war lay not only in protecting the security of the polity but also in providing an arena and proving ground for individual character. Fighting and preparing to fight called upon intellectual and moral traits, particularly the capacity for strategic thought, for a certain kind of courage, for skill, and loyalty. Arendt's language captures the agonal and aesthetic nature of Greek politics, its competitive struggles for heroism and honor. Absent the actual fighting, her image of action would still require some contests by which public character was revealed. That arena is provided in Machiavelli, for example, by the healthy tumult which characterizes competitive factions and parties in politics.

It will be the argument of this book that political representation structured on local geographic districts provides suitable arenas in which the ideal of the citizen might be approximated. Under conditions where the modern citizen is also a person who labors and works, political representation provides a multitiered system that makes public action possible. In the local district, people interact at meetings as individual citizens seeing each other face-to-face as unique characters. Through their local meetings, of assemblies or political parties or single-issue groups, the same people come to know each other over time, and then the media help spread that local knowledge to interested onlookers. People's characters develop from personhood to citizenship as individuals enact, enrich, and understand the rules of the political game. If war as direct combat was one way to gauge a man's character in ancient times, politics as intra-party battle is one way to gauge a citizen's character today. In competing among friends and neighbors to choose one candidate, and then one representative, the people as citizens develop standards of judgment about public character as much as explicit criteria of policy. Then, at the next tier of the system, the representatives talk about justice.

Other political theorists of representation do not see things this way. John Stuart Mill, for example, provides a striking contrast of a nonclassical theory. The public sphere does not serve to develop, exhibit, or recognize the political character of citizens. While Mill speaks of "the public education of the citizens" and has a distinction between private and public life, it is along these lines: the private is the realm of self-interest and individual rights, and the public is primarily the realm of the public interest or justice, understood as fair distribution and protection of the rights of persons and property.[54] There is little arena for the development of the aesthetic dimension of individual citizenship that we found in Arendt. When Mill praises participation, it is participation of individuals as persons; when he discusses character, it is in terms of a busily "active" character animated by instrumental reason, contemptuous of the "passive" character and speculative reason.[55] He seeks the development of a "national character" in representatives who excel in a certain kind of intellectual education and independence of mind,[56] yet this is not the same thing as either civic heroism or civic reverence. Mill values a narrow view of reason and his theory of human nature is backwards: he thinks that human sentiments are "dwarfed" in small environments; that people will be robbed of their rights and interests by others unless they defend them; that reason cannot agree on the ends but only the means of life; that this utilitarian reason can limit the passions through a calculating discipline and an intellectual broadening of the definition of interest; and that individuals of all social classes will be grateful for this guidance.[57]

Thus, Mill advocates a system of political representation based on multimember districts with proportional representation.[58] The Hare system would allow individuals to list their choices for candidates nationwide, and each seat would require a certain number of votes. Once a candidate had either received, or clearly failed to receive, the requisite number of votes to qualify for a seat, any extra or unused votes would be redistributed to the other candidates, first using up the second choices, then third choices, and so on. The merit of this system is that if a significant minority in every area of a country wants the same candidate, they can elect him under this system whereas they will consistently lose under a single-member district system. We will have to consider later whether there are any minorities that warrant this significance over time. The defect of this system, from the perspective of classical theory, is that this participation can occur with little or no emotional interaction among citizens as equals, for the constituency, the people who elected the representative, are spread all over the country; and, too, the constituency theoretically could change every election. Mill argues that this is an advantage, since the representative will be more closely tied to the constituents. Classical theory, I think, would see it as disadvantageous in several respects. The constituents are not tied to each other by any overall interaction, so there is no personal knowledge of their characters as citizens. There is no historical knowledge, no following of personalities over time. Their personal knowledge, insofar as there is any, is solely of their representative, hence leading to patterns of undue deference, assuming he is a good representative. In sum, the ties among the constituents are based on specific interests as people choose to define them at any one point in time, and not on their total association.

Mill did respond to criticism, after the publication of *Considerations on Representative Government* in 1859, that his system would destroy local ties in England. While he had advocated the decentralization of many governmental functions to local representative bodies, and praised participating in local office and jury duty as a "school of public spirit," he did not attribute the same significance to the choosing of national representatives.[59] The Hare proposal had honored local districts only to the extent that votes for the candidate from his own constituency would be counted first. Mill was affected by reading de Tocqueville's *Democracy in America* and so he took account of the importance of localism by modifying his electoral proposals in an 1867 speech to Parliament.[60] While this shows flexibility, representation by local constituencies is incompatible with the rest of Mill's theory, for Mill does not share de

Tocqueville's view of human nature or politics. De Tocqueville sees intense local attachments as primary and valuable and believes that political education occurs through deepening the affections and dispositions of people toward their local political associations, yet within the context of a higher political law as well as divine law.[61] Mill's theory is based on the idea of individuals joined by their social interests into a national interest, instructed by utilitarian reason.

What if we turned to John Locke, an earlier liberal theorist who grounds his theory in natural law rather than utilitarianism and who proposes majority rule rather than proportional representation?[62] Locke does not have much explicit writing on the issue of representation, but his theory is important both for its theoretical stance and its influence on the Americans (although see below n. 66). Locke's social contract does not posit a great difference between the kinds of human action characteristic of the public and private spheres. The government of the society is supposed to protect private interests and the natural rights of individuals. By building natural reason and natural rights into his private sphere, however, Locke gives it some of the characteristics that classical theorists argued could only emerge in the public sphere. Laslett has gone so far as to argue that Locke posits a "natural political virtue" among people that helps explain their transition from the state of nature to the social contract and gives the quality of mutual trustworthiness to all their actions.[63]

When Locke, therefore, says that majority rule is a justified decision-rule, we can interpret this beyond his doctrine of consent, to include also the essential reasonableness of the persons voting. Their natural reason and virtue will enable them to argue until they agree on the ends of politics, and they will then differ only on the means. Since the choice of means involves no ultimate moral issues, the force of the greater part can decide.[64] He trusts that their reason will instruct them not to violate the natural rights of others and their virtue will incline them not to violate the interests of others.

This is a powerful theory which places individual liberty or autonomy within the context of natural law. The question that some modern theorists ask, of course, is whether there really is a natural law and how can we know it; and if not, can we ground Locke's theory in any other way. The answer that modern classicists such as Arendt give is to see individual autonomy as a result rather than as a presupposition of politics and the state. That is, the notion of an evaluative reason that can set the ends as well as the means can only be derived through political speech which, for example, would develop the shared concept of civil and political rights as valuable ends in themselves. Thus, for a classicist, it is not that Locke is necessarily wrong in his values but he "mistakes the cause for the effect." Locke assumes certain communitarian preconditions to his liberal theory which most contemporary classicists are trying to ground in political experience. In particular, Locke's assumptions of a shared evaluative reason or natural law, shared dispositions or natural sociability, and shared history or political units,[65] cannot be taken as given.

It is at this point that the pre-Lockean tradition of civic republicanism enters the picture in an exciting way. Recent scholarship of the past few decades has argued that it was Machiavelli more than Locke who influenced the American founders.[66] Pocock argues that Machiavelli's thought, as transmitted through Harrington and the English Whigs, comprised an Atlantic republican tradition which grounds individual autonomy in a different way. And because Machiavelli was a classicist, there is also a distinct notion of citizen autonomy which is different from Locke and Mill.

Machiavelli posits a sharp distinction between public and private life. Private and social life is the realm of self-interest *and* moral virtue as learned from Catholicism; public life, the realm of interests of the state *and* the public *virtù* of citizens.[67] The citizens of a republic act and speak according to different standards than in private life; their goal is the glory of the republic and their means is heroic virtue, action in the face of fate and time.[68] The prince and citizens use means, such as lies, cruelty, and violence, that would not be sanctioned in private life; they also require traits and gifts, such as courage and honor, that would not be fully possible in private life. In Machiavelli's political theory of the two spheres of life, public and private, each has an existence and value of its own, while each also depends upon and influences the other.[68] When he writes from political exile, "I love my country more than my soul," we believe this yet do not doubt that he believed that men had souls.

Civic republicanism as it developed through English Whiggism in the seventeenth and eighteenth centuries would argue that before entering politics as a citizen, a man must have a "will of his own."[70] He must be his own person, with an autonomous will, following his own lights, not dependent on the will of another. If one were dependent on the will of another in either an economic or social sense, then one was subject to influence, one's vote could be coerced, one could not be an autonomous person.

What preconditions would ensure that a man had a will of his own? In the Putney Debates on extension of the suffrage after the English civil war, English political thought divided in two directions on this issue, and we may wish to return to the fork in the road. The dominant position was that property made a man independent.[71] Ownership in land gave a man both a stake in the society and yet independence from other men. Harrington would later argue that in order to have a virtuous citizenry there must first be an agrarian law to redistribute property to persons.[72] Later English and American Whigs would change the definition of acceptable property to include movable property, even payment of taxes,[73] but a secular civic republicanism required this theoretical basis.

The other position in the debate was that of the more radical Protestants who maintained that religion gave a man his independence and political history gave a man his stake. The left-wing Protestants had an enthusiasm and discipline that formed a conscience more individual than any seen before.[74] And Colonel Rainborough spoke to their stake in society: they had served in the state's army, and therefore deserved the vote as the "birthright of Englishmen."[75] This was not primarily an appeal to the natural rights of man, but to divine law and political service and the historical rights of Englishmen.

But what we also see here is a reversal of the line of causality: a will of one's own is not a precondition of political participation but rather a result of it. For here, first you believe and you serve, then you become free. Civil liberty follows after Christian liberty, liberty to seek the truth. Political liberty is an historical right won in political battle with the state. A will of one's own, in fact, hardly exists in Calvinist theology, such is the power of predestination. But personal autonomy, in the sense of living according to laws one has chosen to accept, does exist. Personal autonomy here follows upon a higher sovereignty, first religious, then political.[76]

Both sides of the debate at Putney continue as parts of the American political tradition. McWilliams argues that the religious ideal of citizen fraternity has existed from the Puritans to the black civil rights movement, alongside the Enlightenment secular belief in the liberty of the person.[77] Contemporary debate continues on whether to interpret the Anti-Federalists, for example, as premodern communitarians influenced by religion, or as radical Whigs quite within the liberal canon.[78] Yet perhaps the language of civic republicanism can cut across this liberal/communitarian debate; but for that we would have to return to civic republicanism at its origins, in Machiavelli's time, before property became defined as the mark of individual autonomy.

How was the person connected to the citizen in Machiavelli's time; how were the relevant people made present in the actions of the city-state? Some say that there was no real representation in the Renaissance, but rather "rotation," a practice midway between ancient participation and modern representation.[79] We will have to investigate this matter further. We shall be asking whether there are not aspects of the activity of representation that are overlooked in the modern understanding of representation when that institution is primarily linked to a national sovereignty of individuals. In turning back from Hobbes to Machiavelli we stay on the threshold of the modern age yet turn to an understanding that was still classical, one that sought citizen autonomy as well as state sovereignty.

We use ancient and medieval terms as well as modern ones because the older words have broad and rich connotations that go beyond our specific situation. Sovereignty, for example, connotes the majesty of a king or queen, as well as the denotation of full and independent power. Autonomy connotes the harmony celebrated in Athenian life conducted out of doors, as well as the denotation of self-rule. Citizenship connotes a warlike heroism, as well as public spirit of a peaceful sort. Even when the historical conditions which provided these connotations are past, people have historical memories which retain these meanings. Thus, to speak of sovereignty can still connote a majestic greatness; autonomy can imply an essential public dignity; citizenship can mean struggle on behalf of what we have in common. The older terms give people a distance from their present situation, one which at the same time names the present but urges them to go beyond it. This, it should also be said, was always the function of such words.

The language that we use to talk about political life affects how we think and act in political life. This study assumes the crucial importance of ideas in politics, and specifically the importance of political speech. The way in which issues are presented can change the terms of debate; the discourse in which argument is conducted frames its very outcome. If one asks what policy will promote people's interests, discussion proceeds along certain lines; if one asks what policy will promote citizenship, it goes differently. Civic humanism of the early Renaissance believed that human conversation provides the bridge between the universal concepts and particular events of life.[70] Civic republicanism of the later Renaissance then tried to build this conversation into the structure of political institutions.

Political institutions are expressive of certain ideas. Institutions stand as symbols of political concepts, even as institutions also cause effects. Thus, in America, for example, counting the votes through the electoral college stands for the federal nature of the union, and proposals for direct election of the president stand for the national sovereignty of the people. The choosing of presidential candidates through intraparty procedures allows other particularistic criteria to enter.[81] Party rules, popular election, and electoral votes may lead, over time, to certain kinds of presidents with certain kinds of characters and policies. These effects occur within the basic symbolism. What, then, does election of the legislature mean? The symbolic meaning of political representation in national, state, and local legislatures is the concern of this study. Specific outcomes from these legislatures occur within a legitimating symbolism; they may enhance it or hinder it, but the underlying symbolism has to be there.

Empirical literature used to see the symbolism of representation as residual. Studies of the effects of different representative systems tested for evidence of human agency, not for the general meaning. Meier and England state this view: "Haunting the large literature on the impact of at-large districts and other urban 'reforms' on black representation has been the question of whether or not representation makes a difference. If it does not, representation becomes symbolic."[82] Symbolism was adjudged not to make a difference; having an effect is assessed in terms of responsiveness to constituents. The criteria of responsiveness can differ, however, as Eulau and Karps point out; they can include: official/constituent policy congruence, following their preferences for general policy for the society; official/constituent service responsiveness, following their desires for particular benefits; allocative responsiveness, including them in collective benefits; and finally, symbolic responsiveness, building constituency trust and diffuse political support.[83] But these criteria raise as many questions as they answer. What is the diffuse support of? What if the constituents do not all have policy preferences, service needs, allocative preferences? What if these preferences conflict? On what does constituency trust depend? One has to have an idea of the overall meaning of citizenship as distinct from personhood for the elaborate fiction of representation to make sense. Human agency has to be seen in the context of representation's symbolism.

Plan of the Book

In Chapter 2 I will present the understanding of representation that grows out of the search for sovereignty: what I call the "transmission belt" theory (after the name for the role the press and trade unions were to play in transmitting demands to and from the Party and the workers in the Soviet state).[84] Representatives are seen as transmission or conveyer belts between the power of the state and the power of individuals and groups, as those individuals and groups are defined in their everyday existence in society. The state's power must be consolidated as sovereign or authoritative by gaining the consent of individuals. Representation is seen as a way of transferring power as control from existing individuals to the state in a way that is legitimate because it accords with their subjective wills or their objective interests as persons.

Recent Supreme Court decisions on voting rights and political districting will be examined in Chapter 3 to show some of the quandaries the transmission belt theory leads to. The explicit language of the "one person, one vote" decisions depends upon transmission belt theory of individual influence and control over government decisions. The Court gets itself into a muddle when it moves to problems of group influence and control, and it also has problems even when it stays with individuals. There are unspoken communitarian preconditions to the Court's assumptions about the meaning of an individual's vote, which cannot be articulated within the definition of citizenship as control.

An alternate perspective on the meaning of citizenship will be presented in Chapter 4 based on interpretations of citizenship as practiced in historical city-states. Two theorists, Marx and Weber, who well understand the modern status of "formally free individuality," find that citizenship was not only a relation of appropriation but also one of association. The condition of both these relations is membership in the polity; how membership is established and affirmed thus becomes a central question. And then, the content of the relations of appropriation and association is something qualitatively new, different from politics as control. Political association, or political friendship or brotherhood, transforms individuals into citizens, and even appropriation, or shared ownership and power, is essentially associative. Citizens seek to affect their environment and they value their mutual relations as an end in itself. This is a communitarian view of citizenship.

Yet classical communitarian theory, unlike liberal theory, has tended to ignore political representation or denounce it as illegitimate. In Chapter 5 I will explore the reasons for this neglect, which have to do with certain significant assumptions in communitarian theory. I will also explore some rather enigmatic figures in classical theory, notably that of the Founder, to see whether the neglect of representation is really total. The founders will be seen to "constitute" the community in fundamental ways; it is an activity that occurs even before leadership can be exercised. We will be moving towards an alternative model of representation as "constitutive" of the shared mores of the polity.

For representation to be constitutive, it has to allow for expression of the significant parts of ethical life. Chapter 6 develops four technical terms for the aspects of modern life, to give precision to the distinction between personhood and citizenship discussed more generally so far. These terms: formal individualism, social individuality, political individuality, and the political whole, derive from my interpretation of Hegel, who as a modern teleological philosopher combined an overarching communitarianism with the liberal moment. That is, the goal of substantive freedom coexists alongside a personal liberty. Our main question throughout continues to be how does the person become a citizen, or achieve political individuality, while still remaining an individual person.

The political experience of early Renaissance Florence is examined in Chapter 7 for its practices of rotation and representation. This city-state is instructive because it combines liberal and communitarian elements: a strong sense of formal individualism and individual autonomy as well as an even stronger sense of political individuality or citizenship. But the citizens chosen to be officials for periods of time are not understood to act for the wishes of the others nor on behalf of their interests; they represent the districts of the polity by being members of those districts and acting for the political whole. The only way we can understand these practices is to move out of the transmission belt model of two-way dichotomies between activity and passivity, and move into a more circular constitutive model which has four different dimensions. We here draw upon Pitkin's conceptualization of the meanings of representation: formal representation, which includes procedures of authorization and accountability, and then substantive representation as descriptive standing for, symbolic standing for, and actual acting for, things not literally present.

While Pitkin in her original presentation of these different connotations of the same word showed how they are incompatible or at least in tension, I argue in Chapter 8 that in a multilayered communitarian theory of the polity all the aspects of representation can, and should, occur, so that the word does have a unity of meaning. The final chapter will show how certain procedures in America—the selection of representatives by plurality rules from single-member districts—can constitute legitimate legislatures whose constituents are citizens. In contrast, say, to multimember districts elected with proportional representation, in which only the representatives become citizens through their interaction in the legislature while their constituents remain solely persons, single-member districts with first-past-the-post election rules promote the face-to-face participation of persons as citizens over general criteria of character and platform. The districts formed by internal boundaries drawn by the state function as microcosms of the political whole and teach the person his or her membership as a citizen. The categories from Hegel will be connected to the categories from Pitkin in a static way; if they make sense of the complex meanings of representation, others may explore their dynamics.

TWO

The Transmission Belt Theory of Representation

Representation is "an instrument of power."[1] It is an institutional technique by which power is structured in a political society. But to say this is only to begin, for what is power? And what does representation do to power—limit it, expand it, share it, create it? And amongst or between whom?

Political representation makes the people present in the actions of the governing power of the state. A few—the representatives—are chosen by the many—the represented—to be the legislature or governing power of the state. Yet "who governs whom in the representational relationship is an empirical question that cannot and should not be answered by definition."[2] Representation limits the power of the king; representation limits the power of the people. A representative legislature stands midway between the executive and the mass, exercising power within constitutional limits. Representation expands the power of the king; representation expands the power of the people. The king cannot act without the consent of the subjects; the people cannot act without the resources of the king. Representation empowers the executive and the mass, expanding the power of the state as a whole.

A society that does not explicitly theorize about power cannot explicitly theorize about representation; this, according to Eulau, is why the ancient Greeks lacked the concept even though they had some of the practices.[3] Modern political society definitely has the concept of power, and so we can think about representation. Eulau claims that Greek political theory ignored power because theirs was an essentialist theory, looking for the true essence of things as they were already given by nature, and because it was aristocratic, pragmatic only up to a point, having no real desire to change the order of things, no felt need for its citizens to "directly engage in the operational control of the physical environment."[4]

Representation in feudal times was seen as "impersonation" of some larger wholes: the church, the estates, the people, the communities. Medieval monarchy, building on concepts from Roman law, began to elaborate the notion of representation as an instrument of power rather than of impersonation. Eulau marks the real breakthrough for a theory of representation as coming with Hobbes's nominalism. "Nominalism, in rejecting 'real' definitions and starting with the individual phenomenon rather than with the whole as its unit of analysis, was an epistemological revolution . . . of critical importance for the emergence of a rudimentary theory of representation as delegation."[5] By being satisfied to name things as they appear, in their discreteness and for their effective behavior in the world, nominalism opened the way to investigating the diversity of individual interests and their causing actions conceived as physical motions. Power here is the ability to cause actions, to cause human events conceived as changes in behavior. Power is then also understood to be effective control of the environment—control over other things and persons.

This chapter seeks to show what happens to representation when viewed as an exercise of this kind of power, power conceived as direct control. We will later be asking whether this is all that power is, and hence whether this is all that representation amounts to. We already suggested, based on Pitkin's interpretation cited in the previous chapter, that even Hobbes saw representation as involving both human agency and a unifying symbolism. Representation is both an instrument of power as well as an elaborate fiction, and the fictional part is not simply the legitimation of power as control. Power is not just the force of direct control,[6] or the direct exchange of force,[7] or the coercive setting of agendas,[8] or sheer domination through oppression[9] and repression.[10] Power is also the constitution of a social world.[11]

Representation as Responsiveness

Two images have dominated the normative discussion of representation—the delegate and the trustee. The delegate is supposed to act on direct instructions from his constituents and the trustee is allowed to act more independently on their behalf. The delegate is supposed to act according to the wishes of the constituents; the trustee according to personal judgment, in a way that will further the constituents' interests, either local or national. The roles of delegate and trustee are contrasting aspects of all theories of representation. While they can go with more collectivist notions of representation, and they did in the origins of modern representation, in their contemporary manifestation in America they combine with individualist notions of representation to form a "transmission belt" theory.

Delegate and trustee, of course, do not exhaust the possibilities of action open to the representative. Recent empirical theory has elaborated further on the many role possibilities here: beyond the "representational role" of delegate, trustee, or politico (a skillful combination of delegate and trustee), a representative might choose a variety of "areal" foci as the origin of delegation or trusteeship: the district or the entire political unit that the legislature covers, or some combination of the two. Furthermore, we could say that the focus for the relevant constituency might be functional or partisan rather than geographical, so that the agent might instead represent a social class, pressure group, or political party. Once inside the legislature, the delegate or trustee or politico might adopt any number of purposive legislative styles, which have been said to include that of "tribune," "inventor," "broker," "ritualist," and "opportunist."[12] Outside the legislature, in relation to bureaucratic agencies, he might even become a "hustler."[13]

Recent empirical literature has begun to label the delegate/trustee model as obsolete, unhelpful to describing the complex realities of our times.[14] In its stead, the most powerful alternative conceptualization has been that of "responsiveness."[15] The representative is supposed to be responsive to the needs and wants of the constituents. Four main dimensions of responsiveness are proposed: "policy responsiveness": "how the representative and represented interact with respect to the making of public policy"; "service responsiveness": "the advantages and benefits which the representative is able to obtain for particular constituents"; "allocative responsiveness": "pork-barrel politics in legislative allocations of public projects [which] involve advantages and benefits . . . to a representative's district as a whole"; and "symbolic responsiveness": less a "behavioral aspect" and "more psychologically based" . . . built on "trust and confidence expressed in the support that the represented give to the representative and to which he responds by symbolic, significant gestures, in order to, in turn, generate and maintain continuing support."[16]

Delegate and trustee set up an either/or model in which the representative was either directly bound to the directing control of the represented, or he was not. Ultimately, of course, the trustee as well as the delegate was subject to the veto power of the constituents, but during his time in office, more power was ceded over to the trustee than the delegate. The idea of responsiveness was supposed to escape the delegate/trustee dilemma because it did not require that we choose between them and instead acknowledged that there is a mutual interaction between the constituents and representative. Responsiveness also could draw our attention to an array of alternative domains of interaction. In each domain, we might say that the representative stands ready to act on behalf of the wants and needs of his constituents.

But, when the concept of responsiveness was operationalized by one of its originators, he and his research associates solved only for responsiveness to the wishes or wants of certain constituents and not responsiveness to their needs or their interests. Eulau et al. acknowledged that they were dropping any "potential for responsiveness" out of the account, as well as excluding a general notion of "the interest of the public."[17] For reasons of empirical necessity, they would take as signs of responsiveness only actions in relation to "expressed interests," which could be found in the "views and expressed preferences of," first, "attentive publics, that is, of identifiable and permanent interest clusters in the community" or, second, "transitory interest groups, . . . or even individual citizens."[18] These characteristics stress only the delegate aspect of representation.

Yet Jewell, whose research builds on the first three categories of responsiveness (policy, service, and allocative), says that policy responsiveness, for example, must take into account "the needs and interests of constituents [which] are often not as clearly articulated as demands."[19] He cites examples where the "needs are clear (better housing, health care, and day care centers)" yet perhaps not articulated.[20] Jewell drops Eulau's fourth category of symbolic responsiveness and replaces it with the category of "communication" in which the representative must "be accessible to constituents," "actively seek to learn about [their] needs and views," and "exercise leadership, educating his constituents and explaining his activities."[21] These requirements reintroduce the role of trustee.

The idea of responsiveness, then, has to incorporate the two aspects of delegate and trustee rather than abandon them. Pitkin included both aspects in her formulation of political representation.

> Representing here means acting in the interest of the represented, in a manner responsive to them. The representative

must act independently; his action must involve discretion and judgment; he must be the one who acts. The represented must also be (conceived as) capable of independent action and judgment, not merely being taken care of. And, despite the resulting potential for conflict between representative and represented about what is to be done, that conflict must not normally take place. The representative must act in such a way that there is no conflict, or if it occurs an explanation is called for. He must not be found persistently at odds with the wishes of the represented without good reason in terms of their interest, without a good explanation of why their wishes are not in accord with their interest.[22]

Jewell also implicitly includes both delegate and trustee dimensions when he states, "We are interested in how representatives respond to both the articulated demands and the unarticulated interests of their constituents."[23] For a representative who responds to the articulated demands is a delegate, and one who responds to unarticulated interests is a trustee.

Representation, the historian J. R. Pole has said, is a prescriptive idea.[24] This means that the very definition of the activity and institution must include some normative ideals of what representation is supposed to do. A definition of representation as "responsiveness" has to state that there will be some linkage between the representative and the demands and interests of the represented. A fuller normative theory of representation as "responsibility" would set the context that defined who the relevant constituents were and what their demands and interests might be. A fuller empirical theory of representation would show the variety of ways in which demands and interests were expressed and discovered, and specify the conditions under which different representative styles might occur.

We shall examine what happens to representation as responsiveness when it occurs in the normative context of radical individualism. Earlier theories of representation arose in contexts that attributed reality and value to corporate and collective entities. A delegate from a Puritan Massachusetts town, for example, was understood to be instructed by the corporate town as a whole.[25] A trustee for Burke's constituency of Bristol, to take another example, was understood to act on behalf of certain collective interests of the constituency.[26] The extreme of the collectivist version of trusteeship is "virtual representation" in which the representative acts solely in virtue of the objective interests of the constituents. But the nineteenth and twentieth centuries saw the rise of a philosophic radicalism which completed the revolution begun by Hobbes, positing that individuals were the primary reality and source of value. Representation is then seen as a "transmission belt" between the sovereign mass of individuals and their state. Representation exists in this model to make people, as individual persons as they exist theoretically in civil society, present in the actions of the state. This model has certain consequences for the practice of representation.

Delegate Version of Transmission Belt Theory

In the delegate version of transmission belt theory, the representative is delegated by others to act according to their wishes, yet in a way that also accords with the good of the whole state. We need to explore how this theory conceives of individual wishes and what kind of power is given to the representative.

Individual subjective wishes are the starting point and ultimate source of value. Jeremy Bentham's utilitarianism provides a coherent model of man and society that he applies to political representation. The individual is conceived as a person who seeks pleasure and avoids pain. Anything that brings pleasure to a person has "utility." The individual constantly engages in a calculation about what will bring the most utility. The individual chooses among policies, persons, and actions on the basis of this felicific calculus; happiness is the goal of the individual will. As for the individual, so also for the society; happiness is the goal of the "universal will." The state exists to further the happiness of society; the universal will is the "national interest." It is calculated as the sum of "the greatest happiness for the greatest number." [27]

The sovereign body in a state is the "whole body of electors belonging to a state"; generally, all adult males.[28] They choose "agents" who are their "deputies." Bentham says he will not call them "representatives" since that might imply they stand for something beyond the wishes of the individuals who deputized them.[29] These deputies are directly "responsible" to the people who can "dislocate" the deputies at will. The deputy is to act for the "aggregate interest" of his constituents, as calculated according to the greatest happiness principle. If there arises a conflict between the "particular aggregate interest" of the constituency and the overall "national interest," the deputy has the duty to vote for the former.[30] The representative remains a delegate, directly bound to the wishes of the individuals in his constituency.

In utilitarianism, individuals may derive pleasure from being public-spirited.[31] Benevolence or sympathy is a real motive. It is "the pleasure[s] resulting from the view of any pleasures supposed to be possessed by the beings who may be the objects of benevolence."[32] Sympathy or goodwill is the motive whose dictates are most in accord with the principle of utility.[33] Thus altruism might be a considerable part of the aggregate interest. Yet despite this attention to the sympathetic impulses, it is possible to see how they came to be neglected in later theories of rational choice. Even for Bentham, the motive is considered "good or bad [only] with reference to its effects in each individual instance" and these effects include principally "the intention it gives birth to" and then "the most material part of its effects."[34] These material effects must be judged on the basis of utility to the individual.

If interest and utility are the ultimate standards, then they must have some specifiable meaning. So that a century later Anthony Downs, for example, in his economic theory of political action in a democracy, makes explicit certain assumptions about human motivation that others have seen as selfish tendencies in utilitarianism. All men seek "income, prestige, and power"; these are the goods that yield utility for the individual.[35] These "private ends" or "selfish motives" are a legitimate basis for rational action in a democracy.[36] As in private life, so in public life—individuals seek government office in order to obtain income, prestige, and power. Political parties are teams of men competing for votes in order to gain power; "political parties in a democracy formulate policy strictly as a means of gaining votes."[37] The electors vote according to the change in their utility incomes which can be expected from government activity; the person views elections as a means for selecting the set of policies most beneficial to him.[38]

Ideally, sovereignty is shared equally by all the electors, now considered to include all adult men and women.[39] The preference of each person is to be given "equal weight" in "fair legislatures."[40] If all actors possess perfect knowledge about the alternative policies, then no one is subject to the influence of another and there is perfect equality of political power. But two kinds of ignorance exist: the government and parties do not fully know the voters' preferences, and the voters do not fully know the parties' intentions and activities.[41] Representatives are therefore needed as communications links between the voters and the governors or "central planning board." Representatives are "agents scattered throughout the electorate."[42] Although they are "sen[t] out" by the government, they are actually agents of the people since their role is "to sound out the electorate and discover their desires."[43] This amounts to being a delegate of the people's desires and hence representation results in a "decentralization of power" from the central planning board.[44] At the moment of the election, the representatives mirror the "political taste preferences" of the voters.[45] If the representatives do not stay in synchrony with the distribution of voters' preferences, then the voters, acting rationally, will replace them at the next election.

In this model of representation, power is individual influence or control over another person's actions. It is Dahl's definition of power as "the ability of A to get B to do what B [might] not otherwise do."[46] The voters (A) have the ability to get the representative (B) to do what they want in public decision-making; if the representative acts against the people's wishes, they remove him. Notwithstanding the insignificance of individual votes in a mass democracy, which Downs discusses in relation to the costs and benefits of becoming a well-informed voter, the whole model is still predicated on the significance and power of an individual's independent preference schedule. The individual is supposed to vote against the representative if he or his party does not follow the individual's private will.

Overall, this model of representation has negative consequences for citizen interaction. Each individual private will deals directly, and vertically so to speak, with the representative. It is neither necessary nor desirable for people to speak mutually, or horizontally, with each other. The power relation is a one-way line of command from voter to representative, in order to serve the end of individual self-interest. Benevolence must be "enlarged" and "enlightened," rather than "confined" and "partial," to accord with the dictates of utility for the aggregate whole.[47] Insofar as citizens are motivated by goodwill or sympathy, it cannot be for specific political allies but must be on behalf of the same object as that of the rational calculus—the whole conceived as a sum. And insofar as there are political parties, they are not objects of social affection but solely instruments to effect the individual's self-interested will.

In addition, what implications does this model have for political districting and the decision rules by which representatives are elected? It depends on what kinds of government policies are believed to be of benefit to the individual. Using the distinction between policy, service, and allocative responsiveness, we might say the following: if the individual's utilities are in terms of policy preferences, there is little need for districts; if in terms of service responsiveness, there should be single-member districts; and allocative benefits seem to suggest either geographic or functional districts.

Policy responsiveness could be achieved by one big national district from which all the representatives were elected (either individually or on party platforms that would assemble specific policy proposals into general programs and ideology), with the number of seats being distributed proportionately according to the percent of national votes received. Proportional representation would ensure that each representative was more closely tied to his particular issue-oriented public, since each representative would have an almost unanimous constituency. Miller and Stokes's study of constituency influence in Congress showed that in single-member districts, congruence between the policy preferences of voters and the preferences and roll-call votes of their representative could be found most clearly in only one of three issue domains (civil rights over social welfare and foreign involvement).[48] Recent studies have shown that "most citizens do not have clear policy demands or well thought-out positions on public issues and that relatively few communicate with their representatives or take any interest in the policy-making process."[49] And if it is the case, then, that clear minority positions on issues get submerged in single-member plurality or majority districts, and, furthermore, that most individuals do not count policy preferences as part of their utility functions, then it follows that, to be responsive to the policy wishes of those who do have them, it would be best to aggregate their preferences so they could be heard rather than submerged in the mass.

Service responsiveness, on the other hand, would seem to require single-member districts. This is due to the particularistic nature of these benefits, the need for which arises in both expected and unexpected ways. Individuals may require "case work" service in dealing with a bureaucracy; groups may want lobbying help in influencing a legislature. Jewell found that state representatives from single-member districts received substantially more requests for service than did those from multimember districts. "The reason for this is the lower level of direct contact between constituents and legislators" in multimember districts.[50]

Allocative responsiveness, the winning of collective benefits for a constituency, would seem to require districting. But it is an open question whether these districts be along geographic or functional lines. Collective benefits such as jobs and transportation might be allocated to class or status groupings rather than geographic areas. Bentham had assumed geographic constituencies; Downs explicitly left it open, that representation could be "geographical or by social groups, depending upon the way society is divided into homogeneous parts."[51]

In the delegate version of transmission belt theory, then, the only reason to have single-member geographic districts is to further the service responsiveness of the representative. Allocative and policy responsiveness might best be achieved in other ways. Local districting, in this model of humans as hedonistic want-satisfiers, serves only the most particularistic ends.

In any case, whatever the nature of the districting, if the representative is to be a delegate he must be subject to the wishes of his constituents. Formally this is accomplished by prescribing fairly short terms or making the representative subject to recall. Substantively, delegate theory seeks ways that the representative can be closely tied, by a large majority of the votes rather than by a mere plurality, to a homogeneous unit whose will he can reflect.

But, since this theory is predicated precisely on the diversity and conflictual nature of human wills (not to mention the structural ignorance built into the model), it is incoherent as a theory of representation unless it allows the representative a certain freedom to act to reconcile the diverse claims. Representatives cannot stay solely at the receiving end of the transmission belt; they must also reverse the belt's direction and become trustees.

Trustee Version of Transmission Belt Theory

In the trustee version of transmission belt theory, the representative is entrusted by others to act according to their interests in a way that is also good for the whole. We will examine how this theory conceives of interests, how the interests are aggregated, and what kind of power is entrusted to the representative.

The trustee version makes more explicit that certain objective interests are the necessary preconditions to a person's being able to realize his subjective interests. James Mill's utilitarianism and V. I. Lenin's Marxism make this explicit, and each author applies it to his theory of political representation.[52]

In Mill, interests are still conceived to be ultimately individual and subjective, as in the delegate version. What a person conceives to be in his own self-interest *is* in his own interest. The individual is, once again, a being motivated by the desire for pleasure and the avoidance of pain. Mill then goes further in the Downsian direction than did Bentham: these desires are infinite, and therefore so are the desires for the means to attain them. The two main means are wealth and power.[53] Behind these desires are the permanent interests of people in modern society, an interest in having security of the rewards of labor, or what we call property. Labor is essential to each person in a society that cannot legitimately enslave any other (slavery being illegitimate, Mill thinks, because it causes extreme unhappiness). Labor is a precondition to material goods, which are "the means of subsistence as well as the means of the greatest part of our pleasures."[54] Security of the results of our labor is essential to society. Government exists "to protect the security of all."[55]

This state is sovereign, and its basis lies in an electorate that is not necessarily equal to all the adults; all those "whose interests are indisputably included in those of other individuals" may be excluded from the suffrage.[56] This electoral body is sovereign for it is "the community itself" and stands for the interests of the community at large.[57] The electors then choose representatives who are trustees in that they must be granted "considerable power" within the government. They need considerable power because they have a lot to do: they need to check the executive part of government, which is assumed to need checking because of all men's insatiable drive to increase their own power.[58] Representatives must also be given considerable leeway in deliberation, trusted to be "competent to the making of laws."[59] The representatives are given leeway for independence of judgment. The mechanism that ensures that their interests will stay identical with the community at large is to give the electorate the ultimate and frequent power to remove them.[60] Representatives are to have limited terms.

For Lenin, interests are not ultimately subjective, either before or after the revolution. The individuals who are to be represented in a socialist state are members of a social class, the proletariat, whose objective interests are to publicly own and control the means of production. This overall political control is to be exercised by a single political party, the Communist Party, which directs society. Yet workers at specific places of work have different desires for higher wages in relation to conditions of work, and these wishes warrant representation and local struggle. Trade unions are therefore allowed to represent the workers in their direct economic activity.

These trade unions are not, however, autonomous; they are limited by the power of the party and the state. Arguing against the Menshevik notion that trade unions should keep their political independence, Lenin writes in 1918: "The trade unions are becoming and must become state organizations which have prime responsibility for the reorganization of all economic life on a socialist basis."[61] By reorganization of economic life he does not mean giving the unions the power to manage the economy,[62] for that power stays with the party and the state. Rather, the unions have the power to transmit the state's policies to the workers through their own elected representatives.

Industrial discipline and productivity are to be encouraged by union leaders. "[T]he principal method for ensuring discipline in industry is persuasion, though 'proletarian compulsion' is 'in no way' excluded; all trade union organs should be elected—but 'of course,' under the 'overall control of the party.'"[63] In 1921 and 1922, Lenin allows that unions may still engage in local strikes to protect workers against state abuses when the state is suffering from capitalistic and "bureaucratic distortions."[64] In strike situations, the union leaders are supposed to act to help resolve the conflict, since, as Schapiro points out, "the object of strikes was no longer the overthrow of class domination but the strengthening of an already established proletarian state."[65] It is the union's duty to resolve the dispute "'with the maximum advantage to the groups of workers represented by them.'"[66] The union leaders act as trustees for the workers.

The notion of power in this version of representation is broader than in the delegate version. There is still the idea of power as control or influence over another, observable in the electors' power of removal: for Mill, "[t]he moment when his constituents begin to suspect him [the representative], that moment they may turn him out."[67] For Lenin, too, the "absolute inviolability of the electoral principle in composing trade union organs" is affirmed.[68] There is also, however, a recognition of what Bachrach and Baratz call the "hidden face of power": the ability to set the agenda, define the issues, set the terms of the conflict.[69] Trusteeship involves a certain freedom to define the issues in new ways. In transmission belt trusteeship, the representative has the power to redefine zero-sum games into variable-sum games.

Independence of the representative could be allowed within a delegate version as well, but it attains more substantial dimensions in the trustee version. Downs had alluded to a second role of the representative—to persuade the voters his party should be reelected—yet saw this primarily as a matter of offering more persuasive "facts" to the electorate.[70] Representatives were also "specialists in discovering, transmitting, and analyzing popular opinion";[71] and presumably if they analyzed that voters' preference structures had radically shifted, they could take the independent initiative to form a new political party. But then, once elected and in seeking reelection, they would function again as delegates courting the people's wills. Bentham had mentioned the possibility of a situation in which the overall national aggregate interest differed from a local constituency's aggregate interest, and thought that in that case the representative should perform his duty to the nation by speaking to change his constituents' opinions while still voting for their view. But it seems that since "the national interest being nothing more than an aggregate of the several particular interests,"[72] this persuading the constituents amounts to little more than telling them that they lost, and not really changing their minds. Mill's theory of the interests of individuals in the security of their persons and property provides a substantive end for representatives to serve. Lenin's theory of the interests of the workers, noncommunist as well as communist, in higher standards of living at particular workplaces, provides a similar substantive end. Within the limits set by these goals, the representatives are then free to choose the means to attain them. These are limited notions of trusteeship, in contrast to the notion of collective trusteeship, say, in Burke, yet they are still real.

Once again, this model of representation discourages citizen interaction. The emphasis here is on leaders controlling their followers, the rank and file. This can be done either through the control of information, through agenda-setting, or through direct coercion. At the same time that Lenin's draft upholds the electoral principle, the party congress also passes a resolution urging "the party organs to undertake a 'renovation' of the leading trade union organs in order to provide them with a complement of suitable communists."[73] In a single-party system, party members are preferable as trustees because they have the correct ideology about that state as a whole.

In a nonrevolutionary context, the implications of the trustee version of transmission belt theory for political districting seem to be even more in the direction of at-large elections than those of the delegate version. The earlier conclusions on the implications of policy, service, and allocative responsiveness would seem to still hold. In general, if the trustee is granted the legitimate right to exercise some independent judgment in the legislature on behalf of three kinds of responsiveness, then he needs to be tied to a local geographic area only in the case of constituency service.

Two qualifications to this generalization are in order. The first concerns the effects of political party competition, in a dual or multiparty system, on representational role. Jewell cites several studies to conclude that: "There is some evidence that the nature of the district affects representational role, with trustees more likely to come from less competitive districts and from at-large rather than single-member districts." [74] A representative who came from a safe seat might feel more free to depart from the direct wishes of the constituents than a representative who came from a seat that was closely contested.[75] So that if it is the case that competitive parties are more likely to exist in at-large districts than in single-member districts, then at-large elections might not encourage the trustee role.[76]

A second consideration that might militate against at-large districts is the educative role of a trustee. Representatives elected at-large have more trouble communicating with their constituents, since access to local groups is harder and access to the media more expensive.[77] Even if trusteeship is taken purely as acting independently on behalf of the constituents, there is some requirement that representatives explain their votes to the constituents, and so communication is a problem. Presumably this could be done exclusively at election time. We have tried to show that transmission belt theory does not put a very great emphasis on educating the constituents; this role will be much greater in another model.

Critique

Transmission belt theory assumes that people are primarily individual want-satisfiers and that society and politics exist to promote those calculations and satisfactions. People's wishes are assumed to be an expression of their interests in situations where people have full knowledge. In the absence of adequate knowledge, a person's wishes may depart from his or her interests. Representatives, acting independently or in political parties conceived as teams, serve as communicators between the people and their government, aggregating their wishes into acceptable compromises and explaining the discrepancy where their wishes depart from their interests.

If the delegate and trustee are two aspects of the transmission belt model, why not then say that a full theory of the representative's role would combine the two aspects into the politico, and leave the matter at that? There are two lines of critique of the model, one internal to the theory, one external.

The internal criticism is that even on its own terms, transmission belt theory has too thin a theory of education. If wishes and interests that inevitably conflict have to be aggregated into acceptable compromises, then the representatives have to communicate to individuals about the choices that were made and persuade them of their legitimacy. Transmission belt theory tends to see political education mainly as a matter of external exhortation, in which the representative explains to the constituents their proper place in the whole, given their present interests. People's minds are rarely changed this way, not only because the model has no external standpoint from which to change them, but also because that is not primarily the way people learn. More thoroughgoing education requires either the arts of indirection, or, alternatively, direct association.[78]

These problems point to the external critique: that transmission belt theory ignores the other crucial aspect of politics—its transformative role.[79] From classical political theory there is the idea that persons might become citizens, having new public characters. In this model, the very wishes and interests of individuals are defined differently. A citizen is an individual who identifies part of his entire being with the political community; he is fundamentally connected to the others in a relation of membership. There is a qualitative distinction between public and private life, in which politics acquires a certain meaning and morality of its own. Private goals are not just redirected but transformed into a commitment to the public sphere itself, treasuring political loyalties and communal glory. Whereas transmission belt theory considers politics to be merely instrumental to purposes given in civil society, an alternative vision takes account of the autonomy of citizens and would conceive of representation in different terms.

THREE
Transmission Belt Theory in Practice

In the beginning there were unequal districts. American state and local political jurisdictions differed in geographical area and size of population, and representatives were selected in a variety of ways. Then came *Baker v. Carr* (1962) and *Reynolds v. Sims* (1964), the Supreme Court's landmark "one man, one vote" decisions, which agreed to consider and then mandated equal ratios of people to representatives between districts in state legislative elections. Soon, in *Avery v. Midland County* (1968), the principle of equal population between districts was extended to general units of local government—city, town, and county. Then, in *Whitcomb v. Chavis* (1971) and *White v. Regester* (1973), the Court considered challenges to the constitutionality of selection procedures within districts, particularly the merits of at-large or multimember as opposed to single-member systems. And then the cases moved below the state level into municipal government, culminating in the Court's decisions of *Mobile v. Bolden* and *Rome v. U.S.* (1980).

Constitutional litigation has been paralleled and intensified by the debates of practical politics. The civil rights movement and its aftermath have revived an older issue in American life—the relation of particular communities to the larger political whole. Ever since the Progressive triumph of good government reform at the turn of the century, most cities west of the Mississippi and many in the East abolished their single-member districts of government and replaced them with at-large elections to smaller councils or city commissions.[1] Yet in recent decades, the tendency is changing as diverse groups form coalitions to press for a return to ward-based districting. Litigation and referenda to this effect have been contested in over ninety-five southern cities (passing in fifty-eight) and in northern and western cities such as Boston and San Francisco.[2] Groups, neighborhoods, localities, and larger districts are asking for more explicit representation in the national polity.

Chapter Three

Before considering the question of representative democracy from the standpoint of the political theory of citizenship being developed here, it is useful to examine the Supreme Court cases themselves. The Court is important because it expresses our mainstream constitutional thought and as such may be expected to reveal some of the complexities of American liberalism set in the context of a federal republic. A political theory of representation might emerge from its decisions on which practices are constitutional. The Court is also significant as an institution of public education enunciating broad principles, such as prohibiting "separate but equal" and mandating "one person, one vote," which then become lodged in the public mind.

This fascinating series of voting rights cases shows the contemporary Court grappling with the concept of citizen equality as it bears on the structure of representative systems. We will find that the Court has pursued the value of numerical equality as an end above all others, without inquiring far enough into the relation of numbers and other factors to political freedom. In extending the Fourteenth Amendment's equal protection of the law clause to local citizens in the general exercise of the suffrage and the choosing of representatives, the Court developed standards to judge whether an individual or group suffers "vote-dilution." Whether or not this standard constitutes a full-fledged fundamental right to equality of representation will not concern us here, although the arguments have sometimes tended in that direction.[3] Along the way, the Court has asked, What does equality of voting rights mean, what does a nondiluted vote look like, and what does a responsive system of representation require? It has struggled with these issues, advancing and retreating as its membership and the times change. But even had this not occurred, the Court would be in a quandary. For we see here some problems of liberal political theory coming up against its own substantive preconditions, or even coming up against a hidden, if limited, communitarian goal.

Summary of Ten Cases on Apportionment, 1960–1980

Ten cases in two decades form the heart of the matter. A brief chronological summary follows to introduce the cases historically and to outline the issues as judicially defined.

The Court first found a local political districting unconstitutional in *Gomillion v. Lightfoot* (1960).[4] The city of Tuskegee, Alabama, had redrawn its boundaries in a way that excluded virtually all the black voters. Frankfurter, for the Court, basing the decision on the Fifteenth Amendment, found the redistricting a device that deprived citizens of the vote because of their race. The justices were unanimous, although Whittaker's concurrence wanted to use the Fourteenth Amendment instead.

The Court moved to the Fourteenth Amendment equal protection clause as a basis for future inquiry into state legislative districts in *Baker v. Carr* (1962),[5] which challenged a 1901 Tennessee apportionment of districts of unequal population size. Without passing on the merits, Brennan's decision stated that if the facts were to establish invidious discrimination (even reflecting no policy), then a justiciable question existed. Frankfurter, with Harlan, dissented, arguing that the matter was still a nonjusticiable "political question" and that there were many other valid bases of representation in America.

The next year the Court struck down the Georgia county-unit system in (Democratic) primary elections of statewide officials in *Gray v. Sanders* (1963).[6] Douglas stated that within the political unit from which a representative is chosen, all the votes have to count equally, and found that here rural votes and counties counted for more. He based "one voter, one vote" on the Equal Protection Clause, though also made passing reference to the Declaration of Independence, Lincoln's Gettysburg Address, and the Fifteenth, Seventeenth, and Nineteenth Amendments. Harlan dissented, citing Frankfurter's dissent in *Baker v. Carr* (Frankfurter had by now resigned) and arguing that the equality principle flew in the face of American history, including the electoral college and other rationally defensible state actions to balance rural as against urban power.

Reynolds v. Sims (1964)[7] was one of six concurrent cases, the progeny of *Baker v. Carr,* that found state apportionment schemes unconstitutional. Here both the existing as well as two proposed plans for both houses of the Alabama legislature were found to violate the Equal Protection Clause. Warren wrote that "legislators represent people, not trees or acres. Legislators are elected by voters, not farms or cities or economic interests," and this requires equality of population between districts. Harlan dissented that the Fourteenth Amendment did not apply to state legislative apportionments and listed ten other considerations which rationally might enter into districting.

Meanwhile, the issues raised in *Gomillion* and *Gray* about intradistrict rules were brewing. In Georgia again, the multimember district of Fulton County (includes Atlanta) was challenged as invidious discrimination against its voters, in comparison to voters in single-member districts in the state. In a summary judgment in *Fortson v. Dorsey* (1965),[8] Brennan wrote that the Equal Protection Clause did not necessarily require single-member districts. But he did suggest the situation in which the constitutionality of multimember districts would be suspect: if they "would operate to minimize or cancel out the voting strength of racial or political elements of the voting population."

This standard was elaborated with regard to racial or ethnic groups in two important cases in the early 1970s. In *Whitcomb v. Chavis* (1971)[9] the Court rejected a claim that Indiana's multimember districts for the state legislature discriminated invidiously within their borders against ghetto residents. Addressing the merits, White asked: Was the scheme conceived or operated as a purposeful device of racial discrimination? Did Negroes have less opportunity to participate in the political process? And did Negroes' interests differ from other voters'? The Court answered no on all three counts. Douglas, Brennan, and Marshall dissented from the left and Harlan dissented from the right.[10] Then, in *White v. Regester* (1973),[11] the Court answered yes to these questions, sustaining a challenge to multimember districts in two Texas counties. White upheld the district court's judgment based on "a blend of history and an intensely local appraisal," finding invidious discrimination against blacks in Dallas County and Mexican-Americans in Bexar County (includes San Antonio). The decision rested mainly on the second criterion of opportunity to participate: minorities' access to the political process, through voting, primaries, and party slating, had been severely limited. Reference was also made to the other criteria: there was discriminatory intent or effect, since the districts and decision-rules "as designed and operated" . . . "invidiously excluded"; and different interests, such as the need for dual languages, were not being represented by white legislators.[12]

Then came a challenge to the boundaries of single-member districts from a new minority group. In *United Jewish Organizations v. Carey* (1977),[13] the Court rejected a claim by Jewish Hasidim of Brooklyn, New York, that their voting rights under the Fourteenth and Fifteenth Amendments had been violated. A state assembly redistricting, to comply with the Voting Rights Act of 1965, had redrawn four districts to give blacks 65 percent of each district, and the Hasidim had lost their one safe seat. White held the redistricting allowable to effectuate the purposes of the act, which requires that any political unit seeking to change its form of government within areas defined as discriminatory [14] has to preclear the change for a judicial showing that it "does not have the purpose and will not have the effect of denying or abridging the right to vote on account of race or color." White stated that benign racial criteria were allowed in districting, as were political criteria. Brennan concurred, but wanted to base it solely on the Voting Rights Act, and otherwise wanted to distinguish between impermissible racial gerrymandering and permissible political gerrymandering. Stewart and Powell concurred, finding no "purposeful discrimination" against whites. Burger dissented, saying it went against *Gomillion*.

The last two decisions showed the Court at a standoff, resolved only by Congress's 1982 amendments to the Voting Rights Act. *Mobile v. Bolden* and *Rome v. U.S.*, handed down the same day in 1980,[15] each dealt with challenges to at-large elections in cities. In *Rome,* the Georgia city wanted to change its government from a nine-person council elected by wards by plurality vote, to a nine-person commission system elected in groups of three in each of three wards by majority vote, along with some annexations. Marshall affirmed that these changes would dilute and submerge the votes of Rome's minority black population, and that the district court for D.C. was justified in refusing to let the city bail out of the preclearance provisions of the Voting Rights Act. Marshall held that under the act, proof of discriminatory effect was enough to invalidate electoral changes. Powell dissented, opposing the preclearance requirement as it applied to whole political divisions and thus violating local sovereignty, and Rehnquist dissented, with Stewart, holding that the electoral changes were not discriminatory state action and the Court's interpretation of the act was overbroad.

In the companion case of *Mobile,* however, the dissenters held sway; Stewart, with Burger, Powell, and Rehnquist, refused to uphold lower court claims that an at-large commission system violated the Fourteenth and Fifteenth Amendments and the city should switch to a mayor-council form of government. Since this Alabama city was not changing its government but rather seeking to retain its 1911 form, the case did not fall under the Voting Rights Act. The Court was therefore able to apply its recent doctrine that proof of discriminatory intent, rather than effect only, was necessary. Blackmun concurred in the result; Stevens concurred in the judgment that asking Mobile to change its form of government was too much, but held that discriminatory effect should remain the operative test and had been found. Dissenting were White, Marshall, and Brennan. White thought intent had been shown; Brennan and Marshall each wrote that only effect need be found and, anyway, intent had been shown. These dissenters alleged, I think rightly, that the Court had retreated from "the totality of circumstances" approach of *White v. Regester.*[16]

The Court's Quandary: Pure Delegate Theory, Modified Delegate Theory, Trustee, and Virtual Representation

The Court finds itself in certain conceptual quandaries in these cases. When it is explicit about representative theory, it uses what we have called transmission belt theory, which sees representation as a matter of messages about action conveyed unilaterally between a mass of discrete individuals and an individual at the other end. In the delegate version of this theory, the representative is bound by mandates from the people; in the trustee version, the representative is granted independence to act and responsibility to report. In both versions, it is a matter of telling the other end of the conveyer belt what to do.

The requirements of pure delegate theory in the transmission belt model are not met by single-member districts. Potter Stewart, a centrist on the Court, recognized this. In his dissent to *Lucas v. Colorado General Assembly,* a companion case to *Reynolds v. Sims,* Stewart wrote, "and if the goal is solely that of equally 'weighted' votes, I do not understand why the Court's constitutional rule does not require the abolition of districts and the holding of all elections at large."[17] He noted that to achieve its goal, such a system would have to use a decision-rule other than the majority or plurality system—proportional representation—yet the fact that PR is not on the American political agenda shows, he says, that Americans still believe in other goals for representation as well. In one of his last decisions, in *Mobile v. Bolden,* Stewart observed that at-large elections were "universally heralded not many years ago as a praiseworthy and progressive reform of corrupt municipal government"[18] and certain "features of that electoral system, such as the majority vote requirement, tend naturally to disadvantage any voting minority."[19] But he explicitly rejects PR: "whatever appeal it may have as political theory . . . The Equal Protection Clause of the Fourteenth Amendment does not require proportional representation as an imperative of political organization."[20]

The Court has veered towards this extreme of at-large multimember districts with proportional representation, yet repeatedly retreats from it as well. It is a nondistrict, as it were, alternative to the American norm of single-member plurality or majority districts; in at-large there is one big district, and with PR the constituency is constantly changing, defined not by geography but by voter preference. Indeed, Rogowski takes the theory to its logical conclusion by arguing that only at-large elections with PR will meet the strong version of "one person, one vote" coupled with the strictures against group "vote-dilution."[21] For if all votes are to count equally and representation is to reflect this, then elections cannot be by winner-take-all rules and people cannot be placed in separate districts where the preference orderings of the populations are different. For then, certain positions count for more in certain districts, and minority positions are consistently forgotten.

In pure transmission belt delegate theory, each individual must have equal influence on the representative, equal power to tell him what to do. The effect of the individual on the representative is crucial. What does it mean for votes to count equally? Formal game and voting theory has proposed a number of definitions.[22] First, there must be universal equal suffrage, equality of voting rights under the law. Second, since *Reynolds v. Sims*, there is what Still calls the requirement of "equal shares—in which each voter has the same 'share' in the election, defined as what that voter voted on divided by the number of voters who voted on it."[23] In addition, some more complicated measures try to assess individual influence. An "anonymity" criterion requires "that the effect of people's votes be independent of the positions they occupy in the electoral structure."[24] And an "equal probabilities [criterion asks that] each voter has the same statistical probability of casting a vote which decides the election."[25] Methods to measure these probabilities were developed by Shapley and Shubik, and Banzhaf, and the Court took judicial notice of the Banzhaf index in *Whitcomb v. Chavis*,[26] although ultimately refused to use the results as too abstractly "theoretical."

Were the results of the test too theoretical, or was the theory wrong? The Court showed an intuition that the logical extreme of its doctrine of individual voting power is wrong by turning to an alternative. In both *Whitcomb v. Chavis* and its successor, *White v. Regester*, Byron White enumerated a set of three questions about minority group members and their relation to the governmental structure, to the political process, and to nonminority interests. Then, based on "a blend of history and an intensely local appraisal,"[27] the Court found different answers in different situations. But this concretely empirical appraisal also rests embedded in a theory, or set of theories. Yet in trying to articulate this doctrine in more general terms—of "no group vote-dilution"—the Court has gotten into some contradictions.

We might consider the principle of "no group vote-dilution" to be a modified version of delegate theory, in which the question is still one of influencing the representative, but now by a group rather than by an individual. "No group vote-dilution" would then require that each group have a political influence commensurate with its numbers in the population (in the relevant area), and also imply that even if a group garners less than a plurality of votes, it should still have representation reflecting its numbers. This would protect against the existence of forgotten or insulated minorities and allow for the aggregation of minority votes between districts (if districts exist).

When the Court confronts the undesirability of having a delegate version of proportional representation for groups, it shifts the representative's initiative to the other end of the transmission belt, to the trustee. Here, the representative is deemed to speak and act for the constituents, on their behalf, by dint of an understanding he or she has of their desires and interests. In Edmund Burke's theory of representation, trustees are a natural aristocracy who act for the national interest;[28] in liberal transmission belt theory, trustees act either for the national or the local interest.

Trustee representation can then easily slide into virtual representation, which contradicts transmission belt theory. The legislator acts "in virtue of" the interests and sentiments of "any description of people" without necessarily being chosen by them[29] (although Burke did assume that virtual representatives would come from local districts in England, this being prudentially necessary to give the representative some stability via a "substratum in the actual").[30] The virtual representative acts on behalf of people in whose name he speaks, such as farmers or academics, always conceived as groups in a national whole. While he may be closely tied in substance to the common interests and sympathies of a group, he is less closely tied to these constituents in terms of the formal exchange of power and influence. Virtual representation is thus a non-transmission belt version of trustee representation. There is no need for "one person, one vote," for the virtual representative can know the interests of the many simply by knowing the interests of the few. This in itself is a respectable theory of representation but it is not consistent with other aspects of Court doctrine.

So in these cases we see the justices experimenting with an idea of group representation, or at least compensatory group representation, somewhere in a hazy area between political proportional representation and functional representation, with a dash of virtual representation thrown in as well. We see a development away from individual delegation to group delegation, then to individual and group trusteeship, and finally to the contradictory result of virtual representation.

The general doctrine as first set forth by William Brennan in *Fortson v. Dorsey* was that it would be unconstitutional for a particular districting to "operate to minimize or cancel out the voting strength of racial or political elements of the voting population."[31] The combination of "racial and political" in the same phase is rather extraordinary, since one is based on ascriptive and the other on acquired characteristics, so presumably each has a different political status; even if both had valid claims to be represented, the nature of those claims would be rather different. Brennan worries about this: while at first, in his concurrence in *White v. Regester*, he is pleased to see his dictum being implemented,[32] by the time of *UJO v. Carey* Brennan is at pains to distinguish political gerrymanders, which are constitutional, from ethnic ones, and to distinguish benign racial and ethnic gerrymanders from discriminatory and therefore unconstitutional ones.[33]

The confusion is not limited to Brennan; Thurgood Marshall relies upon the doctrine, citing a line of four cases that used it, two for racial groups, two for political ones.[34] In the dissent to *Mobile v. Bolden,* Marshall states which minority groups deserve compensatory proportional representation: "only [those] . . . whose electoral discreteness and insularity allow dominant political factions to ignore them"[35] and who have suffered discrimination in the rest of society. And later, "a discrete political minority that is effectively locked out of government decision-making processes."[36] Here again, minority in the sense of race is conflated with ethnicity as well as with political minority, although Marshall does write that a political in contrast to a racial group will bear a "rather substantial burden of showing it is sufficiently discrete to suffer vote dilution."[37] This disclaimer aside, it is hard to see how Marshall's criterion could be applied without upholding the Hasids' claim, at least to community recognition if not to political representation, which they raised in the lower court cases of *UJO v. Carey.*[38]

Political and racial minorities are conflated because the Court ignores the distinctive role of political parties. It makes little distinction between minority parties and minority interests and hence between political PR and PR of societal groupings, whether they be racial, ethnic, or economic. In Europe, PR generally means a system in which majority and minority (or a range of plurality) political parties, and not interest groups, are given legislative seats in proportion to their percentages of the popular vote.[39] Whereas in America, PR seems to connote functional representation of any and all social interests. The American Court is thus wary that a holding "limited to guaranteeing one racial group representation, is not easily contained." White expressed this fear in *Whitcomb v. Chavis* and was quoted again by Stewart in *Mobile v. Bolden*.[40]

Representation of groups in the context of political parties leads to trusteeship; representation of groups without parties leads to nontransmission belt virtual representation. In Europe today where group representation is used without parties—from estates in the Irish upper house to functional interests in German co-determination—one person, one vote in either its delegate or trustee version is left far behind. It is replaced by virtual representation in which a corporate interest, such as agriculture, labor, or management, is considered to be represented by having at least one voice, because then its argument is heard in the deliberative assembly and, beyond that, representation is not necessarily in proportion to numbers.

We can see traces of this view in the Supreme Court's decisions, but it has been overshadowed in the emphasis on numerical equality. John Marshall Harlan was the last justice to vigorously defend it. His dissent to *Reynolds v. Sims* bespoke a trustee view of representation, in which the representative acts on behalf of the shared interests of the electors rather than as the delegate of their aggregated preferences. "People are not ciphers, and legislators can represent electors only by speaking for their interests—economic, social and political—many of which do reflect the place where electors live."[41] His dissent to *Gray v. Sanders* advocated virtual representation, stating as he had in his dissent to *Baker v. Carr* that it might be rational for a state to overrepresent rural as opposed to urban voters if it wanted to protect against the numerically stronger "city point of view."[42]

Yet even without the conservative Harlan, a contemporary version of virtual representation finds its way into *UJO v. Carey*. In rejecting the claim that the Hasidim are losing their representative power in the new black majority districts, White writes that "the white voter . . . in [such] a district . . . will be represented, to the extent that voting continues to follow racial lines, by legislators elected from majority white districts."[43] Brennan questions this "vicarious benefit argument" in his concurrence,[44] although soon repeats it himself: " . . . to the extent that white and non-white interests and sentiments are polarized in Brooklyn, petitioners are indirectly 'protected' by the remaining white . . . districts."[45]

Rogowski has dubbed this "virtual representation by race" and offered a few sarcasms on what Burke would have thought of it.[46] For Burke, oppressed groups such as Irish Catholics whose interests and sentiments have long been ignored may require more actual representation. Whether this allows the oppressor group to be virtually represented is debatable. In any case, race, as a category more ascriptive than religion, would be impermissible as a social basis for representation in Burkean theory as it is in liberal theory. Yet it is also true that race is the precise reason for the genesis of these cases. Be this as it may, the terms the Court uses to address this problem have broader implications for representative theory. In general, it seems that while pure and modified delegate theories are reconcilable with trustee theory, they both are incompatible with virtual representation.

Alternatives: Political Membership and Association as Goals of Representative Districting

So far, the fair representation of minority groups seemed to require either the proportional representation of their delegating power, or, alternatively, the virtual representation of their interests and sentiments. Multimember districts with PR might best serve the first goal, and districts of unequal size might best serve the second. There is, of course, another alternative—the Anglo-American practice of single-member districts with plurality winners. This, rather than PR, is what the plaintiffs in these cases have been seeking, with the result sanctioned in *White v. Regester,* and in *Rome v. U.S.* via the Voting Rights Act. Yet the Court seems to have difficulty discussing and defending this arrangement, widespread though it is. Partly this is due to the fact that the Court is not supposed to legislate local political laws, and even its activists share the reluctance to encroach on state and municipal prerogatives more than is constitutionally necessary and politically feasible. But partly it is due, I think, to the difficulty of justifying the existence of particular districts in terms of the Court's own theory. Note that we are not yet talking about how to draw the districts, but the prior question of whether to draw and respect them at all.

Political boundaries retained a somewhat privileged status after the one person, one vote decisions. Even Earl Warren, in *Reynolds,* allowed that political subdivisions were still "a factor more substantial" than others being overturned that day, although such divisions "still [could] not override the equal population principle."[47] Brennan as well, in *Fortson v. Dorsey,* allowed that "a state might legitimately desire to maintain the integrity of various subdivisions such as counties."[48] Redenius summarized that, "As of 1982, this [state policy of observing political subdivision boundaries] is the only 'rational state policy' for deviation from substantial population equality that has been accepted by the high Court."[49] These opinions for the Court, however, do not elaborate on why internal boundaries are justified, and hence do not provide any reasons for drawing geographic districts within a partially autonomous entity like a state or city. To do so the Court would have to venture outside the transmission belt model to another theory, in which the relation of representative to represented was conceived differently and encompassed in a context of constituency and citizenship. It would involve explicating certain substantive aspects of political life, such as membership, as well as attending to the shared goal of a system of political representation, citizenship itself.

For forays in these directions one has to look primarily at the dissents, which diverge considerably. Most, from Harlan to Marshall, with Stewart and Tom Clark at the dead center, rely mainly on economic corporatism, or an uncertain mix of social pluralism and individual access, without the mediating role of political organizations and institutions. Only Felix Frankfurter and Byron White offer genuinely political defenses of local districting.

Harlan, in his dissent to *Whitcomb v. Chavis,* writes, "The scheme of the Constitution is not one of majoritarian democracy but of federal republics, with equality of representation a value subordinate to many others."[50] These federal republics are comprised of economic interests as much as political ones. Although he tips his hat to "history" once, Harlan relies in the early cases mainly on "economic or other sorts of group interests," "occupation," and other demographic factors as bases for representation. We have seen this in his defense of balancing rural with urban power in dissents to *Gray v. Sanders* and *Reynolds.* These criteria imply a static economic corporatism: there was and is a balance of socioeconomic forces in the good society, and it is the job of political representation to maintain that balance.[51] Harlan takes account of other criteria in a list in *Reynolds* that includes "availability of access of citizens to their representatives" and "the preference of a majority of voters in the state,"[52] but does not accord them as much weight.

Stewart and Clark's dissent to two companion cases to *Reynolds* rests more clearly on a modern social pluralism in which the individual disappears. They see "representative government as a process of accommodating group interests" and want democratic institutions to "accommodate . . . interests and aspirations of diverse groups of people, without subjecting any group or class to absolute domination by a geographically concentrated or highly organized majority."[53] The Equal Protection Clause only requires first, that a districting plan "be a rational one," and second, that it "not . . . permit the systematic frustration of the will of a majority of the electorate."[54]

In contrast, Marshall's main concern is that political life not consistently frustrate a minority. His dissent in *Mobile* cites recent literature on the discriminatory effect of multimember districts[55] and builds a case for compensatory group rights within single-member districts. Stewart accuses Marshall of making an unwarranted leap from individual rights to group rights via some "gauzy sociological considerations."[56] Surely the particular history of black slavery and its aftermath is more palpable than that, as Congress has recognized. Yet, as we have seen, Marshall's theoretical attempt raises some problems.

Frankfurter and White speak to the experience of political rather than social groups. These two justices are significant for tapping into the more communitarian roots of the American constitutional tradition, while retaining the value of individuality. They suggest substantive goals for a system of representation from two different aspects: for Frankfurter, the value of political membership; for White, of more active political participation.

In his dissent to *Baker v. Carr,* Frankfurter defended "local geographic division" as an alternative to equal population.[57] In what he calls practical considerations in addition to the general theoretical one, he mentions "cohesions or divergencies among particular local groups," "the practical effects of political institutions" like the lobby and city machine, "respect for proven incumbents," and "ancient traditions and ties of settled usage."[58] Each of these could be seen as additional theoretical reasons for having districts. Each concerns political relations within the locality—coalitions between groups, membership in political organizations, attitudes towards the representative's character and service, and habits acquired through a shared history. The language is conservative communitarian.

White's decisions (dissent in *Mobile v. Bolden,* and earlier court opinions in *Whitcomb v. Chavis* and *White v. Regester*) are the only ones since Frankfurter to focus continually on the political relations of individual citizens with each other, rather than on the social relations of individuals, relation of individuals to the state, or relation of social groups to each other. White fashions a doctrine of equal "opportunity to participate in the political process"[59] and sustains it. The principle can be phrased in terms of groups but always keeps a focus on individuals: access of members of minority groups to the political process.[60] Not every member of a minority group must participate, but any member who wishes must be able to do so freely.

White is a classical liberal in placing a high value on individual liberty and its exercise, though he is also willing to limit that in the interests of national security or public order, being much less disposed than Douglas, Brennan, or Marshall to honor First Amendment claims. He understands the citizen's right to political liberty to imply a necessity for formal political equality in all aspects of voting; hence, he supported equal shares in representation as Frankfurter did not. For he is also a welfare state liberal in believing that, given conditions of social inequality in civil society, some equalization of opportunity to social and political resources is necessary; specifically in politics this means equal "access to the political system."[61] He puts a high, but again not absolute, value on political participation in representative government—"effective participation in political life, specifically in the election of representatives,"[62]—such activity seen as instrumental to goals given outside of political life, as well as an end in itself.

And in one respect he departs from liberalism, away from those such as Madison, Mill, and the Progressives, who are fearful of political faction. White is the one justice to link these cases to a contemporary failure of political parties to fulfill their role as mediating institutions between the individual and the state. In *Whitcomb v. Chavis* he spoke of the possibility of "political parties . . . as devices to settle policy differences between contending interests . . . [of] minorities, political, racial, or economic."[63] And it is precisely this factor of intra-party democracy that he uses in *White v. Regester* and his dissent to *Mobile* to argue that a challenge to at-large should be sustained and a return to single-member districts mandated.[64]

Within the general criterion of equal opportunity to participate in the political process, White focuses on the practical political institutions that act as intermediaries in politics—representatives and political parties. He does not view the intermediation solely in a vertical transmission belt way but horizontally and communally as well. White values the political relations among constituents, the relations of participation and power among themselves as they also choose who will represent them. In contrast to William Rehnquist, for example, who dissents in *Rome* that the only discrimination occurring there is private rather than governmental,[65] White has a much broader and deeper view of what constitutes the political sphere, without collapsing it into mere social life.[66] "Absence of official obstacles to registration, voting and running for office heretofore has never been deemed to insulate an electoral system from attack under the Fourteenth and Fifteenth Amendments," he argues in his dissent to *Mobile*.[67] In finding that Mobile's at-large system is "denying blacks equal access to the slating or candidate selection process,"[68] he stresses criteria of political association that show "the local political processes are not equally open" to all citizens and, specifically, to blacks acting *as* citizens.[69] White thus moves beyond the sheer individualism of liberalism without embracing the groupism of neo-corporatism, recognizing that people come from social groups and enter into political groups, yet as modern individuals.

Individual Influence versus Communitarian Power

David Mayhew has written that the Court in the reapportionment cases knew "one big thing"—citizen equality—but that there were also three other things to know—compactness, competition, and community.[70] These categories point towards another more political theory of representation.

Compactness involves the geographical shape and density of the district, that it be generally round or square and possess a population center. Over the years there have been some state laws and bills before the House of Representatives that districts be "compact and contiguous" rather than terribly odd-shaped. But compactness does not necessarily have much to do with natural, social, or political community; geographic simplicity is not crucial.

More seriously neglected are the two factors of competition and community. Party competition is important to ensure effective linkage between citizens and government. Representatives must be able to not only "represent by reflection," "standing for" and "acting for" the public in the inter-election period, but also "represent by authorization," "being elected" and "acting for" the public through the election itself and the "accountability" this engenders.[71] Representation by reflection, performed by individual assembly members in the absence of political parties, is a premodern and rather weak form of representative linkage; whereas representation by authorization is stronger, performed by governments composed of political parties that run on platforms and receive the freedom to act decisively in certain specifiable directions. Crucial to this strong form of linkage is "national net partisan swings— the instruments of authorization," for they empower the representatives of a new party and, for party swing to occur, there must be some marginal seats. Hence the necessity of party competition in some districts, although there is also an equally legitimate need for safe seats as well.[72]

Third, there is the factor of community, understood historically as in the example of the Democratic party in Brooklyn granting a congressional district to Bedford-Stuyvesant because of a political pledge made to the area, presumably in return for certain loyalties received. Community may, but does not necessarily, mean compactness; "Bed-Stuy" would still be itself even were it shaped like a "dragon" or a "centipede." Too, community may, but need not necessarily, mean "demographic homogeneity," sameness of social situation. Community is a distinct value which often conflicts with the other three criteria; political districting should seek a mix.[73]

A district or constituency, then, does not depend on geographic or numerical simplicity. It consists rather in the "internal local ties," institutional and informal, which have developed over time in an area, the richness of relations between similar and diverse people.[74] Representatives must be tied to the people in significant and effective ways, for individual messages are only hypothetically or occasionally effective. In constituencies of thousands of people, there must be collective forms of action and interpretation. The two most important collective institutions in representation are party and constituency. These might be seen as necessary constraints on individual autonomy,[75] but we will be arguing that they are necessary preconditions to autonomy and to citizenship.

Some of the Court's decisions on apportionment and districting have continued the tendency to see citizen equality exclusively in terms of "a mechanical counting of discrete noses."[76] In other decisions the Court has stepped back from the abyss (or the ideal, if you want "instant direct democracy," a TV ballot box in every home).[77] In *Gaffney v. Cummings* (1973), for example, the Court refused to overturn a Connecticut bipartisan political gerrymander as long as it only slightly departed from the equal population standard. White defended political districting: "the very essence of districting is to produce a different—a more 'politically fair'—result than would be reached with elections at large in which the winning party would take 100% of the legislative seats."[78] Districting is supposed to have political consequences, promoting interpersonal linkages and loyalties, giving different factions legislative seats. States and localities are free to arrange districting as they wish providing it generally meets the one person, one vote standard and does not violate the goal of "fair and effective representation."[79] But fair representation may be different from equal representation, and so Brennan, Douglas, and Marshall dissented: "Our paramount concern has remained an individual and personal right—the right to an equal vote."[80] For them, even the slightest departure from population equality violates an absolute political right.

When the Court has addressed other important factors in the situation of representative democracy, it has encountered problems. Even when it tries to specify forms of linkage it often does so in a vacuum, speaking a pure theory of the relation of the individual to the state, ignoring the role of party and constituency. Except for White, the other justices, unless they are consistent absolutists like the three above, often come back to measuring individual citizen influence. Thus Rehnquist, with Stewart, dissenting in *Rome*, quotes Harlan from a 1969 dissent: "It is not clear to me how a Court would go about deciding whether an at-large system is to be preferred to a district system. Under one system, Negroes have some influence in the election of all officers; under the other, minority groups have more influence in the selection of fewer officers."[81] If the criterion is solely individual influence on the election of an official, then indeed it might not be clear.

In those instances where the Court has been successful in suggesting how to decide, it leaves its accepted discourse. It seems to lack a language adequate to discuss the associational aspects of local political districting, and specifically the two related issues of political boundaries, or membership, and political action, or power. To see this once more, let us look at two Court opinions, one at the beginning and one at the end of the cycle.

In 1960, in *Gomillion v. Lightfoot,* the Court found that Negroes had been despoiled of "their theretofore enjoyed voting rights" by being districted out of Tuskegee. In a way, Charles Whittaker was right that the case should not have been decided on the basis of the Fifteenth Amendment, for the blacks still had the right to vote; it had rather been shifted to another political division. Since Frankfurter did not believe in using the Fourteenth Amendment for voting rights, he argued instead that Negro citizens had been discriminatorily deprived, as the petitioners claimed, of "the benefits of residence in Tuskegee, including, *inter alia,* the right to vote in municipal elections."[82] How can one treasure the benefits of living in Tuskegee, as opposed to its nearby suburb, without putting a special value on political membership? One cares about being a member of this place as opposed to that one because of having lived a particular history here, and not necessarily because its schools and roads are better, and not merely because of blood ties to the family, *volk,* or soil. In rejecting the volkische set of reasons and embracing the instrumental ones of good schools and services, liberalism has often thought it necessary to reject historical reasons of political membership. Frankfurter does not, but he is not the mainstream of the Court.

And if we look again at the 1980 case of *Mobile v. Bolden,* we see even Stewart straining against the limits of his own formulation. First he argues that Negro citizens have not had their voting rights abridged by an at-large city commission system; the Court does not find adequate proof of discriminatory violation of the Fourteenth or Fifteenth Amendment. Yet then in passing he writes, "It is of course true that the right of a person to vote on an equal basis with other voters draws much of its significance from the political associations that its exercise reflects."[83] He thus acknowledges what he elsewhere denies, that citizen equality has something to do with the political associations one joins, and that power might be, as Hannah Arendt suggested, "the human ability . . . to act in concert."[84]

For a fuller account of what political association might mean, and how it issues in membership and power, we need to turn to other theories.

FOUR

Sources of a Communitarian Theory of Citizenship

Transmission belt theory of representation has a dim view of the citizenry, for it views their role as virtually indistinguishable from that of insecure persons. Individual citizens who are concerned with self-preservation, pleasure, and power are law-abiding and public-regarding only so that the pursuit of liberty by each does not interfere with the liberty of all. Individuals use their representatives instrumentally; public activity is the seeking of individual influence over others in order to get what one already wants.

There are bad citizens and there are law-abiding citizens, but there are few good citizens. The good citizen is different from the ordinary one, according to McWilliams, because he or she identifies with the community and seeks to transform it according to some evaluative conception of the public good.[1] The good citizen may or may not be a political representative or public official; Martin Luther King, Jr., comes to mind. He appeals to what is best in the spirit of his fellow citizens and he transforms what they want. They discover new needs, for dignity and fellowship.[2]

The thin theory of citizenship tends to go with liberal theory in a mass society; the richer conception derives from the classical theory of city-states. The first sees citizenship primarily as the "possession of private rights against the state and against other citizens"; the second regards the citizen as a person "who shares the obligation to govern."[3] Classical citizenship required more intense interaction than liberal citizenship. To what extent can we achieve its qualities in a modern political community?

Chapter Four

Citizenship and the City

Citizenship was first an idea of the city. Classical western political theory arose out of city-states in ancient Greece, and treated citizenship as a status, a relationship, and an activity that could only occur in a certain setting.[4] That setting was bounded by size—larger than the household, smaller than an empire; from a hill one had to be able to take in the city with one view.[5] There was another more stringent requirement—that the city be a self-sufficient unity, containing within itself the possibilities for a varied life.[6] In his analysis of constitutional balancing, Aristotle assumed that a city would be the manifold of social interests and divisions existing in society at the time.[7] Political life would then involve an ongoing contest between the claims (such as wealth, birth, number, merit) of different groups; it would also, if the earlier more heroic mode of Homer and Plato is retained, involve the service and demands of exceptional individuals. But that persons would make their claims in the spirit of citizenship, and not civil war, required two social preconditions: that the community be small enough so that one could come to know the political elite at first hand; and that the city be diverse enough to constitute a social totality, so that the decisions taken there would be considered important and the place deemed worthy to preserve.

Social preconditions alone, however, do not make a city. Citizenship is basically a political relationship, requiring a specific attitude and a specific role. Greek cultural education or *paideia* sought to instill in people a consciousness of being responsible to a polity. The attitude of citizenship included a disciplining of desire, redirecting its energy toward the *polis;* a cultivation of affection for one's fellows as citizens. In Plato's theory, members of each social stratum had to learn to train their private wants onto public objects: the lower classes, from mere carnal appetite onto willingness to adhere to the communal division of labor; the upper classes, from the private desire for wealth or fame onto the military and civic glory of the city. Whereas Plato's main institutionalization of these attitudes is a thoroughgoing system of education, Aristotle's constitutional theory captures the specifically political dimension of a citizen's role, "participation in ruling and being ruled."[8] The citizen receives both the honor and the burden of serving on public bodies: the deliberative assemblies, juries and law courts, and the military. The particular allocation of these privileges and burdens, and the principle by which groups and individuals within the city settle it, concern the ongoing matter of justice. But once people have agreed to debate that question as citizens, justice's prior political condition has been met: the city exists.

City-states had distinctive social relations which can characterize citizenship under ancient and modern conditions, even as aspects of city life change. We can discover these characteristic relations by looking at interpretations of citizenship in city-states of ancient Greece, medieval northern Europe, and early Renaissance Italy. Modern interpretations provide a prism through which to view the older practices, social theory generating new analytical categories. The political experience of the city, understood through these categories, reveals the conditions and essential elements of citizenship.

Participation and Representation

Citizenship in ancient Greece often involved direct participation in politics. If each citizen "shares the obligation to govern," then perhaps all have to actually serve in government office, if not in the executive and administration, then certainly in its legislature. But perhaps not; perhaps there are other ways to engage in public debate and take risks for the polity.

Citizens were persons acting in a public capacity on behalf of the *polis*. Relations between citizens were characterized by political equality or *isonomia*. Euben argues that this meant not only equality before the law but also equality of freedom and power to make the law.[9] Citizens had a "right to an equal say in determining the structure and activities of a common life"; they achieved "individual autonomy through collective action."[10] He claims that this required "the widest participation in the legislative, administrative, and judicial functions of the polis."[11] Political participation was necessary to teach citizens a "sense of responsibility and balance for justice to be achieved" and to cultivate "enthusiasm of a free person to accomplish something for himself"; it "enabled the differences and diversities to appear to others and thereby become recognized, harmonized, and sustained."[12] Political participation was a time-consuming and demanding activity. Political equality was partly the result of this work as well as its precondition.

What kind of representative institutions are entailed in this vision? Some have argued that no representation is entailed at all. They see classical theory as mandating universal active participation in the legislature, if not in governance. Thus Arendt, for example, believes that in a modern republic the mass of people are not really citizens; only the representatives interacting in the legislature function as citizens.[13] I think that this is a misinterpretation of the practice and theory, perhaps for ancient times and certainly for modern times. The qualities that characterized the citizen and sustained the political community could be achieved in ways other than direct legislative participation, such as extraparliamentary politics, although still requiring definite communal political arrangements.

Even where direct participation was expected, it was a right and duty and not a requirement. Citizens were encouraged to attend the mass assembly but attendance was not mandatory, and citizens used procedures to select specific political and administrative officials. If all citizens could not attend simultaneously, then some spoke for the others. And in the case of certain civil and military offices, principles of rotation in office were developed.

While equality or *isonomia* came to figure prominently in public life, *eunomia,* or the "giving each person his rightful due and share according to custom" which sanctioned hierarchy and inequality, continued to prevail in personal behavior.[14] In extrapolating to modern conditions, we will have to ask what political unit provides the diversity that the city afforded, and what political institutions encourage the development of citizen equality while also allowing for *isonomia* in the social and private spheres of life. For these reasons, to meet the need for diversity and to provide time for the citizen as well as the person to seek equality in both spheres of life, a form of representation is necessary.

Legitimacy Relations in the City: Association

Two key political sociologists, Karl Marx and Max Weber, interpret the city-state in ways that are instructive for communitarian citizenship. Both theorists accept the modern condition of free individuality and the search for autonomy, the living according to laws one has accepted for oneself. They do not think it possible or desirable to return to *eunomia,* to a premodern consciousness that accepts unequal social conditions as given. Yet they also understand the weight of historical conditions in shaping persons and citizens; they are not unmindful of social and political experience in affecting structures and events. What is notable for our project is that when they write about the social relations of the city, they do not stress the direct participation of citizens in legislating. They focus on the participation of citizens in two other relations which they each deem crucial to constituting the city: for Marx, property relations, and for Weber, legitimacy relations.

We could consider their analyses of the city in the context of their general theories.[15] Yet the phenomenon of citizenship also raises some interesting problems for each theorist. I will show that Weber, in dealing with citizenship in his posthumously published monograph on *The City*,[16] pushes beyond his former typology of legitimacy, and suggests another understanding. And Marx, in dealing with citizenship in his posthumous *Grundrisse* notebooks,[17] strains against the limits of his concept of property and emerges with an even broader formulation. In analyzing what characterizes a city and its distinctive social relations, both theorists contribute to a modern theory of citizenship.

Weber writes that the city is "above all constituted, or at least interpreted, as a fraternal association" (E&S 1241). It is "actually a revolutionary usurpation of rights" (E&S 1250) whose essence is that it is a "usurpatory urban confraternization" (E&S 1259). The city is a distinct social formation which, while existing in the context of different historical systems, has a nature of its own. He establishes the "ideal-typical" characteristics of the city as such and then compares, for example, the ancient Greek polis and the Renaissance Italian city, and contrasts these with the medieval Germanic city.

Cities exist within larger social formations which, for Weber, are distinguished by their kinds of political legitimacy. He specifies three main bases of political authority—tradition, charisma, and rational-legal criteria—and elaborates a theory of the administrative arm—bureaucracy in its different forms—that accompanies each of them (E&S 212–301).[18] He develops a typology of society's structure that gives importance to status groups (E&S 926–40),[19] and distinguishes between three kinds of economies—the *oikos* or household, the market, and the planned economy (E&S 63–113). These kinds of economy and society and polity can exist in innumerable combinations one with another, although some fit more perfectly than others. Ultimately, the polity or, more specifically, the power struggle between a political leader and his administrative staff, is most influential in shaping other social phenomena (E&S 264).[20] Other factors are of importance insofar as they are used to advance the political power of an individual, status group, social class, political party, or state. Historical change is caused by the power struggle between these actors, and it is a struggle of which the people involved are not unaware.

The city, then, exists within these larger social formations, yet in a distinctive way: it is politically autonomous. While intricately connected with the larger economy and society, it forges its own political independence. The political condition of the city is labeled "nonlegitimate domination," which can be interpreted in two ways. The first meaning is explicit: in the city's origins, leadership groups contest the political legitimacy of the systems of rule that came before and seize power on new terms (E&S 1239, 1250, 1302). Thus, for example, in an early stage of city formation, urban aristocrats challenge rural nobles and, at a later stage, urban artisans exile urban magnates. New status formations, groups of *honoratiores* based on militarily and politically acquired characteristics, arise and challenge older formations. They usurp power and establish new regimes in which their monopoly on the legitimate use of violence is not fully secure.

The second meaning of nonlegitimate is not explicit but is suggested. It has to do with what the new types of legitimacy actually are. In the two examples mentioned above, we can fit each development into Weber's original typology of legitimacy: in the first, traditional authority is being challenged; in the second, group charisma is challenged. But what form of legitimacy replaces them? Here he moves onto new ground and never ventures to summarize it. The legitimacy of the city has some rational-legal elements which are indeed new, but they are not comprehensive. Too many particularistic elements remain. We might fit the city into a fourth category, a subtype he elsewhere suggests to account for the authority of modern mass democracy: "charisma inverted in an anti-authoritarian direction" (E&S 266–67). Yet in some ways, Weber is here pressing up against the limitations of that formulation, and emerging with another kind of legitimacy.

I would suggest that citizenship is the new form of legitimacy produced by the ideal-typical city. By ascribing a certain status to those who are empowered to share in political rule, the city names a new basis for the justice and stability of a government. It is a type of legitimacy that goes beyond the relation of the leader to his administrative staff, but it is not so broad as to encompass his relation to the masses. It concerns the political executive's relation to a political staff that is now broadly conceived to include the body of citizens entitled and encouraged to hold representative office, both civil (executive, legislative, judicial) and military. There is thus a type of legitimacy for the city as such—based on the granting of citizenship—regardless of whether particular regimes in the city define citizenship by oligarchic or democratic criteria. That there is one overall standard for the city is evident in Weber's discussion of those types of regimes—tyrannies and signories—that are illegitimate on the city's own terms. The city's own terms are those of respecting the rights and powers of a body of citizens, however that body is defined.

What constitutes the ideal-typical city, and how does it produce the new legitimacy of citizenship? In his monograph on *The City,* Weber derives five main characteristics from an historical survey of ancient and medieval, patrician and plebeian cities, which he then applies to the actual formation he considers to be the city at its height: the plebeian medieval urban commune. To be a city, it must have (1) a market, (2) a fortress, (3) its own law and its own administration of law, and (4) a related form of association. These four conditions lead the city to have (5) a degree of political and administrative autonomy (E&S 1226, 1322–33).

A city is, first, an economic market, a distinct center for the exchange of goods and services (E&S 1212–20, 1256, 1359). It must be a center for trade, whether between individual households, patrimonial households, economic enterprises, or political bodies. Since the introduction of money, this has meant that at times cities were inhabited primarily by debtors (peasants, the "agrarian burghers" of antiquity), at other times by creditors (the urban burghers of the Middles Ages) (E&S 1261, 1270).[21] The city must also have an urban economic policy (E&S 1328). It must have its own set of market rights, taxes, tariffs, and craft regulations, for example, to ensure the continuance of its market. While at times having the productive enterprises within its borders may make a city stronger, at other times this has not been the case. As long as the city is skillful and powerful enough to "exploit the economic opportunities" (E&S 1329) that lie outside its borders, their incorporation is not necessary. This need not always involve one-way exploitation by the city of rural interests (E&S 1331, 1333). What is required is that the city maintain itself as a commercial center.

The city is, second, a fortress, a defensible place which can maintain a degree of military autonomy (E&S 1220–23, 1323). It may also have a garrison and, if that is extensive enough (as at Sparta), it will not need the city walls (E&S 1221, 1359–60). Historically, cities have fortified themselves in different ways—from the urban castles of the nobility, to the self-equipment of troops via "peasant levies, knightly armies, and burgher militias" (E&S 1261–62, 1222–23). "[T]he oldest specifically civic burdens are guard and garrison service" (E&S 1221). Needless to say, this has special significance in a theory that defines the *sine qua non* of state political power to be "monopoly of the legitimate use of physical force."[22] The ways in which cities change to meet their military needs are crucial to their political complexion; each city at some point redefines the basic units of association away from kinship (ancient) or occupational groupings (medieval) to new territorial and/or military-administrative functional units, and thus paves the way for individuality as a legal status. The most intriguing example of this is ancient Greece, where the city constitution reassembles the family groupings into what it calls tribes in each deme, the new administrative district; yet, these tribes are really artificial creations of the city (E&S 1244–46, 1286, 1311). Military training for a civil militia has consequences, far beyond war, in politics and culture. It may foster the agonal spirit, from the contests in the gymnasium to the contests of dialectical speech (Athens), although it also may not (Sparta, Rome) (E&S 1367–68). But in all cases, military service keeps the citizens involved in "the political fate of the city," (E&S 1319) which concern fades when only burgher interests hold sway.

A city must also have its own law and its own judicial administration (E&S 1325–27). Whereas Asian cities had only fortresses and markets, the Occidental city also had a separate urban law and a separate legal status for its citizens (E&S 1227–29). Urban law specifies that property is alienable and that persons are free. But the condition that a city have its own body of law is more important than the content of the law. Thus in certain matters urban law may have more "irrational," and in others more "rational," elements than the law of the larger society (E&S 1254).[23] For example, English cities had premodern precedent-bound common law which proved more conducive to "capitalist stirrings" than did the more universalistic legal rules of Roman law elsewhere (E&S 976–77). Urban law covers matters relating to land, taxes, crimes, courtroom procedure, and, most significantly, the legal status of persons (E&S 1237–41, 1327–28). It can develop in a variety of ways: sometimes through the communal deliberation of its own assembly, and often through the reinterpretation, by its own judges, of law received from other sources. Even where a larger political entity keeps jurisdiction, for example, of capital offenses, it is essential that the city have its own lay judges, chosen from its midst, to administer and enforce the law (E&S 1325–26). Thus the political condition of the city requires at least some degree of autonomy.[24]

But what is most distinctive about the city is its form of association, the quality of the relations among its citizens. The city is "beyond all this also a sworn confraternity" (E&S 1248) in which the members bind themselves one to another in a collective body. Through a series of institutional practices, a diverse collection of people who had previously been strangers, immigrants to this new and alien place, now become known to each other. There is a ritual joining of people as symbolic brothers, implicated in the fate of others. The rituals include those of "*connubium,* commensality and solidarity against non-members" (E&S 1241). The cultic meals and ceremonies that reaffirm the association always have religious symbolism drawn from the dominant culture, but Weber wants to stress that at heart they are not religious but specifically secular and civic affirmations (E&S 1246–47). In fact the urban confraternity—whether expressed in the Greek *prytaneion,* the common city cultic meal, or the artisan religious unions of the Germanic *confraternitates,* or the sworn city unions of the Italian *coniurationes*—is posited precisely in distinction to the other ties of family, occupation, or religion (E&S 1228, 1242, 1257, 1334). Yet, in a complicated way, civic brotherhood does not completely supplant these pre-political ties, for it affirms them as its precondition and its contrast.

The result is a peculiar mixture of modern and premodern practices that make the essence of the city. In its fully developed form, the city treats persons as individuals with "religious and secular equality before the law" (E&S 1241). In ancient Greece, and at times in medieval Italy, there are gradations of rights among citizens, but their political equality under the law is still the dominant tendency, especially in distinction to noncitizens and foreigners (E&S 1310–11). The special law for the urban burgher sees him as an individual with "a subjective right to an objective law" (E&S 1249). Yet we do not find the characteristics of the individual facing modern bureaucracy. For these citizens are part of a collectivity which has a unique corporate status and has idiosyncratic rituals and communal relations, not necessarily fitting under universal rules (E&S 1228–29, 1240). It is a membership in this place, with this history, with these people, who have the potential for self-rule.

In sum, these four characteristics—market, fortress, autonomous law, and confraternity—make a city politically autonomous or at least partially so. The city exists in its economic as well as its "politico-administrative" concept; it exists as *Gemeinde*, a community (E&S 1220).

Property Relations in the City: Appropriation

Marx regards the city as an aspect of society, which is characterized by its mode of production.[25] There are ancient cities, feudal cities, and capitalist cities, each possessing the main characteristics of the predominant social formation; there is no city as such.

The city is a major element in the social division of labor. The social division between town and country arises soon after the division between handicraft (later industrial) and agricultural labor, and it exacerbates the division between mental and manual labor (GI 410, 443). Cities are not exclusively inhabited by craftsmen; in the ancient form, "Economically citizenship may be expressed more simply as a form in which the agriculturist lives in a city" (PC 79–80). In addition to these two socioeconomic groups, a third is crucial to urban life: commercial labor or the merchants (GI 446). As middlemen in an emerging or established money economy, they facilitate and profit from the exchange of products. The existence of cities shows that a society has moved from production for use to production for exchange, and that it has a surplus to spare.

Marx posits a permanent opposition between town and country, in which the dominant class in one arena will seek to extract the surplus from the other (GI 443). Whether town exploits countryside or vice versa varies, depending on the primary form of property-holding in that historical era and on whether the dominant class in each arena is in the ascendancy or decline. In the ancient city, for example, the rural landowners at first maintain their domination through new forms of rule over the city and its communal property in slaves; only later does the growing class of urban artisans begin to gain economic and political power.

The dominant class in a city seeks to extract surplus from subordinate classes within the city. This dynamic may also occur within classes, so that the upper fraction of a class will exploit a lower fraction. Thus in the medieval city, for example, the artisans of the upper guilds distinguish themselves from lower craft guilds, and they both cheerfully exclude the newly freed serfs from their membership, depriving them of social power and leaving them to be "the unorganized rabble" (GI 444; PC 117).

That cities are in an antagonistic relation to their external environment while also being internally divided can lead to some interesting transient alliances. Often upper strata will ally with lower strata to defeat the middle. Often, too, the lower strata will be used by powers external to the city—rural nobility and nationalizing princes—to defeat the urban burghers. While Weber is better at examining the many coalition possibilities here, Marx does note a few in passing. For instance, the peasants ally with certain national rulers to break the burghers' economic stranglehold, hoping to improve their own lot.

Marx argues that no just balance acceptable to the different classes can ever be struck. The city, like the larger society, is unjust and unstable. This is so both on normative and empirical grounds. First, the subordination of one class to another in economic, social, and political terms results in the lower class's exploitation, alienation, and oppression, all of which are unjust.[26] Second, people's recognition of this injustice leads them to challenge its stability. And third, even if one class's domination of another were accepted as just, it would change in response to changes in the forces of production, leading to new class formations, which would then require new justifying ideologies of domination. Thus, viewed from the perspective of his philosophy of history, the city is ever changing, necessarily undergoing periodic civil wars. Only in the classless society, after the revolution, would the unjust oppositions within the city, and between town and country, be overcome (GI 456–57).

Yet, there is another line of analysis in Marx that tends in a different direction and is particularly suggestive for our understanding of citizenship. On his own terms, it poses problems for his theory which I think he never resolves. For us, it provides openings. A turning point occurs, between *The German Ideology* (1845–46) and *Capital* (1867), in the *Grundrisse* (1857–58) passages on pre-capitalist forms of property and cities. As he struggles to define property more carefully and broadly, to encompass it in any historical era, he moves, I think, beyond his earlier definition and emerges with something quite different.

Influenced by Hegel, Marx was never content to identify a thing as an entity in itself, and so from very early on he defined property as a relation—between persons, and between persons and things. It was a social relation in which a person, as a member of a class, had the right to control other persons and things in order to use their productive resources. Property was a relation that manipulated the productive labor of others; even property in things was ultimately control of the labor of others, labor that was embodied. Essential to this definition of property, and distinguishing it from other definitions, was the stress on labor and its control as the determining activity. There is an active dimension to the relation: labor exerts its powers and in so doing transforms the world.

In 1857–58, Marx moves to an altered notion of property, in which labor is not always its prime or determining activity. He now defines property as "the relation of the working (producing) subject . . . to one's conditions of existence as one's own" (PC 95, and 81, 87–88, 89, 92). The relation is still established by the activity of a working or producing subject, but the definition of what constitutes work or production has broadened considerably. Furthermore, the prerequisites or conditions of one's existence may be organic (such as social organization) or inorganic (such as tools), and one's existence includes not only production but reproduction (of the family, the culture, the social system) as well (PC 69). This is a broad conceptualization which can cover relations as diverse as the ancient farmer's property in land and slaves, the ancient state's property in silver mines, the medieval artisan's property in tool and craft mysteries, and the modern industrial worker's property in his own labor-power.

But most significantly, it includes the ancient townsman's property in his city, in the community itself as a condition of his existence. Property is now defined as a process of appropriation, involving both an activity and an attitude, in which the attitude does not necessarily follow the activity but may precede it, and the activity need not depend exclusively on labor (PC 81, 69). In pre-capitalist cities, the attitude may be a belief in the origins of the city as divine, and the activity may be military service, fighting in war to preserve the city (PC 71). The relation of appropriation, then, can commence with a receptive attitude, which accepts the world as it is, assumed as given, although the property relation must still be affirmed through an activity that seeks to preserve or affect that world.[27]

Marx's discussion of city property leads again to the broader concept. Starting with his orthodox notion of property as depending primarily on laboring activity, we might say that cities in their fullest sense exist only where there is a coexistence of public and private property. In the two social formations where this is not the case, cities are barely mentioned—the Asiatic mode of production, characterized exclusively by public property, and at the other extreme, the bourgeois capitalist mode, where private property reigns supreme. But in the other two pre-capitalist social formations—ancient and medieval—there is a combination of public and private that makes cities more than "a mere multiplicity of separate houses" (PC 78).

The ancient city exists as a "being-together" [*Verein*] and the medieval city as a "coming-together" [*Vereinigung*] (G 483; PC 78). Both exist in definite distinction to, yet in relation with, the countryside. This contrasts with the "undifferentiated unity" of town and country in the oriental mode of production.[28] The ancient city is a "real unity," and the medieval city is a "true association" (PC 78, 80; GI 444); real and true because they bring diverse citizens together in the central aspects of their lives, materially as well as ideally.[29] The medieval city is an "association" because it unites them politically; the ancient city a "unity," which is more, because it is an economic as well as a political whole.

The ancient city defines the rural territory of its citizen landowners as part of itself, so that the rural land and houses as well as the urban houses and market are part of city districts (PC 71). As we have already noted, kinship groups originally join to form cities, and they later regroup for military purposes in the new administrative unit, the deme (PC 71–72, 76–77). While the demes use the language of family, the *phyle* or tribe, these are now political units, based on territory and function rather than solely on ancestral descent. The actual history aside, what results conceptually or structurally is a political community in which the city is believed to exist prior to its individual members, in which one has to be a citizen before one can own property, and in which communal property is deemed prior to private ownership (PC 73).

The medieval city, in contrast, does not include rural territory in its borders, and hence exists in a much more uneasy relation to the country. The Germanic city consists of rural householders who own private property in land, and who then choose to come together for certain communal purposes and define certain property as communal—pasture and hunting grounds, city walls, and market (PC 77–78). Private ownership thus exists prior to communal proprietorship (PC 79). In this city's later development, the urban burghers are completely separate from the land, and they associate together in their positions as individuals to form a communal association. The association comes to be a grouping more inclusive for the burghers than it was for the nobles, encompassing more aspects of their lives. Yet the city is still not a social totality, for its economic life is lived in opposition to, and at the expense of, the countryside.

What, then, is the relationship of property to citizenship? In the ancient city, citizenship is often a precondition to owning private property; in the medieval city, private property is a precondition to becoming citizens. To cover both cases, Marx, almost despite himself, approaches a new position: citizenship or membership in the community is itself one form of property-holding. Membership, first in the tribe, later in the city, is a property relation (PC 90–91). Urban citizenship is an appropriation relation, a holding of public property.[30] Whether this property in the public thing (*res publica*) is considered to predate the individual proprietorship (ancient Greece) or postdate it (Middle Ages), it is in both cases a "relation to the conditions of one's existence as one's own."

Citizenship as a Relation of Association and Appropriation

We must still ask how people in the city come to feel like citizens. What makes them wholeheartedly join the public thing; why would they ever assume the burdens and risks of citizenship?

Marx and Weber give rather different explanations of this, and not the ones you would expect. Neither, of course, is a social contract theorist postulating the proverbial meeting under the oak tree in a Rawlsian original position. Each is a political sociologist, trying to account for what actually happened. But both do grant that one of the things that did happen is that, at certain brief times in history, people believed in the status of citizenship.

The motives of the people founding cities were different from the meaning citizenship later acquired. The origins of cities are found in material interests: for Marx, opportunities of economic exploitation; for Weber, military, economic, and, more broadly, power opportunities. Even Weber admits that the founding of cities was generally a business undertaking. Yet both theorists also concede, if with an element of wonder, that some rather sophisticated men came to believe in citizenship through another route (PC 84, E&S 1246, 1250). Their explanations for the transmission of this belief generally refer to certain segments of the urban social structure, city men with property, who found it to be in their politico-economic interest to reclaim the idea from ancient Greece and Rome and develop it further in order to strengthen the city. In fact, since citizenship often involved a limitation of economic activity, Weber remarks that sometimes burghers did not want to join and were forced (E&S 1253). But once members, they came to honor the idea.

The understanding of the structure of belief seems to hinge on the myth of an origin, the symbolic founding. Through the oath, the common city meals, and the offerings to the city deities, the urban member entered into a cultic community which had an historic existence. At this point there are two rather different accounts of the myth. Marx claims that the myth posits the origins of the city to be divine (PC 69, 73); Weber says that the mythic origins were in man's free will (E&S 1242–43, 1285). It is perhaps ironic that in their respective analyses each finds the opposite of his own intellectual predilections: Marx, the great secular political theorist, finds others positing a belief in divine beings; and Weber, so attuned to the sociology of religion, downplays its influence and sees others stressing an historical event.[31]

It may well be that the role of citizenship involves the threefold human condition of being determined, and free, and in contact with the divine. The myth of an origin is really about the final cause or the purpose of the association. If it is true that such a myth is crucial, there must be ways for the citizen to re-enact that founding, to make it real in his own life. One can conceive of a theory of representative institutions in which participation by the citizen would be a way of recovenanting the original purpose of the community. In this theory, drawing upon Marx and Weber, citizenship would be a relation of rights and duties to a body conceived as a public possession, and a relation to one's fellow citizens as one's own.

The understandings of citizenship that emerge from these analyses are thus remarkably similar, even though couched in different language. Both theorists see citizenship primarily as a relation of association, or civic fellowship, between persons who are formally free. Insofar as citizenship is also a relation of appropriation, or power, among those same persons, this power is distinctly communal or associative power and not individual influence.

We saw this in Marx's analysis of power relations in the city. Despite the class struggle, there is also the ever-present possibility of interclass alliance. More significantly, there is the deeper meaning of property and power in the *Grundrisse,* where property is broadened into the concept of appropriation, which can be established by nonlaboring activity and can start with an attitude rather than an activity. By these moves, Marx makes power or appropriation relations into relations of association, the variety of ways that citizens feel, think, and act towards each other. Citizenship in the city is thus primarily a relation of membership, in which both power and fellowship are shared. Weber's analysis of the terms of legitimacy explore a variety of ways in which governmental power can be shared. If the terms of the state's legitimacy empower a body of citizens, the actual form of the government can be representative. Representation does not diminish, and in fact it may heighten, the associative and appropriative capacities of the citizens.

FIVE
The Neglect of Representation in Classical Communitarian Theory

If citizenship is a relation of association and appropriation, then it requires specific arenas for its exercise. One cannot associate with everyone, save in the mind and spirit of universal brotherhood. One might, it is true, appropriate nature most effectively as part of a cosmopolitan whole, for then the highest technology from all over the world could be pooled. But in a world state, the possibility of direct citizen interaction would be lost. Conversely, a very small polity, like a town meeting or city-state, might so heighten association as to yield direct participation. But that city would have neither the diversity nor the power to be a meaningful totality. Relative to the entire civilization's resources, the group's appropriating power would tend to be meager, and possibilities for diversity of character would be limited. The political places for citizenship must exist somewhere between these extremes, in a variety of bounded settings.

To extrapolate from the city to the nation, since that is the modern unit capable of the diversity we require: the national people, as members of a political whole, express their political will in a variety of ways. This may include, but does not necessarily involve, direct participation in the national legislature. Citizenship can also be voiced through extraparliamentary forums such as declaration and debate in the media, dissent in the bureaucracy, and demonstrations in the streets. Representatives elected in certain ways by the citizens help articulate the political will into legislation. Legislative representatives might, of course, be chosen in ways that violate the condition of shared membership and then their very existence would decrease the political power and fellowship of the people.

America, England, and countries of the British commonwealth tend to use single-member local geographic districts with plurality or majority election rules for representation, in contrast to multimember districts with proportional representation used on the European continent.[1]

America inscribed representation by local political subdivision into its constitutional design.[2] Both the Senate and the electoral college are instances of representation based on internal political boundaries. The early state constitutions honored the principle of representation by political subdivision as much as they honored a proportional population principle. There was "the common guarantee in pre-*Baker* state constitutions of at least one representative per county in one house of the legislature, and a restriction on the number of representatives which may be apportioned to a single county no matter how large its population."[3] Most of the constitutions of the original thirteen colonies had representation by counties and towns in one house.[4] The five state constitutions that emerged from the Northwest Ordinance territories did follow Congress's mandate of representation proportionate to population up to a certain point, but they also allowed some nonproportionate representation of counties and towns. There were similar arrangements in the other state constitutions.[5] As late as 1983, the Supreme Court in *Brown v. Thomson* upheld Wyoming's practice of allowing the smallest county to have at least one representative in one house of the state legislature.[6]

Britain has an even stronger allegiance to geographic constituency (if we ignore its earlier use of rotten boroughs and also the nonlocal practice, now being modified, of candidates nominated by national parties to run in local districts). Britain's periodic Boundary Commissions allow around 22 percent discrepancy in population between parliamentary constituencies in order to preserve local ties and community.[7] In the context of British political experience and ideology,[8] this practice can be seen not necessarily as a commitment to individualist grass-roots democracy but as stemming from a belief that local ties, whether of deference or solidarity, and of political responsibility, are constitutive of the national whole.

How can we account for these practices—what were their origins and what is their justification? The phenomenon is partly due to the historical circumstances of liberalism's emergence, its roots both in feudalism and in the national state even as it challenged their bases of legitimacy. What later became the doctrine of individual liberty was in feudal times a notion attached to corporate bodies. In mid-feudalism the vassal had immunity of his fief from interference by the lord so long as the vassal performed the agreed-upon functions; in late feudalism the societal estates of nobility, clergy, and commoners (landed gentry and, later, urban burghers) tried to preserve and consolidate their corporate identities by asserting spheres of liberties against the encroachment of the crown.[9] At times from the thirteenth to the seventeenth centuries, the local boroughs and shires in England paid their representatives themselves and required local residency, although from the time the latter was written into national law, it seems to have been honored in the breach.[10]

Certain strains of nineteenth and early twentieth century liberalism would so stress the political autonomy of local and nonstate groups as to deny state sovereignty itself.[11] But in the main, Anglo-American liberalism deeply embraced the national state and the doctrine of its sovereignty. As it moved towards the democratic view of basing that state's sovereignty in the national people as a whole, it responded to demands for expansion of the suffrage and for apportionment of representation more in accord with numbers.

Classical Theory and Representation

While Anglo-American political practice may allow, even rely upon, local political units, liberal political thought cannot provide a justification for such districts. The explicit theory of liberalism rejects history or tradition as a guide to political theory or practice—Locke, Bentham, and Mill all being concerned to ground political institutions in a reasoning other than the received sense of custom or even the precedents of common law.[12] The arguments in the recent Wyoming case come from outside the liberal canon, or from its substantive substratum, the concrete political history upon which it depends.[13]

Liberalism denies the reality or political significance of corporate groupings in political society; except for the family, there are no other bodies that have an autonomous personality and fundamentally shape the nature of their members. Individuals associate into groups, but these are passing, transient associations for limited ends. The rejection of caste, estate, and class as the justified basis for social action then extends to the political place and corporation. While the municipal corporation and the joint stock corporation are two significant concepts in the law, they represent adaptations from feudalism which liberalism's explicit theory ignores.

Liberal social contract theory is a systematic theory of a state formed by a national population of free individuals. It sees individuals existing as moral agents prior to the formation of either society or the state. They are presumed to act either on the basis of individually received natural rights [14] or individually generated wants and pleasures.[15] They come to the social arena and enter into one or two contracts forming civil and political society. If there is an intermediary social contract before the national one, it constitutes the civil society prior to the government, and not a lower level of political association. A national state is formed that is sovereign; national sovereignty is sought and assured through the hypothetical mechanism of individuals acting in direct relation to the state. The sovereignty is democratized through the doctrine of consent, explicit and tacit, presumed to be given in activities ranging from participation in elections to simply inhabiting the place under the protection of its laws. The overt political activity of the people vis-à-vis that state is primarily defensive, to protect rights against encroachment, or offensive, to advance interests against others. There is no reason why this model of the state and its subjects should require local political districting.

Anglo-American political practice thus makes ample use of bounded settings in basing much of its representation and administration on local geographic districts. But liberal political thought has not given a theoretical account of such districts and may not be able to do so. Liberalism has a well-developed theory of representation, yet one that would tend to lead to transmission belt theory, which might best be served by elections at-large.

One might reasonably expect, then, that communitarian political thought would provide a theoretical account of political districting and its relation to citizenship. For classical communitarian theory considers the community to predate the individual; the society is deemed to exist prior to individual persons, shaping their characters in fundamental ways. The community has a corporate existence independent of the particular wills of its members; a political corporatism is justified, albeit in a variety of ways. Just as, at the level of the national state, the whole precedes the parts, so, too, at a federal level, intermediary wholes might precede the individuals.

Certain nonliberal communitarian theorists do stress the historical origins of political forms and the importance of locality within a national system of representation. Edmund Burke, for instance, uses history or the theory of prescription to justify present practices; old practices are good ones because they started and have lasted through years of use. The role of the representative is to make decisions of policy to reform in order to preserve a shared system of understandings.[16] Yet while an appreciation of history is important, it alone cannot provide standards for what to conserve when an alternative, such as individual equality, presents itself. History might simply be a record of who won; we need to look for reasons in history. Furthermore, traditionalist communitarian thought, as in Burke, allows incremental action on the part of individuals and representatives, but does not seek to transform individuals into citizens.

Most communitarian theory does not speak of political representatives, much less of political districts. In general, we can see this neglect as stemming from the very structure of such thought. The social whole is seen as primary, if not total, and determinative of the individuals within it. Politics seeks to totally transform people in current society from what they are to what they might be. The people in their present condition are unworthy, not deserving of representation. Insofar as there is a representative, he simply reflects what has been created, after the revolution.

We will consider three communitarian theorists—Plato, Rousseau, and Marx—who, while perhaps at the right, center, and left of the political spectrum relative to each other, are all classical and radical in the sense of wanting their politics to be transformative. They each seek to change a way of life they see as corrupt, regenerating it into a harmonious whole. Membership in that whole is the precondition to achieving their valued goals, and this membership is created by relations of association and appropriation. We will examine their idea of the corporate community, their lack of a theory of representation, and whether the lack is total. Upon closer examination, communitarian theory may reveal the presence of representation, and even of political representatives.

Political Membership Created by Association and Appropriation

Plato's *Republic* is a dialogue about a political whole ordered according to a philosophic vision of reason.[17] The goal is justice in the soul, to be approached through contemplative philosophy as it apprehends the cosmic good, and political philosophy, which tries to approximate its just order on earth. People are placed in three separate strata and required to perform the functions for which they are best suited. Certainly for the philosophers, but also for the warriors and the artisans, this involves a transformation of their previous ways of life. Justice in souls is achieved through membership in a community; membership is established in different ways for the different strata.

For those who possess the capacity for knowledge, membership is affirmed through egalitarian relations not only of association but also of direct participation. The guardians or philosopher-kings share possessions and children in common in a shared social life, they pursue philosophy together, and they share equally in political rule.[18] Since the political power of the community is based on knowledge, all its appropriation relations reflect that assumption: the philosopher-kings rule over themselves and the warriors, the next highest caste, through an elaborate system of education.

For those who are not philosophic, membership is affirmed through inegalitarian association in a communal division of labor; the warrior and laboring classes contribute to the meaning of the whole, the argument goes, without violating their own natures.[19] Human natures have different mixes of reason, spirit, and appetite; the philosophers have a higher degree of reason, the warriors of spirit, the artisans of appetite.[20] But this is relative internally to the other parts of the soul in each stratum; in comparisons between strata it may be the case that the philosophers have more unlimited appetite relative to the appetite of the lowest class. Plato seeks to join that passion—of eros, the longing for completion—to reason,[21] and if his elaborate education is successful, it makes the philosophers able to rule justly over the other two classes, whose needs are more easily met.

Political rule of the lowest stratum, the mass of the people, has a higher element of myth and coercion than the rule of the warriors or the self-rule of the philosophers, yet even the highest level cannot totally dispense with myth and deception in its disciplined preparation for the art of dialogue and the reception of truth.[22] Education offers more incentives to the part of the soul deemed to predominate in each class—desire, or will, or reason; reason is used insofar as people are ready for it. It may be that a member of the masses, like the slave, possesses an eye of the soul that can recollect reason.[23] Thus, "it is better for everyone to be governed by the divine and the intelligent, preferably indwelling and his own, but in default of that imposed from without, in order that we all so far as possible may be akin and friendly."[24]

Reason unites, that they may be joined in civic friendship. Political rule is the exercise of reason over all spheres of life. The state orders all of society: the state and society become one. Politics is mimesis,[25] the art of giving representation to the idea of justice. The people, as they are, are not to be represented.

Rousseau's *Social Contract* is a picture, a theoretical model, of the essential tensions involved in a political community based on freedom.[26] The goal is positive freedom, understood as radical autonomy of the will exercised in the context of public law. Individuals who in the state of nature were unequal physically and equal in their amorality are considered to have entered society by a complicated route.[27] Society "substitutes justice for instinct in [their] behavior, and gives to [their] actions a moral basis which formerly was lacking."[28] Civil society as historically developed has exacerbated physical inequalities and enshrined moral inequality in its principles of political right. Freedom of the will and compassion, two qualities of man in the state of nature and in primitive society, have vanished.[29] The goal of the social contract is to recreate the conditions for the exercise of free will and compassion in the modern situation to which man's self-perfectability has led. The freedom to act and to feel can only be attained or approximated through membership in a political community, for without its restraints, people are prone to the vices and dissimulations of corrupt society.

For the citizens, membership is established through their direct participation in the general will, which is sovereign and makes the law.[30] The general will is their will when they are acting in the interests of the good of the whole; it is present in the intention of every citizen, yet may be present as an understanding of the means of implementation in only a majority or even a minority of citizens.[31] If the minority sees more truly it must convince its compatriots, who will otherwise lose even their good intentions. Membership is reaffirmed through the relations of association, of mutual respect and affection, which that participation both entails and engenders.

There are also, it seems, some who are not citizens, and thereby "slaves."[32] This is partly a metaphor for the tension within the soul of the citizen—slave to his private passions and the will of all, master of his moral being through the general will. That there has to be civil slavery also is an implication of the assumption that the appropriation relations are based on human willpower: social power is the exercise of will—general and just in the case of the state, partial and dominating in the case of society. And the distinction between state and society is to be preserved, for civil society is allowed to continue, although extremes of property and other forms of social inequality are to be moderated.[33] Political life is not architectonic,[34] shaping all the other spheres. Some things and plausibly some people are left out.

Politics is, however, transformative of all members within its own sphere. Participation in the general will changes the will of the citizen, disciplining and enlarging it. Politics creates citizen virtue where previously there was only primitive goodness or civilized vice. It creates a shared language of compassion where previously there had been only a sophistical language that divides. To achieve these ends requires direct participation by the citizens in the enabling experience that makes them free. Sovereignty of their wills is paramount; they cannot delegate either their selfish or their magnanimous wills without violating the condition of political freedom. Representation of the people is illegitimate.[35]

But political community is not exclusively a matter of freedom of the will. So Plato had argued, subordinating the will to a universal reason, and so perhaps even Rousseau argued, implicitly, in his concept of virtue. And so Marx argued, attacking will as alternately impotent and destructive when given free reign in politics.[36] Even if freedom is the highest value among the moderns, it can have a different meaning, as we shall see in the next chapter. And if politics is not solely a matter of free will, then direct participation is not always necessary.

Marx bases political community on the force of human needs, on socialized desire broadly understood. Needs have both material and ideal components; they are created and expressed through sensuous practical activity or labor; they are social and historical, changing over time.[37] Yet at any one historical stage they are fairly uniform and unproblematic. This has consequences for Marx's theory of representation, or rather for the lack of it.

The ultimate goal is unalienated labor and free individuality in the context of socially owned production.[38] Free individuality has more of a liberal moment than in Rousseau; it includes the liberty to develop in any direction, with open-ended creativity.[39] Yet individuality only appears in the context of society, through membership in a political community. "The human being is in the most literal sense a *zōon politikon*, not merely a gregarious animal, but an animal which can individuate itself only in the midst of society."[40] For Marx, as we saw in the last chapter, the mode of production governs all.[41] It determines the shape of society, the contours of social classes, and whether individuality can appear at all. Society determines the state, until the state shall wither away. This can theoretically occur when human needs are all shared and nonconflicting, which is assumed to occur when class division is ended. Reason, now understood as the critical scientific theory of dialectical materialism, will discern the true human needs and social possibilities of the age, and everyone will possess this knowledge.

Membership in a community would still have to be established through the appropriation relations of production; membership would also be affirmed through association relations in production. There is no independent sphere for politics and political friendship.[42] People as workers participate in the division of labor at the workplace; full participation in planning requires plenary meetings of the local work force. Relations of abstract association occur within the one universal class, the proletariat; the union of the associated producers involves a mass feeling of solidarity, of their shared interests and loyalties. A single political party as "selfless instrument"[43] can stand for the working class at the helm of society. Representation is either unnecessary or unproblematic, since any person with theory can understand the needs of the others. There is no obvious role for political representation of the people.

The Transformative Nature of Communitarian Politics

Representation is illegitimate in these theories because they assume that the polity has an underlying common interest, one which cannot be discovered through the practice of representation.[44] For Plato the route to the common interest is the difficult path of philosophy and the rule of philosopher-kings; for Rousseau the way is the perhaps equally arduous process of the general will; and for Marx the path is the hard historical struggle of class consciousness. These are not shortcuts; each has its own vicissitudes. Yet for these theorists, it is worth it, for not only is representation deemed an inefficient way to create the common good, but a positive hindrance, introducing extraneous considerations from the here and now, the quotidian existence of people. For political representation recognizes diversity as real.

These theorists also write as if human life can be made and remade. In Marx this is most explicit: people are social and historical beings, creating the conditions of their own existence and hence their own human nature. Rousseau, too, sees man as social and historical, although certain traits from the state of nature reappear in the good society. Plato works more from an ahistorical theory of the human soul, with given passions and capacities, but something radical happens halfway through his theory and men are never the same after that. Now some readings of these texts take Rousseau and Plato to be arguing for the impossibility of ever transcending man's given nature, but for now we will reject that interpretation and take them at their word.

These theories, then, all consider the political community as a corporate body, having an existence as a whole that is more than the sum of the present consciousness of the individuals composing it, and with a meaning that endures beyond the life of its members. At the same time it is not a whole having an existence truly independent of its parts; the life and spirit of its members, aspiring to the community's ends, constitute the community; and if they do not, irremediable corruption sets in and the community no longer exists. Membership in the healthy body politic is seen as fundamental to defining human character, though membership is established and sustained differently in each theory. So far, these theories are all theories of the whole, requiring or allowing little political intermediation.

They are also unabashedly transformative; they do not play things as they are. Yet they do not rely upon explicit "transforming leadership."[45] There are no figures directly exhorting the people to rid their land of the barbarians and unite in patriotic resolve. There are figures who might be considered trustee representatives—the philosopher-kings in Plato, the magistrates in Rousseau, and the party in Marx-Lenin. Yet all of these are actually executive and not legislative roles. They do not make the law, they only find it and administer it. The sovereign maker of public law lies elsewhere.[46]

How then do the members of the community become receptive to recognizing the true sources of law? Each theory has a figure who does not share in executive rule and who returns to the people and interacts with them at very close quarters. He is both part of the people and beyond them, a tune beyond us, yet ourselves. In Plato, the philosopher Socrates mingles with the serious man in the street; in Rousseau, the personage of the legislator shares his great soul with the people; in Marx and Lenin, the outside organizer comes and then goes. These figures have certain characteristics in common.

The Figure of the Founder

The philosopher in Plato's republic returns to the cave of human experience not only to rule, but to discourse, to engage in dialogue.[47] He starts with received public opinion, and proceeds from there. Those who aspire to know are shown incompatibilities in aspects of their thought and shown the way up to the true, more unitary concepts. Socrates may not know the truth but he is closer to it than the others and he knows a path for pursuing it. The use of logic—contradiction, noncontradiction, deduction, and induction—in the context of dialectical reasoning, helps clear the path towards the ideas.[48]

Now it is also well known that Socrates is a shameless flatterer and ironist, seducing and insulting many an opponent. Often he refutes brilliantly and fairly; often he does not. Sometimes he is a bully. He deals unfairly with Thrasymachus at the end of the first book of the *Republic;*[49] he is "obscure" and "confusing" with Lysis at the end of the dialogue on friendship.[50] Socrates presumes that these people cannot know beyond a certain point what they are talking about, given their life experiences so far, and so when he reaches that point, he begins to address others in the audience. Thrasymachus, although very smart, is still committed to gaining power on any terms; Lysis, although eager and intelligent, is not in love with one who loves him. And so beyond a point each cannot yet see what justice or friendship really is. Words can at best provide the premonition that there is something lacking, and something more to be known. In contrast, Socrates does not often deal unjustly with the brothers Glaucon and Adeimantus in the *Republic*. They are not any smarter than those others, yet they have felt the lack, and aspire to know. Socrates speaks differently to different people.[51]

The legislator in Rousseau seems to speak similarly to all people. He appears on the scene to establish the customs and institutions that enable the general will to appear. He is a wise and perhaps charismatic man who transforms the people so that they can begin to make public law. But how "to speak [his] language to the vulgar"?[52] He cannot use pure reason, since they are not ready to hear and recognize that; in fact it may well be that true public knowledge is a consequence and not a cause of their freedom.[53] He cannot use force, at least not explicitly, since that would contradict the ends of freedom. What is left, in a chapter rife with references to Machiavelli and Hobbes, is the second term of a Machiavellian duo, of force and fraud. Or if not outright fraud, then at least the beliefs and superstition as expressed in popular religion. The chapter on the legislator is ambiguous as to whether politics should serve religion or vice versa; the chapter on the civic religion makes it clear: religion should serve politics.[54] And while the four tenets of the civil religion are the same for all, they are couched in such broad generalizations as to allow different meanings to be construed. All citizens must assent to the general creed, but each person is also allowed his private religious beliefs; here again, Rousseau upholds the separation between state and society. At the same time that intermediary political institutions are condemned, a diversity of religious sects are condoned as long as they tolerate others.

On the crucial question of the moral language used on the path to citizen virtue, the legislator permits a variety of forms of speech. Different metaphors with different symbols are allowed on the path to public knowledge, as the people in their obstinacy or their freedom, or both, cling to their pre-political experience. The legislator also appeals to what he considers to be their best hopes and worst fears for themselves, and makes them uniformly participate in the new political institution of the assembly, forcing them to be free.[55] The legislator is a various man.

The outside organizer in Marxist-Leninism is a similar figure. He works to change the political consciousness of the people. In some sense this change must come "only from without";[56] in another, it must be generated from within, by the people themselves. Marx writes that some members of the bourgeois intelligentsia who can see the workings of the whole will leave their class and come over to the side of the working class; and the proletariat, especially its skilled artisans, can generate self-educated partisans as well[57]: " . . . the workers, and above all the [Communist] League, must work for the creation of an independent organization of the workers' party, both secret and open, alongside the official democrats, and the League must aim to make every one of its communes a centre and nucleus of workers' associations in which the position and interests of the proletariat can be discussed free from bourgeois influence."[58] A view of the whole is necessary but should not be mechanically imposed on the workers; new cooperative institutions "are *only* valuable if they are independent creations of the workers, and not the protégés either of governments or of the bourgeoisie."[59] The political organizer works with the people, encouraging their spontaneity and channeling it.

Lenin intensifies the voluntarist strain in Marx's thought and elaborates a fourfold distinction in the work of political revolutionaries. There is theory, propaganda, agitation, and organization.[60] Theory involves a view of the whole, both the conceptual whole of *Capital* and the practical political whole of all classes and institutions in a nation; propaganda involves the written word, in newspapers and pamphlets, presenting " 'many ideas', so many, indeed, that they will be understood as an integral whole only by a (comparatively) few persons"; agitation involves the spoken word, on a soapbox or in a meeting hall, using a common fact known to the audience for "presenting a *single idea* to the 'masses'"; and organization mobilizes the people to act together publicly against an injustice, engaging them in a variety of "comprehensive political exposures." The igniting spark is the political agitator, who speaks to a specific crowd, taking an example from the entire country and connecting it to something in their own lives. The agitator strives "to rouse discontent and indignation" so that even "the most backward worker will understand, or *will feel*" that there are others distinct from him who also suffer, that there is a larger political situation with which he can identify.[61] The agitator uses speech; to do this well he has to have a superb sense of tactics, of what is happening and what the people are ready to hear. This will vary with time and place.

In each of these communitarian theories, then, there is a powerful figure who works with a diverse people in complicated and indirect ways, using different modes of address. Are these figures representatives?

Representation as Political Founding

Each political figure who returns to the people has need of those people as they of him. They need him to show them the way; in what sense does he need them? The portrayal so far of an outside organizer has suggested manipulation, a necessary element in politics; are the people thereby an inert mass to be worked over by his skillful hands? More charitably, can he be seen as a political artist and they the matter on which he imposes his form? He is a political artist, but not in the manner first suggested here. For the people are not purely passive and material; they have mind and spirit, and so he works differently, on and through a human medium. "The political artist's . . . object is other men. . . . How he views . . . [them] tends to affect the picture he strives to construct in his object."[62] He strives to create a new picture within his object, in their souls. Yet we have not yet answered why he needs to do this.

Plato had written of the contentment of the philosopher who has no desire to leave his contemplation and must be urged to perform political rulership as his public duty; Rousseau had perhaps suggested, although this is more debatable, that the life of the solitary dreamer is preferable to all else even for modern man.[63] Yet Socrates is a character who is driven by his own nature to come back from his contemplation; he cannot stay away. We interpret Plato to mean that philosophers, while privileged to ascend to the mountaintop, must still of necessity return, but now on different terms—no longer aspiring to hold political power for personal ambition. They need to return to the human world because they cannot practice their particular art in isolation. Socrates depends upon dialogue, not monologue, to advance philosophically, even for himself;[64] in this respect his humility is not a pose. Dialectical idealism requires human interaction. So, too, at the opposite pole, does dialectical materialism. Marx writes of the proletariat only finding its completion in a critical philosophy, and intellectuals need a social class to attach to if they are to become organic and their knowledge thus real.[65] Even if we say that by this interactive process Socrates becomes more influential and the bourgeois intellectual more useful, this is not the main point, which is that the political organizer needs the people in some primary way. He cannot use the people as objects, as mere means to his ends given externally. He must treat the people as ends in themselves, generating their own values from within.

For he needs the people as free agents to accord him recognition of what he does and hence, to an extent, of what he is. Insofar as what he does is familiar, commanding work and establishing domination, this recognition could be conferred by a slave.[66] But insofar as what he does is new, it requires interaction with a free being, and one who in principle could also withhold recognition, not grant it. Those who attempt to perform qualitatively new acts, whether in speech or in deed, need a human community to recognize these acts and accustom themselves accordingly.[67] By seeing and affirming the meaning of certain acts, the others confirm the existence and identity of the actor. Each political figure, then, needs an other or a set of concrete others to give him an identity, an identity not just as leader but as member.

Such a figure, moreover, seeks to create the subject matter, the kinds of people, who would no longer need him specifically as a leader. For he is a political founder and not a king starting a dynasty; the founder is singular and mortal, bound to die. By finding and mobilizing the relevant others, enabling them to recognize his gifts, he empowers certain of them to be his equals and makes himself dispensable. Socrates leaves an academy or school, even if a scattered one, among the potential political elite. Rousseau's legislator leaves a constitution, a code and a spirit of the laws, in a general body of people. Since the goal in the

Social Contract is more democratic than in the *Republic*, the means used involve even more indirection than Socrates employs, for the audience is not preselected and not many of the masses are yet receptive to reason. The structure of the problem of political education is also somewhat different in Rousseau than in Plato, because for Rousseau the very language of civil society has corrupted meanings, even for the talented and well-educated. Thus everybody, including the naturally and socially best, need a new public language.

In the case of the modern organizer of mass movements, Marx also provides new political concepts, has the workers read *Capital,* and respects (some of) their members at the First International. Lenin's agitator does not consider the masses competent to understand the theory but does respect their capacity for mass action. His cadres are the least liable to disappear, but at the limit, in his vision of the semi-autonomous soviets, it is still possible.

And in America, where political culture tends to distrust general theory and ideology, political organizing can be seen as the finding of native leadership in a community.[68] The outsider finds the "little Joes" who already have the esteem of their peers in selected arenas, shows them how they can coordinate into a general political plan of action, and then chooses to disappear.

In all of these situations, the leader acts as a founder, starting a community that will continue on its own without him. They are political founders or extraordinary representatives. Yet, as Masters points out, "Since the need for innovation in the laws is ever present, the problem of the founding is thus merely the problem of all government in its most radical form. . . . The possibility of establishing, at a single point in time, lasting political institutions which make men just and free is therefore an 'exception' or 'extraordinary' circumstance which nevertheless illuminates and indeed symbolizes the 'ordinary' problems of political life.'"[69] Political founding is only hypothetically a single act;[70] in actuality it is a continual process. Hence there is a need for more ordinary representatives, doing this extraordinary task.

SIX

Towards a Theory of Political Constituency

The problem of the political founder extends to the problem of citizenship in general. The founder as a special public individual seeks the recognition of others whom he is forging into a political community. Citizenship, their ongoing relationship to him and to each other, involves their mutual recognition. Both the special relation with the founder and the general relations among citizens involve free recognition between members. How can they be members yet also be free?

Freedom has many levels, many stages or moments on the path to citizenship. Freedom depends on membership even as freedom goes beyond membership. We will call the relation of citizenship "political individuality" and show how it has three crucial preconditions—the modern status of "formal individualism," the condition of "social individuality" or membership in social groups, and membership in the political whole. The term individuality is used to describe the individual as free member because it captures both the liberty of the individual subject as well as the group structure of which he or she is a part.

Political representation, then, in its full meaning, will have to take account of four aspects of ethical life: formal individualism, social individuality, political individuality, and the political whole. We will say that the goal of political representation should be citizenship, understood as a kind of membership whose characteristic relations are association and appropriation. These relations comprise political freedom. We can therefore say that political representation should promote political freedom. And to do this, to encourage free recognition among members, representation requires political districting by nonsovereign geographic entities.

Citizenship as Free Membership

One has to consider oneself a member of the political community in order to "relate to one's fellow citizens as one's own." The feeling of loyalty implied in this ideal must come from a definition of oneself as in some way inextricably bound to these others. In private life one might experience this relationship (and with even more intensity) with certain specific others; in public life, ideally, one assumes this relation (albeit in attentuated form) to all citizens as such.[1]

Is membership thereby mute, brute, unselfconscious? Membership means being part of a whole. That whole is often conceived as an organism. In common parlance there is still the usage of a bodily part that has a will but not a mind of its own. In general, a member is an "integral," "vital" part of a larger body, a body in which another part rules.[2] The member is a natural part of this body; the body is born, its parts are born with it and they grow to their predetermined shape. For a brief time, an infant is such a member of a family. To be a member of a body politic in this sense would be to be a fully determined part of a natural pre-given whole. One is born into it and one dies with it; one lives through it and one dies for it. One helps sustain it but one does not change it, except negatively if one fails it, as in a broken arm. This membership is not free.

Membership can become free in several ways. First, one can decide to become part of an organization, but this time as an "independent constituent of a body, structure, or any organized thing."[3] Here one's being exists independently of the membership and then one decides to join. The self is "unencumbered," existing prior to its social attachments.[4] This also means that the body joined is partial, not comprising the whole, since one could decide not to join and still exist somewhere. Thus, people, for example, become dues-paying members of voluntary associations. Although these organizations often have aspects of fraternal relations, they are usually groups for the pursuit of self-interest. They are therefore contractual relations with limited obligations. Since the obligations are limited, they are also more open to being changed by members. And ending one's membership is not an utter failure, a breaking, a severing; it is a leaving, a changing.[5] The member is at liberty to voluntarily decide.

Voluntary membership can thus be of two sorts. It is usually instrumental, for relations of use—to achieve purposes for the individual in which other people and things are means. It can also be what has been called sentimental, or for experience—to feel something pleasurable or interesting, yet in which other people and things still are means.[6]

There is a deeper way in which membership becomes free, through cognitive and spiritual self-consciousness, a movement primarily in thought which only later issues in action. One accepts one's membership in a community of birth, but consecrates it to a purpose beyond the physical world. A natural community becomes a human community by dedicating itself to certain spiritual purposes, ideals not impossible but difficult to achieve. This has been called "covenanted patriotism"[7] and it derives from the Old Testament idea of God's covenant with His people at Sinai.[8] Covenant involves unconditional obligation, membership in a community which defines the central parts of one's being and seeks to keep a faith to certain practices and ideals. The practices are a way to keep an historic people covenanted to God; ideas infuse the practices as custom which teaches, disciplines, preserves and sets apart. Thought also engenders and allows action, although within the limits of critique in the context of community. The community starts with a tribe of families, though it also has provision for incorporation of new members. Becoming a covenanted member involves a turning, in one's soul, towards spiritual purposes. One can conceive of not being a member, as a stranger though not an individual renegade, rather of the whole community falling away, which would be a breaking, an exile, a desolation.

To move from being a mere member to a covenanted member one has to go through a stage of conceiving of oneself as an individual person. In everyday phenomenal life, the three modes of membership seem to trace an ascending path, from the concrete natural membership, to individual voluntary membership, to collective spiritual membership. In the second mode, the individual has freedom of the will, the liberty to decide to join and where to join. Equally significant, he has the ability to conceive of not joining. To say that one is a "human agent as an intentional being urges, if you will, the conceptual inevitability of that form of distraction called 'not belonging.'"[9] This not belonging, or nonmembership, is a theoretical possibility in the mind of any person. In that respect, in the mind, he is free. But is that real freedom? For full freedom involves entering into relation with others, into relations of fellowship and power. Yet unlike the voluntary member, the natural and covenanted members seem unfree; are they not enmeshed in necessity, bound by a sovereignty they are unable to affect?

The Sovereign State

They are bound by sovereign power, and they are in large measure unable to affect it. In what does this sovereignty consist?

In natural membership, the member is bound by the sovereign laws of nature. General laws governing physical processes cause the member to be a certain way; accidents and mutations allow for exceptions, these too dictated by the process and not the person. General laws also govern certain basic emotional processes of the human infant, although the way the person as adult comes to symbolize and direct these feelings is open to self-determination. In natural membership, then, natural laws govern the relations, and humans cannot affect them retrospectively. They can come to understand them through knowledge. The knowledge can be used to build appropriate social structures for succeeding generations.

In covenanted membership the member is also bound by law. In religious language, the sovereign power is God and the law comes as His word and spirit, apprehended by humans. Through reason and through revelation, they come to understand the eternal law—natural law and divine law. Natural law, the fundamental principles of justice among people, is the same for all persons but takes different form as human positive law in different countries according to local circumstance. The political good is prior to the principles of political right, and the good is knowable.[10]

In the absence of religious agreement, men in the modern era have felt they had to establish a secular sovereignty. As discussed in chapter one, this is a response to a specific historical situation—the breakdown of the medieval Christian world view, the heritage of Roman administration, and also the rise of modern science and technology. Some have tried to replace divine sovereignty once and for all; others are more provisional, advancing secular sovereignty in order to enable political communities to act in the absence of religious agreement and to avoid religious civil war. Thus the modern nation-state, made up of peoples of diverse religious and nonreligious beliefs, requires the notion of state sovereignty. The state is sovereign in the sense that, in its internal affairs, it has full and unitary power to make rules for an entire society.[11] The rules are formulated as sovereign law, and this law is formulated by a body empowered to be the legislature for the state. Law is no longer considered to be fully a matter of knowledge, to be found in the order of the cosmos; it is also a matter of will, to be made and created by autonomous persons. Yet I do not think that law can be seen exclusively as the product of human wills. We therefore still say that diverse human wills collaborate in constitutional procedures to discover as well as create the law.

Political representation is a way to constitute national sovereignty. It draws people from the periphery to the center, connecting them to the whole. The naming of the sovereign body within the state defines the representative's role. In the early absolutist states, the monarch claimed the role of sovereign and expanded its meaning beyond medieval limitations. The king claimed to be both the agent and symbol of the community's unified will; he was their representative. But that king had to summon local lords to get their consent and power, and therein lay the origins of representation as an activity by diverse people. Modern representation thus begins as a device of political rule from the center, exercised through local corporate bodies. Its original impetus came from above, in the king's summoning of significant men with local standing to gain their assent to his rules and his levying of taxes.[12] Sometimes these agents held the formal proxy of others, sometimes it was only *de facto*. It was easiest for the central government to govern this way, through established loci of power. Later these local representatives came to realize their "potential powers" in the new national situation— first to assert the liberties of localities and later to assert their capability to make general law, coupled with their new claim to speak for the whole realm.[13] Sovereignty within the state moved from the monarch to the King- or Queen-in-Parliament, and in Britain eventually Parliament itself reigned supreme. The role of the representative in a state with a sovereign legislature is to be a trustee for the people, to find and make the general law for that state.

Sovereignty must lodge somewhere in the modern state, although it need not lie exclusively in the legislature. It can stay in a monarch if that king is a constitutional one, given ultimate power yet required to exercise it within a system of limits.[14] Or, sovereignty can be moved away from the monarch and outside of the legislature, to the people at large. Here, the people are seen as sovereign either as the electors who periodically choose the legislators or, more radically, as the body that empowered the original founders and could once again recall the legislators and call a new founding convention to reconstitute the polity.[15] Sovereignty might also lodge in a judiciary which judges the law the monarch pronounces or the legislature passes, yet insofar as the judiciary is not an inherited caste but rather appointed or elected by another source, its ultimate sovereignty devolves back to the power that chose it.

America's constitutional design lodges sovereignty in the national people at large and secondarily in a system of separated yet balanced and interacting powers—the legislature, executive, and judiciary. Certainly the Anti-Federalists opposed the idea of national sovereignty itself, and their influence is reflected in Federalist thought, so much so that some are tempted to describe America as a "pre-modern polity."[16] But while its separation of powers may seem less modern than a completely unitary state structure, the state still does have a theoretically sovereign body: the people at large and the constitution they are believed to have formed. The consequence for the role of representation in America, of course, is that the legislators must be seen not solely as trustees but in some respects as agents of those who elected them. Yet once in office, these representatives must make general law for a sovereign whole, and that political whole often has its own necessities, its own reasons of state. Political representation will have to be conceived in different terms from agent and trustee in order to capture its diverse aspects.

Freedom as Self-Determination of Character within a Relevant Community

If state sovereignty exists, how then can there be political freedom?

Now one might argue, as does social contract theory, that it is precisely individual freedom that goes with the idea of state sovereignty, and that the one ensures the other and vice versa. Persons enter into a voluntary social compact which furthers their security and secures their liberties. A strong state ensures a stable society which protects freedom of the will.

But this is unsatisfactory, for it gives inadequate weight to the full force of sovereignty and it has too thin a notion of human freedom. First, by giving insufficient due to the sovereign power established, the theory cannot protect against sovereignty's power growing indefinitely.[17] It is impossible for the people in the mass to be sovereign, and so then the *de facto* sovereign becomes the state apparatus. Second, membership in a sovereign state is not simply voluntary. It is covenanted or it does not exist at all. The freedom involved in covenanted membership is a different kind of freedom from the liberty of voluntary membership. It is an understanding that takes into account the full weight of sovereignty in all the spheres of our life.

Freedom can be defined as self-determination. The term self-actualization is often used as an equivalent, but that phrase implies a natural end which exists as potency to be actualized. The term self-rule might also be used, except that it implies a much wider range of choices than our theory, which is heavy with sovereignty. Whereas self-determination contains the paradox of freedom. Self-determination presumes that one knows or is conscious of the self, and in crucial ways the self is determined before and while it determines. One would have to be self-conscious, aware of the forces, internal and external, that are determining you, before you could know the ways in which you could act. Freedom as self-determination requires a rather high degree of knowledge before one can be said to determine one's self.

Self-determination is the shaping of one's own character. There is an identity of the self that can be known; it is one's character. It is not a static but a dynamic entity, yet it has a consistency and unity. Each person has a set of values and dispositions that incline him or her to act in certain ways.[18] The self always exists in a context, and contexts are constantly changing, and so the self has to be self-reflective about what to value and how to act and about how the context has changed the meaning of one's acts. Herself observed, a character changes and grows, yet retains its unity through the unity of a narrative.[19] The self tells a story about her- or himself; the self tells an historical narrative.

The narrative can be seen as tracing a certain cycle again and again. Over the long run, through these cycles the individual makes progress towards a self more unified yet also more complexly differentiated internally: towards a self that is free. In its moral thinking, the self traces recurrent cycles which are similar in form but different in content. In all of these processes, a general moral idea starts out as an abstraction and then differentiates itself into three "moments" or simultaneous aspects. To use terms introduced by Hegel's philosophy, there is first the idea in its "universality," its most general abstract form without a content. Second, there is the extreme contrast to this, the idea rooted in "particularity," a specific, limited content. Third, there is a synthesis of the universal and the particular in "individuality," when a particular establishes for itself its own relation to the universal, or becomes self-conscious.[20]

This self-consciousness, or what has been called the "moral attitude," of being a person with value who is also related to others who have value, requires a notion of a whole existing before the parts.[21] Charvet argues that the individualist accounts of the equal objective value of individuals as self-determining beings is ultimately incoherent, breaking down at the points where their self-determined freedoms do not coincide. He then uses the Hegelian notion of the three moments in the development of the idea of freedom, infusing them with a new content. In the realm of human moral life, the moment of universality is the idea of value itself, and the moment of particularity is the individual as having subjective value for himself. The synthesis, or moment of individuality, comes in the individual recognizing that objective value lies in concrete others.[22]

The individual is a source of subjective value but not objective value. The individual has a will which may aim at whatever it will; this is the individual's liberty and it may have personal meaning for him or her, but there is no assurance that it provides any basis of right or law. Recognition of the individual's moral value as a free person must come from other persons who are also free. We cannot show that this objective value fits into an overarching whole of natural law which ascends up to, or descends down from, one Idea or God. We can at least say that objective value is found in the valuation of concrete others with whom the individual is associated. Freedom as self-determination is manifested in the individual's choosing, and staying by or leaving, a set of concrete others. In our terms, the individual expresses his or her political freedom by becoming self-conscious of covenanted membership in a specific community.

Four Parts of Ethical Life: Personhood: Formal Individualism and Social Individuality; Citizenship: Political Individuality and the Political Whole

In the modern world, this public freedom can only exist alongside private liberty, since all individuals who are citizens must also be persons. Before one is a citizen, one is first a natural member, and then a person; this is the way it is lived in an individual life, even as, actually, one has to have a political whole, a nation or a polity, before one can be either a citizen or a person. There are different levels of individuality and these various forms must be given some place in political representation if the public sphere is to be authentically connected to people's pre-political lives. If representation does not acknowledge these roots, the people who spend their daily existences there will remain simply there, disaffected from the larger sphere of politics and public life.

Legislative representatives must act as morally autonomous individuals, yet these same citizens, when not in office, are entitled to express their pre-political affiliations. Not only entitled, they need to acknowledge their social individuality in politics or else this level will disappear and the state rule its people without intermediation.

The understanding of citizenship being developed here thus differs from the Enlightenment view. Ever since Kant proposed the "categorical imperative" as the basis of moral action, that view of the ideal citizen required that he act as if he were everyman. To be free or autonomous involves acting according to laws one has set for oneself, and for that freedom to be moral, "I should never act in such a way that I could not will that my maxim should be a universal law."[23] Following this rule, to be moral in politics involves acting for the general good by seeking basic categorical principles of public right and wrong, and one does this by conceiving of oneself as universal man and reasoning about universal laws. While this mode of reasoning is valid as the rule of justice, the framing of general public law,[24] it is not the best rule for extra-parliamentary politics, the activity preliminary to and surrounding legislation. For it puts insupportable burdens on certain, if not all, strata of the population, asking them to ignore their private concerns when choosing legislators. This is most apparent in the case of the poor and women and others severely disadvantaged by civil society and the family; to ask them to act immediately for the whole may be asking them to act against their own existence. The demand to be universal man can also be debilitating to privileged groups; Marx argued that the bourgeoisie experienced a split between its public life and private life, in which guilt over the triumph of the private would lead (he hoped) to paralysis of their political will.[25] Members of all social groups, then, experience the difficulty of acting in politics as the abstract citizen should act.

Abstract freedom can be challenged and replaced with concrete freedom. For Hegel, everyman is no longer required to be *any* man, but allowed to be *each* man, or at least *this* man as situated in a definite social context. Each person, to achieve full individuality, still has to move away from his simple particularity towards universality, but now by a different route.[26] Whereas in Kant, "[human] reason mediates between the individual man and that which is universal in him," in Hegel it is "societal forms which mediated between such individual humans and the universal ideas of [a cosmic] reason."[27] Individuality, then, "expressed the particular insofar as it is united with the universal" through the forms of ethical life. In the *Philosophy of Right,* Hegel sets forth an elaborate architectonic structure of three spheres of ethical life—the family, civil society, and the state—each seen as increasing differentiations in the unfolding of the idea of freedom. Each sphere has its own articulation of social roles, and one sphere, civil society, has as its basis the status of pure individualism, of legal or "formal freedom." The logical necessity of these roles, such as "the good father," "the free person," "the patriotic subject," must be comprehended and chosen as duty if one is to be free, if one is to identify the good with one's subjective will.[28]

To the extent that this whole edifice rests on a notion of cosmic reason or spirit and its development in dialectical logic and history, then without it the edifice becomes a bit shaky. Nevertheless several important things can be salvaged. The main one is that freedom requires to be situated: it must start from a defining context in which the individual lives, about which he not only thinks and acts, but also feels and identifies, and this context sets initial purposes for him to achieve, as well as to rebel against and transform.[29] The second important implication is that political society must admit of civic differentiation.[30] This is necessary to protect against the potential power of the state based on a national mass of individuals in the postfeudal world. The radical period of the French Revolution, for example, can be seen as a terror resulting from the attempt by the political sphere to demolish the social sphere completely.[31] Paradoxically, conservative social differentiation is necessary to protect radical freedom. Even if one does not accept the precise lines of social differentiation of the old regimes (such as that the free individual of property join a corporation in civil society without a comparable organization being allowed to the laborer, or that a man but not a woman be entitled to civil rights), the general point remains: that social differentiation fosters the development of individuality, and that one might be able to set forth some general principles about which kinds of social groupings seek universal ends and which do not.

We have, then, certain assumptions behind our conception of political representation. First, that the political sphere, including political activity and the state, is a very significant sphere, with a certain moral life of its own. Second, that nevertheless it depends upon and should not ignore the society of which it is a part, even as it seeks to correct certain societal injustices. Third and fourth (and these are ways of restating the first two points), that "political individuality" or citizenship is a particular status of belonging to a community, from which one gains an identity, and this is posed in contrast to "social individuality" as well as to "formal individualism" in the modern age.

We call the status of personhood "formal individualism" and say that it has to be given a prominent place in representation. It involves the clearest, although not ultimately the deepest, kind of freedom. It entails liberty of the individual who is understood as a private being with his own subjective will. Such an individual enters into the second mode of association described earlier, of voluntary membership. The aspect of citizenship that involves rights in civil society expresses and ensures this form of freedom.

Civil society produces the formally free individual. By acting in a social arena based on the expression of subjective needs, even whims, yet also based on transitory organizational forms which give shape to that diverse activity, an individual person emerges. An individual comes to think of himself as a person who can decide how he will be recognized by others, and begins to shape his field of action, albeit in a limited way, to accord with his personal aims. The individual labors, an activity requiring disciplined subordination to an aim, and makes contracts, involving partial commitments for limited periods of time. He then enters into corporations, which stabilize these relations and focus and limit man's infinite desires. The corporation is a crucial mediating institution. In civil society strictly speaking, corporations are primarily functional ones, although in political society they can be based on territory as well.[32] This, we will see in the next chapter, has consequences for representation.

The formally free individual can also be produced by another route, not via secular civil society but rather by religion, both popular and theological, in civil society.[33] There had been early glimmerings of individualism in the Old Testament prophetic writings; these tendencies were developed more fully by Christianity. St. Augustine articulated the struggle in the soul of the individual as he seeks to find his own right relation to God; the way is different for each person. Catholicism developed the idea of the individual spirit which seeks to reach its ultimate object of adoration by its own authentic route, through a faith infused with love rather than solely by good works. We are by now aware that this doctrine underwent many changes over centuries and suffered a final declension from the Protestant notion of "calling" or "vocation" into a nearly secular work ethic which served as a (rather unsatisfying) sign of salvation. But the notion of individual personhood can be derived from the religious notion of a man's "private occupation"; the impetus towards modern personhood came from powerful religious doctrine, even as that doctrine underwent change. For religious doctrine to affect people it must be institutionalized in religious practices and organizations. The overall political society and its state will still be built upon secular principles, but religious pluralism may be one of its crucial underpinnings, and representation should take account of that.

We call the status of social belonging "social individuality," and accord it a certain, even if not prime, place in representation. Since formal individualism can emerge either out of secular or religious society, we do not necessarily want the functional corporations of civil society to be given representation. Nor do we follow Marx in his inversion of Hegel to require that one key social class "of, but not in, civil society" be represented. Instead, religious or ethnic or class groupings might be the relevant social community to represent. All of these are possibilities; none of them is foreclosed. What we will require is that one of them be represented in any situation, depending on which social precondition is the most salient to the person. The form of membership the individual experiences in relation to his religion, craft, or class is complicated; it is a combination of the natural and covenanted modes discussed earlier. On the one hand, it is a natural given, if one were born into it or it seemed to flow inevitably from one's talents and gifts; on the other hand, it is a higher covenanted membership, for one also knows, in a pluralistic society, that one could leave it, fall away, and so to choose to stay is an act of dedication. The person will not necessarily experience this social membership as a source of formal individualism; on the contrary, at the phenomenal level it will seem to be its opposite, social cohesion. But later (or actually, simultaneously), when posed in contrast to the state, social individuality can be seen as formal individualism's precondition.

The state is the "political whole" within which formal individualism is allowed to exist; the state produces and protects the civil and political rights of the individual. The state is also the whole within which a more "political individuality" is achieved. The main tasks of political representation will be to attend (in ways to be defined in chapters seven and eight) to the existence of the political whole as well as to promote the political individuality of its citizens. These two aspects are related but not identical; they are related as aspects of the dialectic of citizenship, in which, we will argue, membership in the whole is the moment of universality, living in a particular place is the moment of particularity, and the synthesis that emerges when the members of an area decide who will represent them is their political individuality.

The state grants the status of citizenship to certain of its inhabitants. The status includes the rights to civil and political liberty, and the duties of service, obligation, and loyalty. The national state serves as a political society, with a general conception of justice, an overall administration of services, and a national ideal of fellowship. Except for the extreme of mass mobilization in wartime, there is something symbolic about citizenship at this level. Not unreal, but abstract. The state represents the political ideals of the community at the abstract level, yet it needs a set of particular contexts before the ideals can be actualized.

The Meaning of Political Districting or Internal Boundaries: Membership Which Is Free

If citizenship is a relation of rights and duties to a body conceived as a public possession, then there have to be ways for citizens to arrive at that conception of themselves. The state as an organization of legitimate power must be appropriated by its members if there is to be citizenship. They may do this in the most active democratic way, of direct participation in legislative decisions, or they may do this in a more indirect but still essentially political way, in the choosing of representatives. In both cases, the political whole would have to be subdivided into smaller political parts.

A sovereign whole requires division into nonsovereign or semi-sovereign parts if citizenship is to be made real. The significance of internal boundaries within a whole is that they enable individuals to become aware both of their membership and their freedom. If there is only the whole, then one is experienced without the other: membership is experienced as unfree—national citizenship seems a natural given; or, alternatively, liberty is experienced without membership—civil rights are taken for granted as given.

Freedom requires acknowledging those aspects of one's existence that are not open to self-determination, before one can know what is open to change. If sovereignty or full determination occurs at the very top of ethical life (in the realm of ideas, and practically at the level of the state), and at the very bottom (in the facts of social birth), then self-consciousness first requires acknowledging the full weight of these determinations in the moral self, or the self that seeks to be moral. It may be that the only realm of freedom as self-determination lies in the middle, in deciding the path, the way out of the lower realm to the higher one. It may be that only in politics can one be free, as the formal individual seeks to define his or her political individuality, through "the idea of liberty in the intermediate sphere, inhabited by both natural necessity and moral ideals, wherein politics has always dwelled."[34] Yet how does this occur?

One acquires political individuality by choosing how one's intermediate community shall be defined—who the relevant others are, and how they should chart the path. It is a process that cannot be done alone, if objective value comes from agreement with concrete others. It is done with these others in a combination of reason, will, and emotion. The act of defining a political constituency makes one a free or political individual, precisely because the constituency is nonsovereign or intermediate. This is so for several reasons.

First, one is not born into it. One may be born there, but chances are that one was not, and has moved into the district. Or, if one were born there, one has been away for a time and returned. From this mobility comes a sense of the district's uniqueness in comparison with elsewhere. As an adult, citizens become self-conscious about what it means to say they are ward-members or members of this district, in a way that is hard to do for national citizenship. These experiences are available for national citizens only if they have traveled abroad, been in the army, or come as immigrants. They become aware that citizenship is not a natural but a civic fact, capable of being given and taken away by a political state.[35] They become aware of the possibilities gained and foregone in becoming members of a particular community. But for the vast majority who have not been out of their country, this remains an abstract conception. It is not felt, experienced. Membership in semisovereign districts helps teach this.

Second, the powers of a district are contested. The precise lines of its partial autonomy from the state are not set for all time; they are defined in ongoing political debate with that state's constitution; they are contestable. In one era a local district might have some representative functions but only the barest residue of home rule, a few police powers not covered by the nation or state; at other times, when the pendulum swings the other way, it may be granted fuller political and administrative powers. The pendulum does not just swing, it is pulled, and so local autonomy, and the uncertainty of that autonomy, contributes to the self-awareness of the locals as agents. For example, the powers of the municipal corporation as an intermediary body in America have varied, and one might argue that the municipal corporation should seek to regain at law the autonomy that the private corporation gained under the Fourteenth Amendment.[36] Members of a local district, in contesting the constitutional scope of its powers within the national situation, act almost as political founders.

Third, its relations are concrete. Citizenship in a local constituency involves face-to-face relations with specific people; one comes to know their particular personalities as well as their various characters. Obviously one does not know everyone, nor would one want to, but an individual can get to know and assemble a group of people he likes and trusts politically, as well as mark out those he detests. The knowledge of friend and foe at this level is based on a mixture of emotion and judgment, which mixture may admit of some tempering by more Machiavellian political reason as larger issues and coalitions come to be necessary. But this starting point of strong feeling and concrete judgment is essential to political knowledge, and to one's self-knowledge as a citizen. For in the beginning—in the district—as at the end—in the ideal of national fellowship—citizenship has to be a relation of association with people one respects.

Finally, as a result of these conditions, its membership is ironic. Irony describes the stance of one who is at a certain distance, who joins but with a disclaimer, a dissembling. Precisely because one knows that one might not be living here, might not be empowered, and now once living here, might choose not to participate, the local district member can be said to be in "ironic collaboration" with his constituency. It is a different sense of membership from the other modes we have discussed. It is a mode of membership appropriate to a self-conscious individual living in multiple contexts. In ironic collaboration the citizens' "consciousness of belonging is qualified, but not defeated, by their simultaneous consciousness of not belonging."[37]

We are not arguing that membership in the national state is to be conceived this way. Rather, that by becoming aware of the irony at the local level, the citizen might then feel free to surmount it for the whole.

SEVEN
Sources of a Communitarian Theory of Representation

Because social individuality and formal individualism come in so many varieties, and because they should not, even if they could, be pre-orchestrated into an organic whole through knowledge, we need to inquire into how a common whole might be created through political practice. A community's system of political representation is thus crucial to determining whether it has a common political life.

The mode of articulation of smaller units to the larger one affects the quality of relations among citizens. The different values of autonomous individuals and groups or, assuming they share the same ends, their differently perceived means to those goals, may be in tension one with another, yet there is an arena where they can be reconciled. Resolved not for all time (de Jouvenel calls that "the myth of the solution") but continually, in "the activity of ruling and being ruled." Aristotle's concept of citizenship as a sharing in the political whole, with an alternation between ruling and being ruled, prefigures the idea of representation.

Citizenship, we have seen, can be conceived as a complex relation of individual rights and duties to a body conceived as a public possession. Whereas in our era of liberal political theory in the face of the nation-state, citizenship primarily connotes a set of civil and political rights, in the more communitarian city-states of its origin, citizenship was as much a set of duties and obligations the fulfillment of which was considered an honor as well as a burden. The experience of citizenship becomes even more important if one understands political life as an end in itself, not merely instrumental to purposes given in nonpolitical life. In this vision, politics is a sphere with a meaning of its own, which gives even our private actions a moral basis; a process of fellowship and power among members who are free. Politics is a realm of high (and low) drama that no other sphere can attain.

Yet the public thing is also very fragile, and only rarely determinative of other spheres. The political whole and its political parts are not given to us by nature, even if they are our best end. Wolin writes that politics is a created field, and quite ephemeral.[1] It is the collective care of our common concerns, by citizens who are self-conscious.[2] Yet this activity can vanish for long stretches of history. It can succumb to the self-interest of the most powerful part of society; it can also be swamped by bureaucracy. If politics in this ideal sense cannot long last in opposition to social life, what conditions contribute to its appearance? If citizenship is not solely by nature but also by art, what factors attend its creation?

Creating citizenship involves transforming the dispositions and actions of people who nonetheless retain their individuality. Political theorists usually stress one of the two aspects, either attitudes or behavior. Thus Skinner characterizes those who defended the civic life of early Italian cities in two ways—the rhetorical and scholastic humanists—the former believing in the power of leadership and political education, the latter stressing the building of institutions.[3] Obviously, these two aspects together should form a whole: the idea is to have a civic consciousness consonant with political institutions. Yet how they are combined, and the weight and structure given to each, depend on how one views the proper relation of politics to social life.

The distinction between public and private life is crucial to any authentically political theory, although their boundary need not be drawn along liberal lines. I think we need a deeper understanding of what is "public," one which is analytically distinct from, yet still substantively linked to, what is private. Citizenship is a public role in which we each, while remaining also private, take account of our association together. Citizens, or free men and women in their public roles, seek the public good; they seek to create and preserve a shared context of action and affection.[4] Yet this public sphere exists, while contrasting, with a private sphere where people also live. In the view of citizenship and politics being advanced here, politics exists in constant tension with social life in a necessary dialectic. Politics should not seek to be all-powerful and revolutionary, completely remaking civil society and individual personality; it has its own transformative powers, but primarily within its own sphere. But nor, on the other hand, can politics completely ignore civil society, pretending its particularities do not exist.

Citizenship as free membership is primarily a relation of association, secondarily of appropriation. It arose out of city-states and is now situated in nation-states. Yet are we still talking about the same thing? They are not the same experience, yet do have their similarities. Both involve loyalty to a state that is sovereign, or if that sovereignty is qualified it is done so in similar ways, by other states, corporate groupings, natural law, or constitutional law. Both city-states and nation-states are distinguished politically from nonstate spheres within their borders, from families, markets, and churches. Both kinds of states allow the citizens to share in some aspects of political rule, yet both are too large, stratified, and complex for all the people to participate simultaneously in legislating and governing. The vastly greater size of the nation-state is a matter of degree, not new in kind.

The qualitative differences between the classical city-state and modern nation-state are that no persons are now allowed to be slaves, most persons are allowed to become citizens, and a distinction between citizens and private persons exists. These are serious differences which make the ancient situation disanalogous to our own. Yet there is another set of city-states, closer to our time, whose experience is more analogous. Late medieval and early Renaissance cities in northern and southern Europe had strong practices of citizenship and the modern conditions of political freedom (even though not full political equality). Despite differences of scale between these cities and nations, similar qualitative conditions hold. The political practices of these cities suggest ways in which we can stretch our concept of representation to encompass its full meaning.

In examining such a city-state as a source for a communitarian theory of representation, we may ask: how can representative institutions challenge people to express some of their already deeply held private values and feelings as well as teach them new public ones? In sociological terms, how can representative institutions mediate class, status, and ethnic divisions; political science might ask what institutions produce the most legitimate policies and stable polities; and political theory would ask how does politics produce fellowship and justice, the best political leadership, and citizens who are free? Our special focus is, how does a public sphere emerge that treats people and issues differently than in the private sphere?

Citizen Rotation in Office in Early Renaissance Florence

The political experience of early Renaissance Florence sheds a special light on these questions. Florence, "that bedazzling array of conflicting loyalties," also managed to form a polity with a coveted status of citizenship.[5] A citizen might belong to a neighborhood, family, church, and political party, as well as a trade guild, local militia company, lay or religious confraternity, and political faction. Yet by the beginning of the 1400s, the political commune and its citizenship was the acknowledged center of these loyalties, practiced and celebrated in the public philosophy of "civic humanism."

Florence as a republican city-state existed at a crossroads between the medieval and modern worlds, between feudal corporatism and modern individualism. It thus provides an example of how a political system might cope with the claims of particular group traditions and universal rules of justice, achieving a new synthesis between them. The late Middle Ages itself had that tension in the contrast between the concrete obligations of feudalism and the concrete and abstract obligations of Christianity. Pocock has argued that Florence forged a new kind of knowledge, a specifically political philosophy of human interaction, which began to bridge this antimony and eventually leave it behind.[6] By the time of the fall of the republic, her political thinkers had issued a new ideal of human action—the concept of political *virtù*—set in a theory of republican mixed government and a cyclical theory of history. Political *virtù* was that public action that created a republic of free citizens and saved it from destruction in time. This *virtù*, of great leaders and citizens, had a different morality from the Christian virtue of the people upon which it also depended. Politics had thus acquired a certain meaning and morality of its own. Its end was republican liberty, its extraordinary means was political *virtù*, and its ordinary practice was citizenship—understood as a competition to share in political magistracy, with the mutual affection, conversation, conniving, deliberation, and discipline that entailed.

The Machiavellian tradition put great stress upon the political education of its citizens, "not so much the machinery of government as the proper *spirit* of the rulers, the people and the laws, which needs above all to be sustained.[7] The character of citizens, their inner resources for both virtue and *virtù*, was the thing, rather than the structuring of an efficient governmental system that would coordinate corruption or private vice into a public good. Yet it is still the case that political institutions were seen as an important element in the political education of the citizen; public spirit was acquired not just through following the example and exhortation of a prince, but through participation in republican institutions.

We wish to consider the contribution of one set of political institutions to the emergence of civic humanism. The geographical division of Florence into local political districts and the increasing array of communal activities performed through them, especially the nomination of citizens according to district for public office, promoted the growth of civic spirit.

The period 1250–1433 saw "Florence in transition," moving from a medieval commune to a modern territorial state. A centralized political authority acquired sovereignty, wresting it from external powers (emperor, pope, other city-states), and from internal corporate bodies (nobility, church, family, guild). Exactly how the city did this, and what relation it forged between political and civil society, is significant, for it did not move directly in a unilinear direction of the state confronting an undifferentiated mass of individuals. While it is true that the nobility and church were subdued as alternate sources of power, the same cannot be said so simply of the guilds, families, and neighborhoods. In some ways these were weakened, but in other ways their energies were increased and encouraged, while channeled in a political direction. One of the institutions that performed this political taming, as it were, was the electoral system.

Florence had complicated and oft-changing ways of admitting citizens to the polity and choosing citizens to be officeholders. It was a system of citizen rotation in office, a practice midway between ancient participation and modern representation. These procedures embodied definite, if unarticulated, principles of who should rule, in what manner, and for what ends. While theoretically citizens for high office were chosen by lot, the actual lottery involved certain assumptions. Steps were later added so that Cosimo de' Medici, sometimes called the greatest political boss of all time, could artfully manipulate the outcome favorable to his family's rule. But for almost two centuries before, the system combined certain structural principles of what was to be represented with relatively open procedures of who was to rotate in office.

Florence Observed: Guilds, Districts, and Commune

Three organizations, the guilds, districts, and commune itself, played a major role in deciding who would be chosen for high office. The guilds and wards represented relations of appropriation in their power over productive and military resources, respectively. The commune as a whole combined these sources of power, with their accompanying fraternal ties, into the status and activity of citizenship, a new associative tie among members of the city. The dynamic between the guilds and districts lent a vitality to the representative system, issuing in a political corporatism that produced citizens.

A snapshot of the governmental structure in 1343, midway in the period, captures the essential offices. The three highest offices (*Tre Maggiori*) were the Priorate or Signory and its two advisory colleges. The Signory had eight priors plus a standard-bearer of justice (Gonfalonier of Justice), the most prestigious post in the commune. Two collegiate bodies with voting rights advised the Priorate: the Twelve good men or worthies (*buonuomini*), and the Sixteen standard-bearers (*gonfalonieri*) of the militia companies. Citizens served in the Signoria for two months, the Twelve for three months, and the Sixteen for four months. The Signoria was the executive; it had "general responsibility for internal administration and the conduct of foreign affairs . . . [and only it] initiated legislation."[8]

Membership in the guilds was generally required for citizenship and high office. At first this meant that a man had to practice a trade in one of the citywide trade and artisan associations to exclude nobles whose livelihood came from elsewhere; this requirement was soon relaxed to mean that one could have a formal or former membership in a guild.[9] If one were a "new man" not born of a citizen, there were also other hurdles to pass before being admitted to the polity,[10] yet the guilds remained the main gateway to citizenship. The entire citizenry was equal to the membership of the guilds (save for the proscribed magnates, members of one hundred families notorious for resorting to private vengeance), and the Signoria would from time to time call special mass assemblies (*parlementi*) of the whole guild community.

For a brief time the guilds had direct political representation in the government. Three and then six Priors of the Guilds, who were consuls of the main guilds, served as the chief magistracy,[11] and later the priors were chosen by "independent nominations from each of twelve guilds and [that] allowed no more than one Prior from any guild in each term of office."[12] Unit representation of individual guilds, however, did not last. What did continue was the requirement that the Signoria offices be distributed along the lines of the seven upper and fourteen lower guilds. The statutory proportion varied and was the occasion for political battle in the Signory and the streets, the outcome usually allowing the lower guildsmen one-quarter of the seats. Thus the guild community remained not only a gateway to citizenship but to high office as well, and the distinction between greater and lesser guilds provided a structural principle about what interests were to be given greater weight in public affairs.

But the guilds were not the only gateway and they no longer provided the electoral units, which moved to the commune as a whole and its political parts. Even in the regimes where the guilds held the greatest power, the commune always required that the Priors be distributed according to a second principle—equal division among the geographical districts of the city. Medieval Florence had been divided into quarters, and when the city became an independent commune it divided into sixths (*sesti*). Two consuls from each *sesto* formed the central magistracy, and the choosing of consuls or priors by sixths was continued in subsequent regimes. Then in 1343 the districts were redrawn to quarters. It is said that the Oltr'arno quarter of Santo Spirito threatened to secede from the city and destroy the bridges across the river if the redistricting did not go through. Each quarter—S. Spirito, Santa Croce, San Giovanni, and Santa Maria Novella—had a distinctive character, with certain kinds of industries and crafts predominating, and each had a diversity of social classes and political factions.[13] The poorest workers tended to be concentrated in S. Croce and S. Spirito, and some of the commune's most powerful families resided there. The populations of the four were not equal; for example, in 1382, they ranged from 8,869 to 25,255.[14]

Florence was further divided into sixteen wards (*gonfaloni*), each with its own banner with a mascot—Red Lion, Unicorn, Black Ox, and other diverse creatures—and standard-bearer, the *gonfaloniere*. The wards were military in origin; as Machiavelli chronicles, they formed the basis of the popular militia system: "With these ordinations, civil and military, the Florentines established their liberty."[15] The first popular regime established twenty armed companies of citizens in the city and ninety-six companies in the countryside. Unlike the rural companies, the ones inside the city walls did not correspond to parish lines, not only because there were so many parishes in town (two to ten per ward), but also because the commune was trying to establish itself as a force independent of the church.[16] *Gonfalon* lines sometimes cut parishes in two. While the parish remained in some senses the center of associational life, gradually two larger geographical areas came to predominate: what Cohn has called the "cluster" for social relations of marriage endogamy, and the formal gonfalons and quarters for politics and revolution. After the defeat of the Ciompi, unorganized workers who wanted to form their own guilds and share in political power, the noncitizen working classes would retreat to the parish once more.[17] By that time, the wards and the commune had been consolidated as the basis of associational life for the citizen.

The wards and quarters became the basic units in the selection process for government office. The gonfalonier of each ward put the names of citizens in for nomination, and then a citywide council nominated some of them according to ward or quarter, depending on the office. Officeholders were chosen by lot according to quarters, in a few cases by wards. Equal numbers of citizens were chosen from each district;[18] this was never contested.

In theory, offices were to be rotated among all citizens of all factions. By statute, citizens for the *Tre Maggiori* were chosen by lot rather than elected by hand, *a mano*. At a middle stage of the process, however, officials passed on citizens' eligibility for office and did a bit of arranging of the selection purses. A special citywide Scrutiny Council[19] met every three or five years and by a two-thirds majority decided which citizens were eligible for the lottery, approving one-tenth to one-fifth of citizens.[20] This public scrutiny (*squittinio*) was the one stage in the process where it was legitimate to bring "political and economic interests" to bear in "the actual appointments to office," and this only occasionally lapsed into corruption.[21] Another step was added that was not written into statute "for the simple reason that elections *a mano* of the Signoria were unconstitutional."[22] Special electoral officials appointed by the Signoria, the *accoppiatori*, were allowed to put names in the purses according to new numerical limits and, in forming this shortlist of sorts, they came to exercise great discretion.

Throughout these changes the geographic districts remained the basis of the final sortition, the choosing of names from the purses. The Signory and the Gonfalonier of Justice were allotted in a complicated manner, which only Rubinstein can describe succinctly. "In the sortition of the Signoria, a total of eight bags was used: one for the Gonfalonier of Justice, the office rotating among the four *quartieri;* one for the two artisan members, for the *quartiere* which happened to provide the Gonfalonier; and six for the remaining three *quartieri*, that is three from each of the two kinds of bag from which the Priors' names were drawn, the *borsellino* and the *borsa generale*."[23] The Gonfalonier of Justice had to be an upper guildsman and come from the quarter that provided the two lower guildsmen, and six other purses were for upper guildsmen, one little bag of specially selected names and one general bag for each quarter. Clearly there was an effort to keep the highest political power evenly matched among the quarters, for not only was numerical representation of priors equal between districts, but an approximation of class power as well, in the rough equation of two artisans plus the Gonfalonier being equal to two richer commoners (*popolo grasso*). And the more local the districting, the more diverse the social base of candidates. The college of the Twelve *buonuomini* was also chosen according to quarter, three to a district. The college of the Sixteen *gonfalonieri* was chosen according to wards, and this was the most democratic magistracy of the *Tre Maggiori*, in the sense of having the highest proportion of new men.[24]

Neighborhoods Not Natural But Created

Nomination of citizens according to wards steadily grew in importance until the wards became the sole source of candidates for the scrutiny. After the guilds lost their monopoly on nominations, two other organizations gained the power to put in names: the captains of the Guelph party and the gonfalonieri of the wards, and some statutes only mentioned the gonfalonieri.[25] While occasionally a gonfalonier "might use his influence to help friends who were not also neighbors," by and large the neighborhood became the basis of political networks; even the Medici family had to build a base in their home district first.[26] Although some wards were dominated by powerful families, usually there was turnover in the families who predominated and these families were more diverse socially than those who controlled the Guelph party.[27] Diaries attest that the new men worked at gaining access to the various cliques in their wards and gaining the patronage of the more powerful men and the ward's gonfalonier.[28]

The wards were important and relatively democratic units because of this political function and also because of their military origins and administrative role. Militarily, they represented a democratization of the city's fighting forces, from an exclusive dependence on nobles to a new involvement of commoners (*popolani*). The armed companies of the wards infused the *sesti* themselves with a popular character; the commoners marched under the gonfalons of the commune, rather than as previously under the gonfalons of the guilds. (Due to the distrust between the people and the magnates, they marched under different leaders.) Political districts soon fought together; in one battle a leader led men of his district and they were all "covered with glory."[29] Military patriotism affected civic loyalties; citizens now became attached to their wards. When a duke tried to change a procession of the festival honoring the commune's patron saint by having people march behind the gonfalons of the guilds instead of the wards, he met with an uproar.[30] The civic militia, while it lasted, had the effects that Machiavelli celebrates: it taught the *popolo* some aristocratic virtues—the pursuit of honor and glory, the art of war, the courage to fight and to sacrifice. It also taught the nobles some popular virtues—the taming of family loyalty, the discipline of communal endeavor, the restrictions of public control. Eventually the civic militia was abolished by the Signoria, the use of mercenaries having increased, yet the militia left a heritage of local patriotism.

Socially and politically, this is evident in various statutes.[31] One law legitimated a practice in which a magnate could change his status to a *popolano* and hence be eligible for high office if he renounced his family name and its armed *consorterie*, and moved to another section of the city.[32] One sees here the belief, based on reality, that the wards were a powerful influence on a man, and that families were strong in the wards. The commune also exercised its sovereignty, while acknowledging the importance of the districts, in its requirement that a citizen who wished to move from one district to another apply to the commune for permission.[33] Families were often self-conscious about building their power base in one ward, or sending out a few family members to colonize another ward, and this kind of political maneuvering is something the commune might well have wanted to keep its eye on.

The second development contributing to the politics of the wards was their emerging administrative role. Now the republic's need for money—for its foreign wars, mercenaries, public works, and public debt—made it democratize further, opening citizenship to the prosperous new men who were settling in the city and starting families. When the city consolidated all its outstanding debts into one *monte* or "mountain of indebtedness," it listed eight thousand communal creditors, citizens listed in a registry by the quarters of the city.[34] (This is almost three times the number nominated for the scrunity that year, showing the degree to which citizenship exceeded nomination, and certainly rotation, in office.) In collecting indirect taxes such as the *prestanze* or forced loans, a quota would be imposed on each quarter of the city and hamlet of the countryside, which, if one citizen did not pay, the others had to step in to fulfill.[35]

Ward cohesiveness was enhanced by a procedure developed in preparation for the first direct tax on property. A commission formed with members from each ward to draw up an *estimo,* a schedule of estimates of the property worth of each citizen. The tax was not instituted for fifty years, but when it was, local committees of assessors were in place ready to work.[36] This system lasted another half century until the *catasto* was imposed, the first completely direct tax where the individual filed directly with the state his assessment of the worth of his personal and real property; only here did the sovereign city-state confront the mass of its citizens directly, without social or political intermediation. For years before that, little groups of citizens had been sitting down to assess the worth of their neighbors' property, and filling the ward's quota if a neighbor defaulted. This led to various stratagems of appearing poor. Cosimo de' Medici's austerity in his living style was probably due as much to political prudence as to religious or economic motives, but for the more average new man who would not excite such great envy by his wealth or political ambition, the desire to acquire and conceal was more simply economic. A merchant "wrote his wife to spread the word that ships carrying his merchandise had been lost at sea," and another urged his sons to sneak their farm produce into their townhouse at night and lie about their wealth to members of their *gonfalon*.[37] Yet these merchants were very successful and were also given to great bursts of public generosity through donations to the guilds for public works and loans to the state through the *monte*.[38] Like most people of all eras, they chafed under and schemed at direct taxation, but they generally paid. The ward-based *estimo* put them under public scrutiny in a pre-political sense, so that by the time they were established enough to reach the political *squittinio,* their neighbors knew a thing or two about their characters.

Representation by Districts Signifies a Political Corporatism

The structure of political representation in early Renaissance Florence contributed to citizenship and civic humanism. A specially selected body of citizens, chosen not only by chance but also by diverse power considerations, acted in the name of something other than themselves; in this sense, they were political representatives. They were not, to be sure, modern delegates elected for longer periods of time to express the wishes of a mass of voters. To some extent, Florence knew about these alternatives and rejected them, prohibiting longer and continual terms of office and only allowing elections *a mano* for lower office. The Florentines certainly knew about the diverse desires of a tumultuous, violence-prone, conspiratorial populace. They just did not think it would be particularly helpful to have those differences directly reflected in the polity and therefore they constructed an electoral system more suited to what they wanted to achieve.

These political procedures of citizen rotation ensured that individuals would consider themselves members of the polity. The ideas of political representation implicit here help us to appreciate the overcoming of a person's particularity versus a state's universality in the synthesis of a citizen's political individuality. Since in theory all citizens were eligible for the scrutiny, and since the names were not drawn from the purses until actually needed, every citizen could harbor the hope that he was one of the political elect. This lifelong uncertainty about "the secret of the scrutiny"[39] led to a sense of belonging even for those who were not chosen. Actual participation was not essential to active identification with the goals and methods of the polity,[40] understood as a corporate commune subdivided into geographical political parts which put in the local names.

Pitkin has written that all representation is "the making present of something which is nevertheless not literally present."[41] That "which is not literally present" at this moment but predates it—as citizen's wish or heritage or goal—is "made present" by the representative, who presents it again, or even for the first time. In the case of Florence, the high officials represented a political corporatism, the commune as a political body constituted of four geographical quarters composed of sixteen geographical wards. These were the units given equal representation and the key role in nominations; for all the other contests in those years, these divisions were rarely challenged,[42] and only twice redistricted. Geographical areas that developed into neighborhoods with a political existence were the units of representation; to an extent they had existed, to an extent they were created.

This political corporatism differs, then, both from individualism and functional corporatism. There was never representation of individual people, or even of individual citizens. Kent finds that the number of citizens cleared by the scrutiny from each quarter in 1382 and the years following tended to be equal, and surmises that this was intentional.[43] Thus the commune came to accord equal nomination and representation to each of the quarters; despite differences in area and population, each quarter was deemed an equally valuable part of the whole. Yet if individuals were not represented, neither were functional groups, the corporatism in which representatives act in virtue of specific interests of civil society. Except for one brief period, at no other time did the commune allow high office to individuals chosen by particular groups—the family *consorterie,* the church, the guilds, or the Guelph party. While not utterly vanquishing these groupings, the state increasingly required that they direct their political energies through the units of the commune, its wards and quarters.

Aspects of Representation: Authorization and Accountability, Descriptive and Symbolic Standing For, and Acting For

This political corporatism meets all of Pitkin's meanings of representation, as well as the creative dimension she sees in specifically political representation. For Pitkin, there are five different meanings to representation: the formal aspects of "authorization" and "accountability," and the substantive aspects of "standing for," in a descriptive and also a symbolic sense, as well as the substantive dimension of "acting for."[44] Florence's political corporatism is stronger on the substantive than the formal aspects because of what it wants to represent, but all the aspects are there. Whereas the original analysis of these categories finds them to have alternative and often incompatible meanings, I think this is due to the transmission belt situation. In a complexly differentiated communitarian polity all the aspects of representation could coexist.

Formal representation involves one person willing instead of another, in his stead, by grant of formal authority. "Authorization" to do so may occur at the beginning of representing; "accountability" occurs at the end, or at intervals, in the process. Florence gave authorization to its high officials; the Signory was legally empowered to sign treaties, make policy, pass legislation. Formal authorization was very limited, however, to those extremely short terms of two, three, four, sometimes six months. Yet despite the high turnover of citizens in office, there was considerable continuity of policy. This was partly due to the continuity provided by the advisory councils whose opinions the Signory respected, and by the upper civil servants of the bureaucracy; the civil humanist chancellors Salutati and Bruni and civil servant and diplomat Machiavelli are outstanding examples. Limited authorization worked also because continuity existed in the minds of the citizens; officeholders changed rapidly but through the wide rotation in office men were socialized, to an extent, to its necessities.

For those who were not so inculcated, there was accountability. Procedures of accountability occurred mainly in the extreme: citizens would be exiled from the city or banned from holding office. During certain crises, these were frequent; the exiling of Cavalcanti and Dante are poignant examples. Later the Guelph party would issue proscriptions declaring certain citizens unfit for public office on the grounds that they had treasonous intentions and connections. This tactic got out of hand, prompting the Signoria to pass various reforms (especially urged by the ward-based Sixteen), which toned down the party and "shattered permanently the threadbare myth" that the party equaled the commune.[45] After that, the commune returned to more normal procedures of accountability: the quinquennial nomination procedures held previous officeholders to account, deciding whether they were entitled to be nominated again.

Whereas in formal representation the representative wills "instead of another," in substantive representation he wills "for another," so that in some way their wills can be said to coincide.[46] Rousseau argues that since the will is absolutely free it can never be represented by another, and so only formalistic representation is allowed. But most theorists save substantive representing by arguing that a person can be expected to will what is in his interest and wants to have that interest represented; insofar as his will goes against his own interest, that is part of his liberty but he would not want that to be given representation. Whether the theory of interest posits the ubiquity of subjective interests or the existence of objective interests has consequences for the role of the representative, as we have seen: if only individuals can know their own interests, then their representatives tend to be delegates of their instructing; if there are objective interests that can be known by others, then the representative is freer to act in virtue of his understanding of these interests.[47]

Florence's political corporatism involved substantive representation in its three aspects: descriptive and symbolic "standing for" as well as "acting for" something not literally present. The theory of interest underlying their conception of political life tends more towards the objectivist pole; hence citizen officeholders are deemed to stand and act more for a set of goals and a shared way of life rather than for the particular wishes of a set of people. Yet the goal is republican liberty and fraternity in the context of a sovereign commune, and so those very goals give a certain scope to individualism.[48]

Political representatives descriptively stood for two mediating structures deemed crucial to the polity: the guilds and districts. Citizens in high office spoke and acted as individuals yet could be expected to give not a mere reflection but an "articulate" "rendering" of the interests of the members of those organizations.[49] They could be expected to have the "intention to depict" the interests of the guilds and districts because they themselves were members of these bodies, the citizen members of these bodies were considered political equals, and they had been chosen in the public sortition according to these bodies. In the case of the guilds, the citizens stood for two layers of civil society, upper and lower guildsmen, in the proportions political struggle allotted them, usually three to one. Representation here was of wide horizontal groupings, citywide functional interest. The prosperity of the guilds was thought to be coterminous with prosperity for the city; if one part of the commune started to go bankrupt, another part of the guild community moved to bail it out.[50] After the revolt of the unorganized workers, when the guild community refused to expand further and the oligarchical regime breathed a sigh of relief, both the guilds and the commune made a mistake, for thereafter the identity of interests began to fall apart. Soon the guilds exercised no significant independent role in political affairs; the dynamism all went to the family-based wards. By losing a citywide network of industrialists, merchants, artisans, and workers in a secular fraternal organization, the commune could become easier prey to the rise of a powerful family faction and eventually to Medici despotism. That the triumph of the district over the guild system was *so* complete is the one way in which, in the long run, it helped undermine one of the bases of civic humanism.

Meanwhile and nevertheless, the wards became and remained the locus of that "veritable trilogy" of associations—*parenti, vicini e amici*— kinsmen, neighbors, and friends.[51] These three relations were basic to the Florentines as free citizens, proud of many private aspects of their own personalities and knowledgeable, if not always so proud, about the public characters of their compatriots. It is important to note here, however, that these neighborhoods did not exist as preformed wholes; the system of political representation helped create them. "Men of their neighbors become sensible"[52] when the politics of the ward encourages them to do so; otherwise, neighbors tend to remain strangers. While historians often list the neighborhood as an ancient loyalty alongside other corporate groupings predating the republic, there is a sense in which the neighborhoods were really not such ancient loyalties at all. Maybe for the old *magnati* families with their armed tower societies, but even there the family ties across district lines proved stronger than neighborhood if it came to a conflict. Political, military, and economic policies by the state created and consolidated the neighborhoods in a new sense, empowering them as local political communities with specific representative and administrative roles.

The political corporatism of the electoral system also played a symbolic role. Behind or beyond the structures of the guilds and districts were the values to which they aspired. That the guilds were the gateway to citizenship meant that the status of productive work was high; it had come a long way from its low status in ancient Athens as well as its uncertain status in medieval Catholicism. While not yet heralded as the methodical path to divine salvation, work was now celebrated as one path to earthly glory. Civic humanism encouraged the economic activity of its members, and the guilds competed with each other to provide the funds for the most beautiful statues for public buildings. A second way in which the guilds had important symbolic meaning was in providing that stake in civil society considered a necessary precondition to citizenship. Whereas for Aristotle, real property provided the proprietary interest that would lead to prudence in politics, the Florentines were more modern in moving not only to movable property but to property in one's labor itself as the essential precondition.[53] If one had a craft and joined a guild corporation one could be counted upon to have a recognized status in civil society and a dependable interest in the prosperity of the city. Rather than property in land or urban realty, the essential stake came from the restraints felt by those who treasured a trade.

What the districts symbolized is more complex. At the same moment, they represented the unity of the commune as well as its internal diversity. That the sixteen wards in four quarters were coequally grouped together, interdependent under a sovereign government, there was no doubt; yet there was some suggestion that each geographical area also represented in some way a microcosm of the whole. Not that they were exact replicas, but at least in the general fact of social diversity of classes and legal strata, all districts shared common dilemmas. At times they all were divided by political factions which cut across class lines. The ward system affirmed that these political factions were healthy so long as kept within lawful limits of political coexistence (no mean feat in Florence). Skinner has traced the change in the attitude towards faction from prehumanist to civic humanist thought; whereas the prehumanists were fearful of faction and sought to achieve a public good by having individuals immediately equate their own good with that of the whole, the humanists accepted that faction was itself part of the very liberty they sought, for individuals could express their love of the republic by joining with others who shared their political views.[54] Becker describes the change in civic consciousness in different, yet parallel, terms: from the poets' hope in a "gentle *paideia,*" a community bound by the love of brethren, in the context of divine love, to the humanists' teaching of the "stern *paideia,*" a community bound by a legitimate coercive state, equality before the law, and the discipline and respect of citizens.[55] The significance of the districts for political life is that they symbolized the ideal of a polity that was a harmony, not a simple unity. This was Aristotle's metaphor and they were aware of it. The districts, in their internal diversity, allowed for that healthy tumult which gave energy and vitality to politics; it allowed a structure within which people could group, win, lose, regroup again.[56] To use our terms, they allowed for political individuality, for as citizen of the ward the individual found a status and activity within which his particular personality might make contact with one aspect of universality, the glory of the commune.

Finally, there was representation in the sense of acting for others. But here there was little or no sense that the representative should act for his particular geographical constituency. Once selected, while the individual citizen might "stand for" his particular ward in both a descriptive and symbolic sense, he was supposed to "act as" an individual and "act for" the whole. There was a change in the quality of debate in the Signoria and its advisory councils so that by the regime of 1411 a new language had emerged.[57] Compared to a century and even a half century earlier, the leaders were no longer speaking in received rhetorical formulae and solely in terms of their corporate associations. They had moved to a new individuality, a more analytical mode of reasoning that also increasingly drew upon the city's own history as a unique source of experience and judgment. In short, the priors were speaking more like statesmen, speaking and acting for the interests of the political whole.

There remained, of course, a tension between the public and the private lives of the citizens holding high office. Yet "[t]he public world was no less real because its values were not completely internalized."[58] In fact, the tension between the two spheres is what created the possibility and necessity for civic humanism. Capponi prefigures Machiavelli by a century when he urges his sons to elect those men "who love the commune more than their own welfare and even their own souls," and yet he also advises them to "maintain the closest ties with your neighbors and relatives, and serve your friends at home and abroad."[59] The Florentine system of political representation made it possible for the citizen to inhabit both the public and private worlds; other representative systems can widen their distance to an unbridgeable chasm. Representation by guild and by district allowed a man to begin his politics at work and in his ward, with family, neighbors, and friends. If it sometimes required that he break with them in the interests of communal liberty, this was due to the representational, and teleological, nature of politics, which strives to make present that which is not yet present.

EIGHT
Constitutive Representation

The dynamic between wards and guilds in Renaissance Florence assured a connection between public and private life, producing public-spirited citizens. Each person admitted to a guild had his productive existence recognized politically in the role assigned to the guilds in choosing representatives. A citizen could be assured that his material self-interest would be taken into account, even if it sometimes had to be weighed against other class interests or the material interests of the commune as a whole. A citizen was also someone much more than a guildsman, for the guilds were trained to exercise their political energies through the wards. Territorial districts gained political and administrative powers which made them arenas both for material interests as well as schools in civic dignity. This dignity was a new creation, a secular status sometimes involving power and glory and always involving association and equality.

What comparable dynamic between organizations could we find in modern America to achieve a similar result? We actually have more alternatives open to us because of the versatility of the modern mass political party. So that in addition to a symbiotic relation between, say, labor unions or trade associations and districts, there can be the dynamic between political parties and districts. A party may serve as either an associative or appropriative tool, or both. What seems important to the formation of citizenship is that there be two organizations that interact, one that clearly represents the polis and another that bridges the public and the private spheres. The articulation of these two organizations helps produce an integrated and differentiated citizen.

Yet in America an influential current of thought has often denied the importance of these mediating organizations. Early twentieth-century Progressives attacked all special interest groups and devalued political parties and districts, considering them special interests akin to the others;

it sought to reform, perhaps to destroy, them. The National Municipal League had a view of good government in which elected representatives would directly represent the public interest. As we saw earlier, to this end they advocated replacing local ward-based representation with at-large elections, in which all representatives to smaller legislatures would be chosen by entire cities; they succeeded in this for 60 percent of American cities, and also validated similar practices for some state legislatures. Their argument was that whereas politicians elected by local districts act on behalf of parochial and private-regarding interests, and in personalistic ways riddled with patronage, the officials elected by the political unit as a whole are public-regarding, dignified, and adhering to impersonal canons of merit.[1] In this we can now see they were Kantian; the representative was to act as if he were everyman, and could attend to the public interest by thinking in general categories about the issues at hand.[2] Not only the representative but also the voting citizen was to act as if he embodied the whole, in choosing a few representatives who best personified the whole.

It is generally agreed that at-large elections contributed to the weakening of traditional party organizations and resulted in a different kind of representative being elected. In contrast to the rather tumultuous period of mid- to late-nineteenth-century American history, representatives now came more uniformly from the dominant ethnic and class groups—Protestant as opposed to Catholic or Jew, white rather than black, and salaried and self-employed rather than wage-earning. Members of these groups had greater ability to win at-large elections because they had the kind of articulateness recognized as the common denominator of the society and greater access to the funding required for larger campaigns. Whether this kind of representation better serves their constituents and the polity is debatable. Whereas the kind of petty corruption that characterized the machine regimes decreased, the overall quality of socioeconomic policy has been the same in both systems, specific policy responsiveness may vary, and minorities feel excluded from such systems.[3] Efforts by coalitions to return to district elections continue.

The political debate on the merits of district versus at-large elections has been conducted mainly in terms of discrimination. This is not surprising in view of the historical legacy of black slavery in America and, too, the nativist prejudices evinced against urban immigrant groups. We have seen how the Supreme Court stresses the terms of discrimination in its decisions on litigation surrounding the Voting Rights Act, and argued that the theory of discrimination is not adequate to discussing the issue. For there are other crucial aspects to the matter, most notably the question of which system of representation best promotes citizenship. Perhaps the Court cannot be faulted for sticking to narrow constitutional doctrine to decide these issues, since it is not within its scope to decide what "a republican form of government" shall mean for the states and localities. Nevertheless, when the Court has tried to bring in considerations that inform the situation of representative democracy, it has gotten itself into problems, sometimes tending towards the ideas of one person, one vote in one big district with proportional representation, or of functional representation and virtual representation by race. Even if these alternatives have not usually appeared as doctrine in decisions, they are characteristic of current American nonjudicial thinking on the issue— tendencies either towards a highly abstract good government or towards an ethnically particularized neofeudalism.

Late twentieth-century popular political thought is questioning progressivism and turning to conservative corporatism, as exemplified in a little pamphlet by Berger and Neuhaus published by the American Enterprise Institute.[4] It criticizes what they see as Enlightenment liberalism's exclusive reliance on the state and individual, and proposes instead a "paradigm of pluralism" in which social policy would focus on four mediating structures: neighborhood, family, church, and voluntary association. These institutions are important for "they exist where people are," in contrast to the state, capitalist enterprise, big labor, and educational and professional bureaucracies, which are excluded because they are "megastructures." People lack a general political will, but "On matters of family, church, neighborhood, hobbies, working place, and recreation, most people have a very clear idea of what is in their interest." "Liberation," they assert, "is not escape from particularity, but discovery of the particularity that fits."[5]

While at first this sounds rather like our critique advanced in earlier chapters, a closer examination reveals its deficiencies. It has an indiscriminate theory of "particularity," little notion of formal "individualism," and no notion of political "individuality." Its particularism is indiscriminate in that it ignores the sphere of civil society, the realm of "needs and labor." It is hard to see how a theory of mediating structures after Hegel and Marx can ignore the second ethical realm, between the family and the state, the sphere of free contract and alienable property and labor, and of membership in corporation and craft. Surely this too is "where people are," where they express much of their creative energy as well as find it thwarted. Berger and Neuhaus fail to acknowledge the modern individual, in his and her status as a legally free person and in their yearning for disciplined self-expression. Insofar as they do notice it, they imply that this liberty is expressed mainly in leisure-time activities of life-style, ideology, friendships, hobbies, recreation, and charity.

They also have no notion of a whole person apart from one's particular determinations; yet, lacking an architectonic theory, they overlook the possibility of a person's particularities coming into role conflict, which might then require moral choice or autonomy. There is no way here of achieving what we have called individuality, of experiencing a significant joining of particularity with universality. As Price points out, they continually see universality and particularism as necessarily opposed, failing to see the ways in which they can sometimes connect.[6] For example, in liberty of religion, each of its forms reaches for the universal; this contrasts to, say, liberty of hobbies, in which none of its forms do. By failing to perceive the kinds of knowledge and human activity that can bridge particularities horizontally at the local level and bridge the particular and the universal vertically between levels, they deny the possibility of human freedom, both abstract and concrete.

Put another way, and here we add our fuller notion of communitarian politics to the vacuum left by the collapse of Hegel's cosmic reason, neoconservatism is distinctly antipolitical. It is explicitly antistate but also implicitly antipolitics. Even though Berger and Neuhaus are at pains to remind us that there are things "public which are not governmental,"[7] they also assert that people never have a general political will about anything other than defense of their partial social groupings, and hence politics is reduced to social pluralism. Family and voluntary associations are praised, but political clubs, movements, and parties are not. They exalt existing social institutions without seeing that poor people are barely connected to those structures and they ignore the community-building aspects of political organizations. That, obviously, is partly an empirical question, but the normative issue remains: whether one thinks that political activity can ever be transformative, between citizens seeking fellowship and justice in community.

The state is not the family writ large, recent appeals notwithstanding. Neither the patriarchal nor the mothering family is an appropriate image for the relation of citizens. In searching for alternatives to the liberal ideal of the polity, we must not retreat to pre-political conceptions.

Constituting the Parts: Political Districts

The structure of a representative system can contribute to the formation of citizens, for the institution itself embodies and promotes certain understandings of politics. "Organisation is the form of mediation between theory and practice," organization more fundamental than ideology because organization embodies ideology and because organization affects which ideological carriers will predominate.[8] The structure of political organizations is as determinative of political outcomes and values as are other factors.[9] If glory and diversity amidst fraternal membership are desired outcomes, then district representation promotes these values more than other arrangements.

Political representation can be conceived as an ongoing founding, as the constitution of community. Founding: to create a constituency, to constitute it, and hence to define oneself as well.

Political founding traditionally involves the giving of a constitution to a people, bequeathing them a set of institutions, laws, and spirit that makes them a polity. The origin of the word is the Latin verb *constituere*, to constitute (from *con* plus *stitum*, a combining form of *statuere*, "to make stand or set up").[10] The noun *constitutio* thus meant "the way in which a thing is set up." Specific *constitutiones* were enactments from the Emperor, yet in its usages at the end of the Roman republic as a general noun, *constitutio* meant "the establishment of the state order," or "the total composition, the shape or form of the state," "the gradual establishment of the state through the evolution of its institutions," and "the nature or form of a republic." Constitution has always meant both the empowerment of government as well as its limitation, and there is an historical continuity in usage from Cicero to today.[11]

The etymology of the word in English introduces two further variations in the nouns. As in Latin, the base is the verb *to constitute*, one of whose early written occurrences in the late 1400s means "to set up, ordain, appoint."[12] The general noun *constitution*, from middle English, appears in a general political sense in the early 1600s: "the mode in which a state is organized." A slightly different meaning for the verb also occurs in that period: "to frame, form." In the seventeenth century, the verb acquires more specifically political connotations, especially through its usage by Hobbes. Two new specific nouns also develop. First, the *constituent*, "one who constitutes another his agent or representative." Then, "one of those who elect another as their representative; an elector, loosely, any inhabitant of the place so called." The eighteenth and nineteenth centuries name the *constituency:* "a body of constituents, the body of voters who elect a representative member of the public body; in looser use, the whole body of residents in a place so represented, the place itself." And finally, the verb *to constitute* acquires its most abstract meaning: "to make (a thing) what it is."

There is an interesting progression in the linguistic development here which parallels a dialectical cycle. First there is the verb, the activity of constituting, the constant going over of one thing into another. Then there is the formation of the whole, a constitution for the polity. Only then is there the naming of the individual parts, the electors, and finally the identification of the collective parts, the constituencies. At a formal level, these concepts go from universality (constitution) to particularity (electors) to political individuality (constituents in constituency). We must now explore their substance.

Representative democracy has political significance as "the periodic reconstituting of political authority." Consent of the governed, which is the basis of democratic political authority, is periodically reconstituted or reaffirmed through elections of representatives, where citizens actively renew their membership. First, the individual person reaffirms his membership in society, "says to the rest that he is still one with them and with their common purpose." Second, the people as a whole body of citizens, "the group of individuals . . . reexpresses its voluntary corporate character."[13] Kateb remarks that once democratic political authority is constituted, whereas the unit of obligation to the law continues to be the individual, the unit of consent to the law and public policies becomes the group, that group which is the "ever-changing majority" of the people.[14] The representatives making the laws and policies owe their offices to a "contest" in which each makes a successful "choice of the relevant constituency."[15] This choice itself makes a special contribution to political reconstitution; it is a choice akin to a founding. Thus the leaders as well as the voters, not to mention those who participate in other ways (such as striking, demonstrating, and civil disobedience) contribute to the process.[16] Yet "[w]ithout the existence of the electoral procedure, supportive and participatory activity would have no starting point, no framework, no source of articulation, no coherence, no focus, no ultimate object of attention, passion and aspiration."[17] The choosing of representatives is one of the surest ways to "preserv[e] . . . the frame of action, a constitution."[18]

How do you frame and form a people, making them what they are? A constitution may be handed down from on high, but it must be understood by individuals as citizens in order to be realized. The institution of political representation provides a way of doing this, of periodically reconstituting the polity. It is a process in which a people makes a choice about how it will be recognized politically, and hence becomes self-conscious about who they are collectively.

The division of a country into districts "constituting the people, in their wards, a regularly organized power, enables them by that organization" to stay connected to their representatives "regularly and peaceably."[18] So wrote Jefferson, arguing that only through the division of counties into wards with political and administrative functions would the people retain their status as citizens. Whereas with at-large elections the people might for a time retain their anti-tyrannical spirit, they would not have the means to effect this short of civil war.[19] In order to keep their representatives from usurping power, to keep them as one of their own, local districts were central. Wards or townships with electoral and other roles, such as jury duty, "by making every citizen as acting member of the government, and in the offices nearest and most interesting to him, will attach him by his strongest feelings to the independence of his country, and its republican constitution."[20] Ward republics did not require that every citizen serve as a representative, but that he be able to attend meetings in person with the representative.

Representation is constitutive, and to do this to the greatest extent, it must be rooted in local constituencies. In countries where there are not single-member constituencies, voting and meeting and watching the political process have a different significance and politics has a more ideological and instrumental value.[22] "The choice of a relevant constituency" within a set of settled constituencies is most conducive to reconstituting a polity of citizens. Single-member districts best encourage the development of political individuality, the civic status of being a citizen who retains his or her own particular loyalties yet acknowledges membership in the whole. By having set boundaries to a district one defines a relevant constituency not just by one aspect of its life at a moment in time but rather by the totality of its political life over the years. In the shifting constituencies of at-large elections the constituency itself is determined by one or two issues, while in an established constituency there are many issues, and not only issues but characters. Settled constituencies have historical memories about themselves and their representatives, and they bring this important kind of knowledge to bear on politics. Only within such a framework can the political covenant be sustained.

Chapter Eight

Connecting the Parts to the Whole via Representation

Constitutive representation can be conceived as an activity that promotes the "political individuality" or citizenship of its constituents, while preserving their "formal individualism" and "social individuality." Understood in this manner, it will be seen to reconcile the various aspects of representation, rather than leaving them incompatible as in the transmission belt model. Constitutive representation preserves individualism through its formal aspects of "authorization" and "accountability," enhances social individuality through its substantive aspect of "descriptive standing for," promotes political individuality through its "symbolic standing for." And finally, when the representative substantively "acts," he or she acts for the political whole or sovereign.

As we summarize each of these four aspects, we will be dwelling on the connecting role of representation in an almost static sense. There is also, of course, a more dynamic way in which representatives connect the parts to the whole, by mobilizing minorities, new people and issues, into politics. Creating constituencies out of people who never before considered themselves together is the work of political organizers and leaders, and in the modern era the prime agents of mobilization have been political parties.[23] Parties, of course, can coexist either with district or nondistrict systems; parties can also be ideological or nonideological. Parties can be single, dual or many; party discipline can be strong or weak among the legislative political elite; party identification can be strong or weak within the mass electorate. The interplay of party systems with electoral systems is a vast and important topic beyond the scope of this book, and the interaction between them affects the nature of political representation. What we want to assert here is that single-member districts are a necessary building block in instituting citizenship as political individuality. While most of our discussion focuses on America where there are two nonideological parties, it can also apply to other single-member district systems like Britain, which has two or three ideological parties, and France, which has many ideological parties with a second round of voting to ensure a majority. Our analysis excludes electoral systems that elect many representatives per district, whether by plurality, majority, or proportional representation rules, and whether by individual candidates or party lists, because these systems do not produce the same meaning of citizenship.

Authorization and Accountability of Formal Individualism

Constitutive representation is based on the formal individualism of its constituents through procedures of authorization and accountability. When a constituency votes for the candidate at the beginning of the election period, it authorizes him or her to act on its behalf, and when it holds another election at the end of the term, possibly throwing the incumbent out, it holds the representative to account. In developing these categories, Pitkin saw them as opposing views of formal representation, each embedded in different conceptions of what the representative is supposed to be and do in relation to the represented.[24] Now it may be that in transmission belt theory they are incompatible, insofar as the formal authorization/accountability distinction tends to turn into the substantive trustee/delegate debate, in which the representative either is free to act independently of voter preferences or is not. But they are not necessarily incompatible in a communitarian model. It would seem rather that, as Mayhew has suggested, they are two endpoints of a process of "representative linkage," one at the beginning and the other at the end of the election period.[25]

In both transmission belt and constitutive representation, the represented say in some way, "We will authorize you; we will hold you accountable." But in transmission belt theory, the communications and instructions flow along a set of single lines, from individual to representative: "I send you; I revoke you," or, "I send you; he (another constituent) revokes you," as the case may be. In constitutive theory, the communication comes in a different form, from a circle conceived as a limit, made up of a set of individuals who have mutual relations: "We define you; we surround you." The representative is empowered to act within the boundaries set up by the circle; public opinion serves as a limit, as V. O. Key put it, outside of which the representative may not go, but within which he is quite free to act.[26] The formal acts of authorization and accountability set the boundaries but not the content of public will and sentiment that the representative must respect.

Given this circular imagery, constitutive representation has different requirements for how to determine the "we" than does transmission belt theory. In this first respect, its requirements are less stringent. Since transmission theory sees society as made up of individuals as persons and distrustful of one another, it cannot trust that majority rule will be adequate, even if the majority does not abuse minority constitutional rights. The logical outcome of a consistent atomism is that even political minorities must be given some weight and hence proportional representation is mandated. In constitutive theory, on the other hand, majority vote is legitimate because a majority is taken as evidence, however weak, that an underlying "we" has been formed. Even a plurality is valid because it at least attests to the fact that no other group has been able to muster such a collective expression. Perhaps this can only occur in societies that are not severely divided and in which constitutional mores are so strong that certain minority rights will not be abused. Under these conditions, majority and even plurality election rules contribute to the coalition-building that goes into forming a "we," in contrast to proportional representation that allows and enshrines these divisions in the electorate.

In constitutive theory, the "we" is formed in a process of mutual association, among the constituents as well as between them and the representative. Formally free individuals enter into associative relations that are not of necessity, though they may be natural, if man is a *zōon politikon*. The relations may be informal, based on *amici e vicini,* friends and neighbors who get along and trust each other. Or they may be more structured, as in the *confraternitates,* fraternal clubs of artisans, and in the local branches of the mass political party. Parties based in districts are a strong form of representative linkage, binding the constituents and representatives together more clearly in between the moments of authorization and accountability than do weaker and individual kinds of linkage.[27] This is especially true in responsible parties which generate ideological platforms and seek to organize governmental power in specific ways. However, at this first formal level of procedures of authorization and accountability without any specified content, it is also true that parties may perform only a "constitutive" function, as Lowi has argued. They might not stand for any ideological differences, and instead be congeries of people who get along in other respects and agree to fill offices, recruit leaders, slate candidates, and deliver specific services through these organizations; in short, "to perform a 'constituent' or 'constitutional' function . . . necessary in the formation of the whole."[28] While I think that this assessment of American parties is a bit far-fetched, since even ours contain some ideological differences, it does highlight this other aspect of political life: the forming of a "we" as an end in itself.

What does this model require in order to preserve the status of formal individualism? The modern juridical concept of "formally free individuals" requires legal equality, equality of individual rights under the law. In the public sphere, the main political rights implied by individualism are freedom of speech, association, and suffrage.[29] Individuals must be able to exercise these rights to appear in public. As many have commented, these rights do not guarantee equality of outcome—achieving equal power, or equal influence, or even equality of being listened to. They are rights to equal opportunities, the opportunities to make a mark in a variety of public forums. Nor must these opportunities always be taken.[30] Mutual association, for example, may be natural but is not of necessity, and so formal freedom implies that men and women are free to reject their true political natures, free to choose not to participate. The teleological theory assumes, trusts, hopes, that people can be wooed back to politics by skillful founders, but knows too how hard it is, given life's other attractions. And the political rights of speech, association, and suffrage may be justified in nonteleological terms anyway, for they are entailed in a certain conception of the person. This philosophy is of humans as bearers of rights and duties, capable of dignity and understanding the significance of actions in a social context.[31] It follows that political representation in a democracy involves "responsibility" but not direct responsiveness to the voters; the voters must be able to see whether the representative is acting in ways they understand and on their behalf, yet not necessarily according to their every wish. Responsibility thus involves accountability to the voters in the sense of their gaining confidence in, more than influence upon, the representative.[32]

Formal individualism in the context of constitutive representation requires "one person, one vote" to this very general extent: each individual should have an equal opportunity to have his vote count as one in the formation of the whole. Each representative must represent the same number of people, or rather, the weight of the representative's vote in the legislature should be proportional to the number of his constituents. Without yet considering the substantive aspects of representation, there are two ways to achieve this goal with local constituencies: first, equality of population amongst the districts, as in recent Supreme Court decisions; second, inequality of population between the districts but weighted voting for each representative in the legislature depending on the size of the constituency. This was proposed, for example, to save the constitutionality of New York City's Board of Estimate, with one representative for each of the five boroughs.[33] This weighted voting alternative is more conducive to social and political individuality; however, it can raise problems for the political right of association, discussed more fully below.

Descriptive Standing for Social Individuality

Constitutive representation promotes the social individuality of its members in its substantive aspect of descriptively standing for them. Representatives elected from single-member districts are able to stand for the dominant social groupings there. The easiest way to achieve this "representation by reflection"[34] is for the representative to actually be a member of those groups; he or she can be counted on to embody some of their major defining characteristics. Given all the other things a representative has to be and do, this literal reflection is probably the best way for the representative to echo certain group aspirations and metaphors. But actual membership is not absolutely necessary; what is crucial is the "intention to depict," to give an accurate rendering, of the interests and metaphors of the represented.[35]

Two kinds of social individuality are fundamental: family and class or status. These are the essential building blocks in society on the path to political life, pre-political training grounds in ethical life for the citizen-to-be.[36] Whereas Aristotle had stressed the preparation in moral mastery for the head of a household, Hegel extends the education to moral reciprocity among equals in civil associations of corporation and craft. Burke's theory of representation stressed that representatives must stand for the interests of civil society, which he took to include the great families, civil corporations and associations, and Church (and political corporations and associations, see below). Marx plunges further into modern political economy for "the anatomy of civil society," dropping the family as a unit of analysis or representation and stressing solely the social and political association of the proletariat. Hegel remains pivotal; theoretically poised between Aristotle and Marx, he keeps the two moments of family and class (while also, we have noted, excluding religion) as direct and necessary preconditions to politics and political personality.

Modern social groupings that have fundamental significance for politics and hence deserve descriptive representation are those that derive from the two categories of family and class. Obviously, neither direct family line nor inherited social position is now completely determinative of who one socially is. But their modern extensions, ethnicity and socioeconomic status, are affiliations that still shape people's social lives in basic ways. Ethnicity is the collective culture of a set of families in which they pattern their ongoing relation to birth, life, and death, the values and metaphors they choose to inherit and transmit. While ethnic origins may be national or religious, the basic social unit of transmission is the family (and secondarily the Church and clubs). Race, while strictly speaking different from ethnicity since one cannot personally convert into it, is still on the whole an ethnic category into which one can intermarry and then culturally transmit its sensibilities to the generations through families. Even sexual preference or gender is a variation on the theme of family, as direct challenge or alternative, although whether it is a culture capable of transmission is contestable.

Socioeconomic status is a wider more diffuse category than either class or status, leaving purposely open (for both the participants and the observer) whether its definition depends on income level, style of life, mode of payment, nature of work, job control, rights of ownership, or the distinction between being employed and unemployed.

The political representative should descriptively stand for the dominant social groupings in the constituency. If the district is predominantly working class Polish, for example, the legislator should be the same, or at least able to speak to their hopes and fears in their metaphors. If the district is majority black, the representative should be black; if predominantly white Baptist, then the same. Note that we are not asserting anything about what the representative should do, but rather what he should seem to be or stand for. He or she stands for where the people have come from in their pre-political lives. Having the representative embody some of the history of these social groupings helps preserve the people's sense of themselves, their social constitution, as they make the transition into politics. It helps preserve social individuality in an intangible but definite way, by contributing to their pride. It also contributes to the initial sense of trust between the constituents and the representative.[37]

What if, as often happens, there are two or more forms of social individuality in the district that could marshal a majority? And in particular, what if the two main categories of family and class cannot both be met? Then the representative should stand for whichever division is more salient. Or, to put it the other way around, those constituents who care more intensely about one social affiliation can try to promote a representative of that dimension. Lijphart has found that, in European national party politics, voters tend to choose party representatives on the basis of religion (first) and language (a strong second) in situations where religion, language, and class are competing factors; whereas representatives when in office tend to form party coalitions, when these are necessary, more on the basis of socioeconomic issues than on the religious dimension, in situations where these both exist.[38] Similarly, Converse and Pierce found that French voters' political attachments and choices were more strongly based on religious divisions, plus attitudes towards the leader de Gaulle, than on class divisions, even though at the national level managing the economy was a more central preoccupation of the representatives.[39] I would expect this to hold even more strongly at the district level in America—that ethnicity would be more salient than SES at the constituent level, whether urban, suburban, state, or congressional. One can also think of exceptions—if a significant part of a district has just been thrown out of work because of the closing of a steel plant, the rest of the constituency may feel impelled to vote along class lines. The studies suggest in general, however, that socioeconomic concerns translate more into questions of ideology and action only at the level of the representative's actions for the whole society, while ethnic identifications remain an essential dimension of voter behavior at the local level. Furthermore, ethnic and SES divisions are often quite compatible; salaried white-collar workers in an area may tend to be Protestant; blue-collar ones, Italian Catholic. Where there is a variant on the family theme, as in the political clout of San Francisco's gays, it seems to replace other ethnic categories but not the class dimension (e.g., the Harvey Milk Gay Democratic Club was "younger, less wealthy, less professional" in its membership than the Alice B. Toklas Memorial Democratic Club).[40]

The great American exception to this sanguine view—of safely shifting self-identifications between family and class in the democratic mood of the voters—is the category of race. Race has had a salience, for prejudiced whites certainly and hence for blacks, that overshadowed all others; whites of the most diverse family and class affiliation would continually join together to keep blacks out of political power and social recognition. Racial hatred and distrust left a legacy of an entrenched majority continually overpowering a minority. In America, the exceptional history of slavery has justified exceptional legislative, administrative, and judicial remedies. So that in areas defined as historically discriminatory under the Voting Rights Act of 1965, local constituencies were to be drawn with 65 percent black population, in order to bring their number of representatives in line with their percentage of the general population in the area.

This policy cannot be required for other ethnic groups, as the Court declared in *UJO v. Carey*. It cannot mandate it as a matter of compensatory right because no other group suffered the extreme wrong of slavery and its deep aftereffects. And it also cannot require it because of practicality, for it would be impossible to know which groups to district into majorities where two or more groups or cross-cutting cleavages existed. Nevertheless, the idea of having political districts that generally conform to existing ethnic divisions at the local level is a legitimate one. If there exists a majority or plurality ethnic community with a set of social institutions, that social basis should, all other things being equal, be respected in order to further the purposes of descriptive representation. There will be ample opportunity in the other aspects of representation for group conflicts to be mediated and issues to be reconciled; at this starting level of the representative process, the differences should be seen.

Symbolic Standing for Political Individuality

And yet a local constituency represents something more than the existing social divisions while something less than the political whole. The representative of a district can be conceived as standing in a symbolic sense for the political individuality of the constituents. He or she now stands for them in their political interactions and aspirations, their political way of life, their decision to be citizens. The representative symbolizes the attempt to move beyond social divisions and form a political community. The existence of one representative for a diverse constituency, one which is known to contain formally free individuals and social majorities and minorities, is itself an emblem of their current agreement to coexist without civil war, a symbol that they are trying to define what unites as well as divides them. And that their own representative symbolizes something slightly different from the next ward over, preserves their political individuality as well.

For a person to achieve political individuality, the experience of citizenship, he or she must inhabit an area with a distinctive character. Political individuality, we argued earlier, is a civic role of recognition and fellowship wherein an individual achieves a synthesis between the particular aspects of his personality (needs, whims) and the universal aspects of the political whole (national security, justice, and ideal fellowship). Citizenship understood in this sense is an activity of autonomous individuals (with opinions and principles) who acknowledge that they are "at one with each other" and reaffirm their "voluntary corporate character." Yet what does it mean to be at one with each other if they are formally free? It means either that they share the same purposes or a mutual affection, or both. In either case, this sharing requires that they actually know each other over time, and as this knowing occurs, it must acknowledge difference and idiosyncracy. Symbolically, a single representative attests to the fact that the constituency is composed of political individuals who have collectively defined themselves as distinct from other wards. Niemi et al. have shown that congressional candidate recognition and recall by constituents is greatest when district lines coincide with community boundaries, and suggests that local media markets are an intervening variable to explain "the relationship between district congruity and political knowledge."[41]

The district then is both microcosm and unique. It is a microcosm of the political whole in its formal structural respects and in certain general political values which all must share. It is unique in its particular mix of pre-political conditions as well as in its choice of which secondary values in the tradition to stress. And while only the political whole can bestow the formal gift of citizenship, only the political part can make that grant effective.

The locality is a microcosm of the whole in two very general senses. Structurally, it, like the nation, is heterogeneous, characterized by social divisions, even if the particular mix of groups differs, and by political divisions, citizens who are free to form political factions. The legal rights of these factions, their conditions of entry and growth, are crucial to the political freedom of the area. In order to be a true political microcosm of the whole, it will have to satisfy certain requirements of political freedom (see below). Normatively, the district is a replica of the whole insofar as its inhabitants share the dominant political values of the national constitution.[42] In America, for example, that now includes a commitment to political equality as a core value.

The districts forge their distinctiveness out of two related conditions. First is the particular mix of social groups and idiosyncratic characters who inhabit the area. Structurally, if there is a vast majority of one group rather than a polyglot mixture of several, the district will conduct its politics in different terms.[43] Substantively, and this is related to but by no means determined by the structural condition, the constituents may choose to exalt different values in the secondary pantheon of values of the political culture. In America, for example, this may involve stressing fraternity to a greater degree in one locality, and liberty to an extraordinary extent in another. One district appreciates an old style politico who gives patronage and deals in the elaborate byways of political friendship; another favors a representative who looks to his own conscience for the springs of action.

The political character of the constituency depends upon the condition of political freedom. Political freedom encompasses the two meanings of liberty as understood in the classical republican tradition. In its positive aspect it requires that individuals be free to enter into associations with others of their own choosing and that these associations have the possibility of gaining governmental power. In its negative aspect it requires that individuals be at liberty to leave those associations and find or form others, or not join them at all. What Berlin has called negative freedom is the civil liberty to be at one with oneself and one's pre-political household and friends, and positive freedom involves the eventual joining of political liberty to power, what Arendt has called "the human ability . . . to act in concert."[44] We have argued that exercising positive freedom is crucial to self-determination of character.

The political freedom of the ward depends on its being open to the formation of new political factions that have the possibility of gaining majority assent. Political factions (groupings and parties)[45] are salutory because they represent efforts by citizens to redefine the things that unite them specifically in relation to political power rather than along the lines of social cleavage.[46] They organize disagreement along the lines of opposed political values and sensibilities, and contribute to that competition which is one of the essential aspects of politics. Plurality and majority vote as the rule that empowers a faction, giving a single representative the authority to act for the whole, is desirable because it leaves some people free to disagree yet also encourages lesser groupings to band together in coalition to achieve these pluralities and majorities. Ethnic and class groups are encouraged to work together, moderating or creatively melding their demands into a political formation that can appeal to many. Minority rights are here defined dynamically as the ability to build majority power.

What does this political freedom require in the way of political equality? It does not require that each district have the same number of people, the same quantity of voters. It does require that the quality of associational life within the constituency be such that any individual has a real opportunity to build majority power. Here we move beyond formal equality into more substantive enabling conditions of power, particularly equal access to media and equally open parties. Competitive parties tend to offer the greatest possibility for an individual to woo a few constituents to form a new majority. But this is also possible within a single party in a one-party district, if there are procedures, whether formal or informal, for the recognition of intra-party factions. And while I think that political parties play a crucial mediating role in the formation of political consciousness, it is also true that nonpartisan elections might meet the general conditions set forth here—that the political process be open to the "instigation of emergent authority."[47] There must be equal opportunity to participate in the crucial early stages of the political process, way before the voting occurs. These are the processes enumerated by Justice White in *Whitcomb v. Chavis* and *White v. Regester*: assuming the existence of parties, then party membership, primaries, and slating of candidates must be open to political contest. Equality of these rights, the equal opportunity to become a political activist in a faction, is as important, if not more so, than equality of the later mass individual vote.

It follows that districts can vary in size if it serves the purpose of associational vitality, and then equality of mass voting power can be met by having weighted voting of representatives in the legislature. While it is true that in a very large district as opposed to a very small one, the opportunity for a group of citizens to grow from a minority to a plurality or majority is diminished, this is not necessarily the case between two districts that vary, say, by 20 percent in population. Consider a situation in which a smaller district has little or no social group cohesion and a nonpartisan political structure, versus a larger district characterized by cohesive social groups and political parties. Assuming that both districts meet the requirements of formally open procedures for choosing the representative, then an insurgent faction may have an easier time building a winning coalition in the larger ward. For it will be able to call upon the received social and political loyalties of the constituents, their sense of identification with institutions they trust, their sense of participation in metaphors they share. Fenno's study of congressmen's home style shows this reliance on existing local groups.[48] Obviously a new faction challenges part of that universe of understandings and introduces new personalities and issues to the political arena, but it can also depend upon the parts it leaves unchallenged to tap into reserves of support through circles of political friends and neighbors. Whereas in a completely unorganized constituency, the individuals have all to be reached anew.

Acting for the Political Whole

While the constitutive representative stands for where the people have come from (their social individuality) and where they are now (their political individuality), he acts for where they are going, the goals of the political whole. He or she acts on behalf of the political telos—fellowship and justice in the context of a sovereign association. Insofar as the constituents' preferences depart from this, the representative is obliged to remind them of the significance of the departure; they, in turn, are free to accept or reject his definition of the peril, but in rejecting, must choose another who also defines the whole in some way.[49] To promote and preserve the larger context, the representative has to keep in mind two things, often hard to balance: the external security of the country and its internal conditions of association and appropriation. But he or she is free to make these judgments on his or her own, or in the context of a political party, and not at the behest of the constituents.

If the representative finds that the interest of the nation differs from the perceived self-interest of the constituents, he should act for the whole. He of course must do this skillfully, so that he still gets re-elected, speaking to his people so they do not lose face nor their trust in him. The range of rhetorical skills are open to him, from startling new wisdom to a simple wink while he does other good deeds. In order to remain citizens, his equals, and not be debased to mere persons in relation to the representative, the constituents have to know they are involved with him in an effort to redefine wants and needs, goals and means. Even if they do not know the details of every compromise he negotiates, in principle these must be comprehensible to them, valid in their search for new, if temporary, harmony.

Note how in this substantive respect, constitutive representation's requirements are more stringent than transmission belt's.[50] Bentham, we recall, thought that in the case of a clash between district and national interest, the representative should speak on behalf of the national interest but vote on behalf of the policy conducive to the local interest.[51] In this, he was faithful to the transmission belt model of representation yet clever in dealing with one of its dilemmas: constituents might entrust their representatives' public voice, yet those same representatives should ultimately vote as delegates. But the theory of representation as constitutive cannot allow this; legislators must act as virtual representatives, for the whole exists prior to the parts, as their formal and final cause, and as an entity qualitatively different from the parts. Not that the political whole is ever fully formed or set, but its definition is sought and contested on its own terms by the citizens and is conceptually prior to the parts. Hence the legislator, in this view, must have complete freedom to speak and to act for the existence of that whole.

When we say that the representative is to act on behalf of the good of the national whole, we mean this not only in a static but also a dynamic sense. Statically, the representative is the conserver of the arrangements that have worked so far. He or she acts in virtue of those institutions and interests that characterize the nation as a political whole—broad appropriative interests such as labor, service, agriculture, and commerce, and deep associative interests such as cities, states, churches, and schools. The representative speaks and acts for these yet is independent of any one of them, especially if he belongs to a political party. For party encompasses diverse interests and institutions within its ken, joining them through key principles, ideologies, and programs.[52] The party representative thus has a virtual independence of the constituency when he speaks and acts, yet must have his base in a particular place, in that locality of affection which is the starting point of political knowledge and action.

Dynamically, representatives can articulate new values and enable political formations to develop and change.[53] In a political constituency, social groups, individuals, and citizens all can respond to creative leadership, interaction, and membership. The districts are not merely contractual bodies whose charter has been set for all time by a state, but are also organic entities "conceived as possessing a[ny] living power of self-development" . . . "like a person" with "a mind or will of her own."[54] They have a "real inward life" with "inherent rights of self-development" which may depart from the original terms negotiated with their members. Societies are not "mere collections of individuals who remain unchanged by their membership," but rather "means by which the individual comes to himself." "[P]ersonality is a social fact" that is "changed by this fellowship."[55] Substantive representation in the constitutive mode speaks and acts for these fellowships. Individual persons are not the basis of representation, since it is impossible to represent another's free will. Instead, representation should act for the common purposes of associations of people. "[A]ll true representation . . . is not representation of persons but [only] representation of common purposes."[56] The representative acts for what the people want to become, "the object at which they aim."[57]

This notion of substantive representation as acting for the political telos of the association requires that the legislature be conceived as a deliberative or general purpose assembly.[58] The parliament is seen as a place of public speech in which the representatives consider which general principles are to inform their actions. The mode of knowledge is practical political wisdom informed by a prudence or judgment about which means are most apt to reach which ends; but the main debate should be about the nature of the ends, their definition and redefinition. The legislative assembly is not to be the mere rubber stamp of a legislating executive, nor the bureaucratic repository of all the ways and means. It can depend upon the executive for some initiative in timing, and depends on committees for the mass of expertise on implementation, but it is supposed to decide the general principles. The deliberations of the assembly in the context of its necessities give it a political character of its own. "Men who were not by nature political animals were made such by parliamentary discipline."[59] The discipline may be structured through informal networks of friends and allies or the formal organizations of political parties.

The Art of Political Representation

Political representation is the standing and acting for an objective entity—a constituency of citizens—which is constantly in the process of becoming itself. The representative's role should be to encourage the formation of community among the constituents, doing this in a way that preserves their individuality. The constituency itself is a "socially objective" entity, to use Marx's terms: it occurs within given historical conditions, is characterized by definite social relations, and is malleable to human agency. It has a material base, of concrete people in a specific place with definite interests. Yet it also has an ideal reality, for, in Weber's terms, people characteristically have not only material but also "ideal interests": in the modern political sphere they aspire to freedom in association. This goal is objective, deriving from what it means to be

Chapter Eight

human in the modern age; the ways to reach it are various, depending on the particular histories of the people involved. The constituency is continually being created because the goal is never met for all time.

The political representative is not a mere transmitter of individual desires nor a purveyor of the needs of the whole. Insofar as she is a member of a defined geographical community which chose her, she is a citizen among others, embodying their values and working to realize them. Just as there may be conflict within an individual over priorities and strategies, so too in a local constituency; the representative can make explicit the moral reasoning and choices involved in political action.

Theories that value political community as an end in itself have been lacking in a concept of representation, and theories that value political community in the service of goals higher than civil society (religion or philosophy), notoriously so. But we have seen that in each of the great communitarian political theories there is a figure who returns to the people and interacts with them in a more intimate manner than the external educator of the transmission belt model. These unusual, enigmatic personages—the philosopher in Plato, the legislator in Rousseau, the organizer in Marx and Lenin—speak and act in public and behind the scenes in ways that change people's consciousness. These leaders also need the people in some sense, to recognize them and tell their "stories."[60] Politics is indeed the manipulation of real things, of goods and services and war and booty and immigrants; yet one of the real things is people's histories as citizens, the stories they construct about their lives together. Political representation can write these stories large.

Marx and Weber's writings on the city-state remind us of what the real preconditions of citizenship are. They do not necessarily involve a self-sufficiency of production, continually growing standard of living, and constant political participation. They do involve the community as a commercial center, with some shared production structured into public and private property, and a political life characterized by its own partially autonomous law, administration, and forms of association. Citizenship, we argued, could be conceived as a complex relationship of rights and duties to a body conceived as a public possession. These rights and duties are not necessarily instrumental to other goals given outside of political life; they are part of the meaning of membership in a political state. Weber showed how and why the legal status of citizenship is deeply indebted to voluntary fraternal associations: rights and duties were embedded in structures of affection. Marx showed how the political status of citizenship depends upon an institutional context in which both public and private property coexist; privileges and immunities are posed in a context that allows a contrast. A political community is characterized, then, both by relations of affection and relations of shared power, relations of association and appropriation. These are the essential, if very general, conditions to be preserved and enhanced, the goals of the political whole which the representative should serve.

Representation by single-member constituencies makes it possible to connect the parts to the whole through an actual person who is the bearer of our shared power and affection. Either as an individual politician or as member of a political party, the representative serves as more than a transmission belt, for he or she is a leading participant in the creation of the whole. "The substantive common interest is only discovered or created in democratic political struggle, and it remains contested as much as shared."[61] That common interest is not necessarily opposed to the particular local interest, just as the public good is not necessarily opposed to the personal good, although both may require sacrifice.[62] The politician's genius may be to redefine the situation so as to make the connection between them, to "discover connectedness— [and] forge new connections—with others."[63] Traditionally, we have called this building a base in the constituency, and to keep that base, in a context that is constantly changing, requires the political art. Political representation by districts allows the representative to depict things as they really are, in their plenitude.

Notes

Chapter One

1. Hanna Fenichel Pitkin, *The Concept of Representation* (Berkeley: University of California Press, 1967), pp. 144, 237.
2. Ibid., pp. 2–3, 241. See also Alexander Hamilton, John Jay, and James Madison, *The Federalist* (New York: Modern Library, n.d.), no. 14, p. 81; and no. 63, p. 412.
3. J. G. A. Pocock, *The Machiavellian Moment* (Princeton, N.J.: Princeton University Press, 1975), p. 521.
4. Herbert J. Storing, *What the Anti-Federalists Were For* (Chicago: University of Chicago Press, 1981), p. 55.
5. Gordon S. Wood, *The Creation of the American Republic 1776–1787* (New York: W. W. Norton & Co., 1972), p. 164. See also *Federalist*, nos. 10, 14, 63.
6. Alfred E. Zimmern, *The Greek Commonwealth*, 5th rev. ed. (Oxford: Clarendon Press, 1931), pt. 2, ch. 6.
7. Ibid., pt. 3, chs. 7–12.
8. Aristotle, *Politics*, trans. Ernest Barker (New York: Oxford University Press, 1968), bk. 1, 1252a–1260b; bk. 3, 1274b–1275b, 1277b.
9. Werner Jaeger, *Paideia*, trans. Gilbert Highet, 2d ed., vol. 1 (New York: Oxford University Press, 1974), chs. 1–9.
10. Fustel de Coulanges, *The Ancient City* (Garden City, N.Y.: Doubleday Anchor Books, n.d.), bks. 1–3.
11. Charles A. Beard and John D. Lewis, "Representative Government in Evolution," *American Political Science Review* 26:2 (April 1932), pp. 230–31; Pitkin, p. 244; Edmund S. Morgan, "Government by Fiction: The Idea of Representation," *Yale Review* 72:3 (April 1983), pp. 324–26.
12. Gianfranco Poggi, *The Development of the Modern State* (Stanford: Stanford University Press, 1978), chs. 3 and 4, esp. pp. 43, 49–50, 61, 71, 77–84.

13. Alexander Passerin d'Entrèves, *The Notion of the State* (Oxford: Clarendon Press, 1967), pp. 75–79, 89–93; John B. Morrall, *Political Thought in Medieval Times* (New York: Harper & Row, 1962), pp. 64–65.

14. Beard and Lewis, pp. 232–35; Morgan, p. 326; Alfred de Grazia, *Public and Republic* (New York: Alfred A. Knopf, 1951), pp. 15–49.

15. Helen Cam, *Liberties and Communities in Medieval England* (Cambridge: Cambridge University Press, 1944), ch. 16; May McKisack, *The Parliamentary Representation of the English Boroughs during the Middle Ages* (London: Oxford University Press, 1932), pp. 82–99; Bernard Bailyn, *Ideological Origins of the American Revolution* (Cambridge, Mass.: Harvard University Press, 1967), pp. 162, 164.

16. Francis William Maitland, "Introduction" to Otto von Gierke, *Political Theories of the Middle Age* (Boston: Beacon Press, 1959), pp. ix–xi, xviii–xxi.

17. Pitkin, pp. 245, 251.

18. Gierke, pp. 64–66, and Maitland, "Introduction," pp. xxx–xliii.

19. Thomas Hobbes, *Leviathan* (New York: Collier Books, 1962). Pitkin has an interesting note that one theorist considered "the principle of representation incompatible with the Hobbesian doctrine" (p. 255, n. 1).

20. d'Entrèves, p. 100.

21. Hobbes, ch. 14; Michael Oakeshott, "Introduction to Leviathan," in *Hobbes on Civil Association* (Oxford: Basil Blackwell, 1975), pp. 18, 30–36.

22. Hanna Pitkin, "Hobbes' Concept of Representation," I, *American Political Science Review* 58:2 (June 1964), pp. 328–40.

23. Pitkin, *The Concept of Representation*, pp. 17–18, 35.

24. Ibid., pp. 19–20, 33; d'Entrèves, pp. 106–8.

25. Hobbes, ch. 16, p. 127 [emphasis his].

26. J. R. Pole, *Political Representation in England and the Origins of the American Republic* (Berkeley: University of California Press, 1971), p. 196.

27. For recent discussions questioning whether later liberal theory and practice can justify any restrictions on immigration, see Joseph H. Carens, "Aliens and Citizens: The Case for Open Borders," *Review of Politics* 49 (Spring 1987), 251–73; and "Nationalism and the Exclusion of Immigrants: Lessons from Australian Immigration Policy," presented to the American Political Science Association, Washington, D.C. (August 29, 1986), 38 pp.

28. Wood, pp. 345, 350, 353.

29. Bailyn, pp. 201–2.

30. Wood, pp. 347, 350; Pole, pp. 391–94.

31. Wood, p. 353.

32. Ibid., pp. 362–63, 599.

33. Ibid., pp. 510–11, 195.

34. James Madison, *Federalist*, no. 10.

35. Wood, p. 357.

36. Pole, p. 350.

37. Hannah Arendt, *The Human Condition* (Garden City, N.Y.: Doubleday Anchor Books, 1959), pt. 2, sec. 5, pp. 29–30.
38. Aristotle, *Nicomachean Ethics*, trans. Martin Ostwald (Indianapolis: Bobbs-Merrill, 1962).
39. Sheldon S. Wolin, *Politics and Vision* (London: Allen & Unwin, 1961), p. 5.
40. Hanna Fenichel Pitkin, *Fortune Is a Woman* (Berkeley: University of California Press, 1984), p. 95; see also p. 300.
41. Carol Pateman, *Participation and Democratic Theory* (Cambridge: Cambridge University Press, 1970), p. 25.
42. Jean-Jacques Rousseau, *The Social Contract*, bk. 3, ch. 15, in *Social Contract*, ed. Ernest Barker (New York: Oxford University Press, 1976), p. 262.
43. The ideal is still a harmonious rule of reason free of domination, but sometimes we know not that route and willful domination is necessary.
44. Arendt, Wolin, Pitkin, (see above nn. 37, 39, 40); Wilson Carey McWilliams, *The Idea of Fraternity in America* (Berkeley: University of California Press, 1973).
45. Pocock (see n. 3 above).
46. Arendt, pt. 1, sec. 2, pp. 13–18; pt. 6, secs. 41–42, pp. 262–78.
47. Ibid., pt. 6, secs. 35–40, pp. 225–62.
48. Ibid., pts. 3 and 4, pp. 71–153.
49. Ibid., pt. 5, pp. 155–223.
50. Hanna Fenichel Pitkin, "Justice: On Relating Private and Public," *Political Theory* 9 (August 1981), pp. 327–52.
51. Nancy C. M. Hartsock, "Masculinity, Citizenship, and the Making of War," *PS* 17:2 (Spring 1984), pp. 199–200; Arlene Saxonhouse, "Men, Women, War and Politics," *Political Theory* 8:1 (February 1980), pp. 66–67.
52. Saxonhouse, p. 68.
53. Pitkin, "Justice," pp. 339–42.
54. John Stuart Mill, *Considerations on Representative Government* (South Bend, Ind.: Gateway Editions, 1962), ch. 15, pp. 286, 298. So that serving in political and administrative office is "the indirect schooling of grown people by public business" (p. 305).
55. Ibid., ch. 3, pp. 63–70.
56. Ibid., ch. 7, pp. 157–61.
57. Ibid., and ch. 3, pp. 51, 58, 55; see also Mill, *On Liberty* (Indianapolis: Bobbs-Merrill Co., 1956), ch. 1, p. 14; ch. 2, esp. pp. 21, 24–25, 44, 58, 64.
58. Ibid., pp. 148–62. See also Douglas W. Rae, *The Political Consequences of Electoral Laws*, rev. ed. (New Haven: Yale University Press, 1971), pp. 36–38, 110–11, 113.
59. Mill, ch. 3, p. 73.
60. Dennis F. Thompson, *John Stuart Mill and Representative Government* (Princeton, N.J.: Princeton University Press, 1976), pp. 103, 109 and n. 64.

61. Alexis de Tocqueville, *Democracy in America* (New York: Vintage Books, 1945), vol. 1, pp. 198–205, 326–30; vol. 2, bk. 2, pp. 104–32.

62. John Locke, *An Essay Concerning the True Original, Extent and End of Civil Government* (Second Treatise) in *Social Contract,* sec. 6, pp. 5–6; secs. 25–26, pp. 16–17; secs. 61, 63, pp. 35, 36; secs. 95–96, pp. 56–57.

63. Peter Laslett, "Introduction," to John Locke, *Two Treatises of Government,* rev. ed. (New York: New American Library, 1963), pp. 122–30.

64. Locke, secs. 95–96, pp. 56–57.

65. Ibid., sec. 158, pp. 93–94.

66. Pocock (n. 3 above), ch. 15, esp. pp. 506–7, 527, 545–46, 551–52. Pocock draws on the works of Bailyn, Wood, Pole (see above nn. 15, 5, 26), adding his own interpretation.

67. Niccolò Machiavelli, *The Prince and the Discourses,* trans. Luigi Ricci (New York: Modern Library, 1950); Stuart Hampshire, *Public and Private Morality* (Cambridge: Cambridge University Press, 1978), pp. 49–52.

68. Pocock, chs. 6–7; Pitkin, *Fortune Is a Woman,* chs. 2–4.

69. See also Thomas Nagel for the suggestion that each, while distinct, may be dependent on a larger unity, in "Ruthlessness in Public Life," in Hampshire, pp. 78–79, 82–83, 86, 90.

70. Pole, p. 184 and n. 2; 246, 272, 419; see also C. B. Macpherson, *The Political Theory of Possessive Individualism* (Oxford: Oxford University Press, 1962), pp. 148, 134.

71. Macpherson, ch. 3.

72. Pole, pp. 7–9. Large estates could also "feed an army"; thus Harrington also wanted to redistribute land in order to limit the power of wealthy lords who might raise arms against the state.

73. Pole, pp. 173–78, 266, 271–72, 314, 321, 328.

74. A. D. Lindsay, *The Modern Democratic State* (London: Oxford University Press, 1969), ch. 5, pp. 115–21.

75. In this characterization I am stressing the religious and ignoring the secular Levellers. Thomas Rainborough in the Putney Debates (1647) in A. S. P. Woodhouse, *Puritanism and Liberty* (Chicago: University of Chicago Press, 1951), p. 67; Macpherson, pp. 121–27; 134–36.

76. McWilliams, (see n. 44 above), chs. 5, 6.

77. Ibid., chs. 8, 9, 20.

78. Herbert Storing, (see n. 4 above), p. 83, n. 7.

79. Pocock, p. 519.

80. Pocock, pp. 64–65.

81. Outside the formal Constitution, the choosing of presidential candidates through intra-party procedures that take account of certain ascriptive criteria (such as sex) and certain acquired criteria (such as political office), as well as numerical and geographical criteria, stands for the legitimacy of particularistic criteria at lower levels of representation.

82. Kenneth J. Meier and Robert E. England, "Black Representation and Educational Policy: Are They Related?" *American Political Science Review* 78:2 (June 1984), p. 401.

83. Heinz Eulau and Paul D. Karps, "The Puzzle of Representation: Specifying Components of Responsiveness," *Legislative Studies Quarterly* 2:3 (August 1977), pp. 241–47.

84. Robert W. Campbell, *Soviet Economic Power*, 2d ed. (Boston: Houghton Mifflin Co., 1966), p. 25. Otto Kirchheimer also uses the phrase in characterizing the role of political parties as "transmission belts between the population at large and the governmental structure." "The Transformation of the Western European Party Systems," in *Political Parties and Political Development*, ed. Joseph LaPalombara and Myron Weiner (Princeton, N.J.: Princeton University Press, 1966), pp. 177–78.

Chapter Two

1. Heinz Eulau, "Changing Views of Representation," in *Contemporary Political Science: Towards Empirical Theory*, ed. Ithiel de Sola Pool (New York: McGraw Hill, 1967), p. 62.

2. Ibid., p. 80.

3. Ibid., p. 62.

4. Ibid., pp. 59–64, and quoting Benjamin Farrington.

5. Ibid., p. 65.

6. Steven Lukes, *Power: A Radical View* (New York: Humanities Press, 1975), ch. 2.

7. Michel Foucault, *Power/Knowledge*, ed. Colin Gordon (New York: Pantheon Books, 1980), pp. 88–89, 91, 98.

8. Lukes, ch. 3.

9. Ibid., ch. 4.

10. Foucault, pp. 91–92, 118–20.

11. Sheldon S. Wolin, "Democracy and the Welfare State: *Staatsrason and Wohlfahrtsstaatsrason*" (Paper presented to Faculty Seminar on Democracy and the Welfare State, Project on the Federal Role, Princeton University, December 12, 1985), p. 2.

12. John Wahlke, Heinz Eulau, William Buchanan, and LeRoy Ferguson, *The Legislative System* (New York: John Wiley, 1962), chs. 11–15 and Appendix 1.

13. Heinz Eulau and Paul Karps, "The Puzzle of Representation: Specifying Components of Responsiveness," *Legislative Studies Quarterly* 2:3 (August 1977), p. 244.

14. Heinz Eulau, "Changing Views of Representation," in *Contemporary Political Science*, pp. 81, 78; Malcolm Jewell, *Representation in State Legislatures* (Lexington: University of Kentucky Press, 1982), pp. 119–20.

15. Eulau, pp. 78–79; also, Heinz Eulau and Kenneth Prewitt, *Labyrinths of Democracy: Adaptations, Linkages, Representation and Policies in Urban Politics* (Indianapolis: Bobbs-Merrill, 1973), ch. 21, pp. 424–25.
16. Eulau and Karps, pp. 242, 243, 244, 246.
17. Eulau and Prewitt, p. 426, drawing on Hanna Fenichel Pitkin, *The Concept of Representation* (Berkeley: University of California Press, 1967), pp. 209–10; 221–22.
18. Eulau and Prewitt, p. 427.
19. Jewell, p. 18.
20. Ibid., p. 83.
21. Ibid., pp. 18–19.
22. Pitkin, pp. 209–10, and cited in Jewell, p. 17.
23. Jewell, p. 18.
24. J. R. Pole, *Political Representation in England and the Origins of the American Republic* (Berkeley: University of California Press, 1971), p. 350.
25. Pole, pp. 38–39, 53, 233.
26. Edmund Burke, "Speech to the Electors of Bristol" (Oct. 14, 1774), in *Burke's Politics,* ed. Ross J. S. Hoffman and Paul Levack (New York: Alfred A. Knopf, 1949), pp. 114–17.
27. Jeremy Bentham, "Leading Principles of a Constitutional Code" (1823), in *Bentham's Political Thought,* ed. Bhiku Parekh (New York: Harper & Row, 1973), p. 218. See also Bentham, *The Principles of Morals and Legislation* (1789) New York: Hafner Publishing Co., 1948); and "Constitutional Code" (1830), in *The Works of Jeremy Bentham,* vol. 9, ed. John Bowring (Edinburgh: William Tait, 1843).
28. Bentham, "Leading Principles," pp. 207, 216.
29. Ibid., pp. 202, 207–8.
30. Ibid., p. 217.
31. Ibid., pp. 112–13, 166.
32. Ibid., p. 36.
33. Ibid., p. 121.
34. Ibid., p. 120.
35. Anthony Downs, "An Economic Theory of Political Action in a Democracy," *Journal of Political Economy* 65:2 (April 1957), p. 136.
36. Downs, p. 137.
37. Ibid.
38. Ibid., p. 138.
39. Ibid., p. 141.
40. Ibid., pp. 138, 139, 144.
41. Ibid., p. 139.
42. Ibid., p. 140.
43. Ibid.

44. Ibid.
45. Ibid., p. 142–45.
46. Robert A. Dahl, "The Concept of Power," *Behavioral Science* 2 (1957), pp. 201–5.
47. Bentham, pp. 120, 129, 135.
48. Warren E. Miller and Donald E. Stokes, "Constituency Influence in Congress," *American Political Science Review* 57:1 (March 1963), pp. 49, 51–52, 56. See also Philip E. Converse and Roy Pierce, *Political Representation in France* (Cambridge, Mass.: Harvard University Press, 1986), pp. 503–11, 518, 727.
49. Malcolm E. Jewell, "Legislator-Constituency Relations and the Representative Process," *Legislative Studies Quarterly* 8:3 (August 1983), p. 306; Converse and Pierce, pp. 256, 286, 296, 313–15.
50. Jewell (see n. 14 above), pp. 146–47.
51. Downs, p. 140, n. 12.
52. Neither Lenin nor Marx starts from the assumption of radical individualism in his analysis of capitalist society; rather, social classes are the bearers and creators of value. For Lenin only a vanguard political party can represent the consciousness of a class (see ch. 5 below, "The Figure of the Founder"). Yet Lenin's theory of trade union representation, which is all we shall be considering here, is of man as an individual want-satisfier, which meets the premises of this chapter.
53. James Mill, *Essay on Government* (1820) (Indianapolis: Bobbs-Merrill, 1955), pp. 62–63.
54. Ibid., p. 48.
55. Ibid., pp. 49, 51.
56. Ibid., p. 73.
57. Ibid., pp. 67, 82.
58. Ibid., pp. 67–69.
59. Ibid., p. 83.
60. Ibid., pp. 67, 69–71.
61. Leszek Kolakowski, *Main Currents of Marxism*, vol. 2, trans. P. S. Falla (New York: Oxford University Press, 1978), p. 488.
62. Ibid., p. 489.
63. Leonard Schapiro, *The Communist Party of the Soviet Union*, 2d ed. (New York: Vintage Books, 1971), pp. 205, 339.
64. Kolakowski, p. 489; Schapiro, pp. 202–5, 336–40; Mary McAuley, *Politics and the Soviet Union* (Harmondsworth: Penguin Books, 1977), pp. 60–63.
65. Schapiro, p. 338.
66. Ibid.
67. Mill, p. 72.

68. Schapiro, p. 339.
69. Peter Bachrach and Morton S. Baratz, "The Two Faces of Power," *American Political Science Review* 56 (1962), pp. 947–52.
70. Downs, pp. 139–40.
71. Ibid., p. 140.
72. Bentham, "Leading Principles," p. 217—which is also why Bentham allows the deputy to still vote for the constituency: "There is *not* a *majority* in the legislature, his vote will be of no effect; and to the national interest, no evil will have been done by it" [italics his].
73. Schapiro, p. 339.
74. Jewell, "Legislator-Constituency Relations," p. 311. See also Wahlke et al., pp. 291–93.
75. While this interpretation accords with our intuitions, Converse and Pierce show that the opposite holds in America and France: representatives from safe seats tend to act less as trustees and more as delegates than do representatives from competitive or marginal seats. (All districts in these studies were single-member, and other intervening factors are suggested to explain the results.) Converse and Pierce, pp. 743–59, 762.
76. The question of the relation of political party systems to the issues discussed here is significant and deserves further formulation beyond the scope of the present work.
77. Jewell, *Representation*, pp. 56–57.
78. Carol Pateman, *Participation and Democratic Theory* (Cambridge: Cambridge University Press, 1970).
79. Obviously Lenin is a transformative theorist. His theory of the political party accounts for how revolutionary change occurs. His theory of the trade unions, however, is by and large nontransformative.

Chapter Three

1. See Ch. 8, n. 1 below.
2. Robert Mundt and Peggy Heilig, "District Representation: Demands and Effects in the Urban South," *Journal of Politics* 44:4 (November 1982), pp. 1037, 1039 n. 4, 1040. And in the North, for example, in Atlantic City, New Jersey, in 1982, an alliance of the local NAACP with white, middle-class homeowners succeeded in persuading the voters to replace their at-large five-member city commission with a mayor and nine-member council, with two-thirds of the council from local wards.
3. Charles Redenius, arguing that it does. "Representation, Reapportionment, and the Supreme Court," *Political Studies* 30:4 (December 1982), p. 530.
4. *Gomillion v. Lightfoot*, 364 U.S. 339 (1960).
5. *Baker v. Carr*, 369 U.S. 186 (1962).
6. *Gray v. Sanders*, 372 U.S. 368 (1983).

7. *Reynolds v. Sims*, 377 U.S. 533 (1964).
8. *Fortson v. Dorsey*, 379 U.S. 433 (1965).
9. *Whitcomb v. Chavis*, 403 U.S. 124 (1971).
10. Harlan dissented to another aspect of the case that found a population variation between districts to be too great.
11. *White v. Regester*, 412 U.S. 755 (1973).
12. The Court was unanimous on this part of the case and divided on another part that allowed a departure from mathematical equality between districts, on which Brennan, Douglas, and Marshall dissented. Harlan had resigned in 1971.
13. *United Jewish Organizations v. Carey*, 430 U.S. 144 (1977).
14. The southern states and three counties of New York City included. The 1975 Voting Rights Act Extension (HR 6219) expanded protection to jurisdictions with certain language minorities, but the action of this case began before that, in 1974, and the amendments would not have affected this case anyway.
15. *Mobile v. Bolden*, 446 U.S. 55 (1980) and *Rome v. U.S.*, 446 U.S. 156 (1980).
16. The 1982 Voting Rights Act Extension (HR 3112) adopted the "totality of circumstances" approach. It specified that discriminatory intent did not have to be shown, and a showing of discriminatory effect was adequate.
17. *Lucas v. Colorado General Assembly*, 377 U.S. 713 (1964), at 750.
18. *Mobile v. Bolden*, 446 U.S. 55 (1980), at 70.
19. Ibid., at 74.
20. Ibid., at 75.
21. Ronald Rogowski, "Representation in Political Theory and in Law," *Ethics* 91:3 (April 1981), p. 429.
22. Jonathan Still, "Political Equality and Election Systems," *Ethics* 91:3 (April 1981), pp. 375–94.
23. Ibid., p. 378.
24. Ibid., p. 382.
25. Ibid., p. 380.
26. *Whitcomb v. Chavis*, 403 U.S. 124 (1971), at 144–46.
27. Ibid., at 769.
28. Edmund Burke, "Speech to the Electors of Bristol," in *The Philosophy of Edmund Burke*, ed. Louis I. Bredvold and Ralph G. Ross (Ann Arbor: University of Michigan Press, 1967), pp. 147–48.
29. Burke, "Letter to Langriche," in *Burke's Politics*, ed. Ross J. S. Hoffman and Paul Levack (New York: Alfred A. Knopf, 1949), p. 494.
30. Ibid., p. 495. See also Hanna Fenichel Pitkin, *The Concept of Representation* (Berkeley: University of California Press, 1967), pp. 170–78, 184–88.
31. *Fortson v. Dorsey*, 379 U.S. 433 (1965), at 439.
32. *White v. Regester*, 412 U.S. 755 (1973), at 773 n. 1. Although note that White for the Court does not directly quote it.
33. *UJO v. Carey*, 430 U.S. 144 (1977), at 170–75, esp. 171 n. 1 and 176 n. 4.

34. *Mobile v. Bolden,* 446 U.S. 55 (1980), at 119–20.
35. Ibid., at 122.
36. Ibid., at 123.
37. Ibid., at 120 n. 19.
38. Marshall did not sit on that case, and I wonder how he would have dealt with it had it not come under the Voting Rights Act.
39. Douglas Rae, *The Political Consequences of Electoral Laws,* rev. ed. (New Haven, Conn.: Yale University Press, 1971), pp. 28–39.
40. White in *Whitcomb v. Chavis,* 403 U.S. 124 (1971), at 156–57; Stewart in *Mobile v. Bolden,* 446 U.S. 55 (1980), at 78. "It is expressive of the more general proposition that any group with distinctive interests must be represented in legislative halls if it is numerous enough to command at least one seat and represents a majority living in an area sufficiently compact to constitute a single-member district. This approach would make it difficult to reject claims of Democrats, Republicans, or members of any political organization in Marion County who live in what would be safe districts in a single-member district system but who, in one year or another, or year after year, are submerged in a one-sided multi-member district vote. There are also union oriented workers, the university community, religious or ethnic groups occupying identifiable areas of our heterogeneous cities and urban areas. Indeed, it would be difficult for a great many, if not most, multi-member districts to survive analysis under the District Court's view unless combined with some voting arrangement such as proportional representation or cumulative voting aimed at providing representation for minority parties or interests."
41. *Reynolds v. Sims,* 377 U.S. 533 (1964), at 623–24.
42. *Gray v. Sanders,* 372 U.S. 368 (1963), at 386–89.
43. *UJO v. Carey,* 430 U.S. 144 (1977), at 166 n. 24.
44. Ibid., at 171 n. 6.
45. Ibid., at 178.
46. Rogowski, p. 424. Burke, in his theory of society, polity, and empire, gave evidence that he thought the interests of entities such as class, municipality, church, and nationality should be represented, but not those of race. Social interests acquired through experience and education, hence involving human volition even if transmitted through tradition, were deserving of representation. A social category ascriptive from birth like race was not worthy of representation unless it took social or political expression through legitimate human institutions.
47. *Reynolds v. Sims,* 377 U.S. 533 (1964), at 580.
48. *Fortson V. Dorsey,* 379 U.S. 433 (1965), at 436. (And thus change some single-member to multimember districts in order to meet the new equal population rule.)
49. See *Mahan v. Howell,* 410 U.S. 315 (1973). Redenius, p. 521.
50. *Whitcomb v. Chavis,* 403 U.S. 124 (1971), at 166–67.

51. On contemporary manifestations of corporatism, see Philippe Schmitter and Gerhard Lehmbruch, eds., *Trends Toward Corporatist Intermediation* (Beverly Hills, Calif.: Sage Publications, 1979).
52. *Reynolds v. Sims,* 377 U.S. 533 (1964), at 623.
53. *Lucas v. Colorado General Assembly,* 377 U.S. 713 (1964), at 749.
54. Ibid., at 753.
55. *Mobile v. Bolden,* 446 U.S. 55 (1980), at 105–6 n. 3.
56. Ibid., at 75 n. 22.
57. *Baker v. Carr,* 369 U.S. 186 (1962), at 300.
58. Ibid., at 323.
59. *Whitcomb v. Chavis,* 403 U.S. 124 (1971), at 149.
60. *White v. Regester,* 412 U.S. 755 (1973), at 765–66.
61. *Whitcomb v. Chavis,* 403 U.S. 124 (1971), at 155.
62. *White v. Regester,* 412 U.S. 755 (1973), at 769.
63. *Whitcomb v. Chavis,* 403 U.S. 124 (1971), at 158–59. Criticism of at-large plurality and majority elections, he writes, "is rooted in their winner-take-all aspects, their tendency to submerge minorities and to over-represent the winning party as compared with the party's statewide electoral position, a general preference for legislatures reflecting community interests as closely as possible and disenchantment with political parties and elections as devices to settle policy differences between contending interests. The chance of winning or significantly influencing intraparty fights and issue-oriented elections has seemed to some inadequate protection to minorities, political, racial, or economic; rather, their voice, it is said, should also be heard in the legislative forum where public policy is finally fashioned."
64. Having said this, I should add that White is not sure that the best alternative to at-large plurality seats is necessarily single-member plurality districts rather than, say, small multimember districts with PR.
65. *Rome v. U.S.,* 446 U.S. 156 (1980), at 216–17.
66. On this distinction see Hannah Arendt, *The Human Condition* (Garden City, N.Y.: Doubleday Anchor Books, 1959), esp. chs. 2 and 5.
67. *Mobile v. Bolden,* 446 U.S. 55 (1980), at 102.
68. Ibid., p. 97.
69. I am here drawing on the distinction made by Rousseau between the "will of all," each individual acting as a self-interested person, a member of civil society concerned with his private ends, and the "general will," each citizen acting as a public-spirited member of the political whole. Jean-Jacques Rousseau, *The Social Contract,* trans. Gerard Hopkins, in *Social Contract,* ed. Ernest Barker (New York: Oxford University Press, 1962), bk. 2, ch. 3.
70. David R. Mayhew, "Congressional Representation: Theory and Practice in Drawing the Districts," in *Reapportionment in the 1970's,* ed. Nelson W. Polsby (Berkeley: University of California Press, 1971), pp. 249–85.
71. Mayhew draws on Hanna Pitkin's categories, which he then rearranges

creatively. Pitkin, n. 30 above. For my further elaboration on Pitkin, see Chs. 7 and 8.

72. Mayhew, pp. 274–77.

73. Political scientists have proposed mathematical models to maximize the mix of certain values in political districting, mainly voter equality and party competition, not community. Edward R. Tufte, "The Relationship between Seats and Votes in Two-Party Systems," *American Political Science Review* 67:2 (1973), pp. 540–54; Richard G. Niemi and John Deegan, Jr., "A Theory of Political Districting," *American Political Science Review* 72:4 (1978), pp. 1304–23.

74. Mayhew, pp. 271–72. See also Janet K. Boles and Dorothy K. Dean, "'Communities of Interest' in Legislative Redistricting," *State Government* 58:3 (Fall 1985), pp. 101, 103, 104.

75. Dennis F. Thompson, "Representatives in the Welfare State" (Paper presented to Faculty Seminar on Democracy and the Welfare State, Project on the Federal Role, Princeton University, November 7, 1985), pp. 20–33.

76. Mayhew, p. 255.

77. See, for example, Robert Paul Wolff who is a philosophical anarchist and places an absolute value on individual liberty. No representative system, or any decision-rule short of unanimity, is politically legitimate. Wolff, *In Defense of Anarchism* (New York: Harper & Row, 1976), pp. 22–67.

78. *Gaffney v. Cummings,* 412 U.S. 735 (1973), at 753.

79. Ibid., at 748.

80. Ibid., at 781.

81. *Allen v. State Board of Elections,* 393 U.S. 544 (1969), at 586. See also Gerhard Casper, "Social Differences and the Franchise," *Daedalus* 105:4 (Fall 1976), pp. 105, 107–8, 110, 112–13.

82. *Gomillion v. Lightfoot,* 364 U.S. 339 (1960), at 341.

83. *Mobile v. Bolden,* 446 U.S. 55 (1980), at 78.

84. Hannah Arendt, "On Violence," in *Crises of the Republic* (New York: Harcourt Brace Jovanovich, 1972), p. 143.

Chapter Four

1. Wilson Carey McWilliams, "Civil Disobedience and Contemporary Constitutionalism," *Comparative Politics* 1 (January 1969), p. 223.

2. Michael Ignatieff, *The Needs of Strangers* (New York: Penguin Books, 1986).

3. Dennis Hale, "What Was Citizenship," in *American Political Science and the Meaning of Citizenship* (Ph.D. diss., City University of New York, 1977), ch. 1, pp. 21, 11, 29, 33. See also his essay, "The City as Polity and Economy," *Polity* 17:2 (Winter 1984), pp. 205–24.

4. The root for the words *city* and *citizen* is the Latin *civitas,* as developed

in Roman law. The ideas of the city and citizen are of earlier origin, in the *polis* and *politēs* of ancient Greece. The Roman conception leads towards the liberal idea of citizenship as the possession of civil rights by an individual against the state (and potentially as part of a universal society). The Greek conception is more communitarian, stressing collective membership and individual participation in political office. See A. E. Zimmern, *The Greek Commonwealth*, 3d ed., rev. (Oxford: Oxford University Press, 1922); Raphael Sealey, *A History of the Greek City States* (Berkeley: University of California Press, 1976); H. Mark Roelofs, *The Tension of Citizenship* (New York: Rinehart & Co., 1957), ch. 3, esp. pp. 120–33; and Michael Walzer, "The Problem of Citizenship," in *Obligations* (New York: Simon & Schuster, 1970), pp. 205–6, 210.

5. Robert Dahl and Edward Tufte, *Size and Democracy* (Stanford, Calif.: Stanford University Press, 1973), pp. 13–15.

6. Aristotle, *Politics*, I, 1252b; VII, 1326b.

7. Ibid., III, 1280a–1283b.

8. Plato, *The Republic;* Aristotle, *Politics*, III, 1277a–b; Hale, Intro., and ch. 1, pp. 1–7, 8–80.

9. J. Peter Euben, "Political Equality and the Greek Polis," in *Liberalism and the Modern Polity,* ed. Michael J. G. McGrath (New York: M. Dekker, 1978), pp. 211, 213, 216.

10. Ibid., p. 208.

11. Ibid., p. 218.

12. Ibid., pp. 213, 215.

13. Hannah Arendt, *On Revolution* (New York: Viking Press, 1965), pp. 229, 253–58, 272–73.

14. Euben, pp. 210–11.

15. See Nancy L. Schwartz, "Communitarian Citizenship: Marx and Weber on the City," *Polity* 17:3 (Spring 1985), pp. 530–48.

16. Max Weber, "The City: Non-Legitimate Domination" [*Die Stadt*], trans. Claus Wittich, in *Economy and Society* [E&S], 2 vols., ed. Guenther Roth and Claus Wittich (Berkeley: University of California Press, 1978), vol. 2, ch. 16, pp. 1212–1372.

17. Karl Marx, *Grundrisse: Foundations of the Critique of Political Economy (Rough Draft)* [G], trans. Martin Nicolaus (Harmondsworth: Penguin Books, 1973). Most of the passages relevant to our topic were published earlier in English, Karl Marx, *Pre-Capitalist Economic Formations* [PC], ed. E. J. Hobsbawm, trans. Jack Cohen (New York: International Publishers, 1965).

18. Weber, "The Types of Legitimate Domination," in E&S, vol. 1, pt. 1, ch. 3, pp. 212–301.

19. Weber, "The Distribution of Power within the Political Community: Class, Status and Party," in E&S, vol. 2, ch. 9, sec. 6, pp. 926–40.

20. Weber, "Sociological Categories of Economic Action," in E&S, vol. 1, pt. 1, ch. 2, sec. 1–14, pp. 63–113.

21. Additionally, cities may be primarily "producer" cities—the artisan communes of the late medieval/early Renaissance—but for Weber this is not essential to the definition of a city (E&S 1341, 1350). Compare Henri Pirenne, who specifies that a true city—at least a medieval one—has to be an industrial as well as a commercial unit. Pirenne, *Medieval Cities* (Princeton, N.J.: Princeton University Press, 1969), pp. 189, 212.

22. Weber, "Politics as a Vocation," in *From Max Weber,* ed. H. H. Gerth and C. Wright Mills (New York: Oxford University Press, 1958), p. 78.

23. On the different kinds of rationality within the law, and within religion and politics generally, see Weber, "Politics as a Vocation," in *From Max Weber,* pp. 118–19, 123; and "The Sociology of Religion" and "The Sociology of Law," in E&S, vol. 1, pt. 2, ch. 6, and vol. 2, ch. 8, esp. pp. 656–57. See also Nancy L. Schwartz, "Max Weber's Philosophy," *Yale Law Journal* 93:7 (June 1984), pp. 1387–89, 1396.

24. The city can have some legal autonomy even in the modern national situation. Gerald Frug, "The City as a Legal Concept," *Harvard Law Review* 93:6 (April 1980), pp. 1057–1154.

25. Our first understanding of the Marxian analysis of the social forces that constitute and transform cities derives from the theoretical framework he and Engels developed in *The German Ideology*—the idea of a mode of production. Marx and Frederick Engels, "The German Ideology" [GI], in *Writings of the Young Marx on Philosophy and Society,* ed. Loyd Easton and Kurt Guddat (Garden City, N.Y.: Doubleday Anchor Books, 1967), pp. 409–10, 413–14. In this scheme, there are three spheres of social life—forces of production, relations of production, and social consciousness—and these interact in specific if complex ways. The forces of production refer to the natural and social resources at hand, including the available technical knowledge and technical division of labor. The relations of production are the social and legal relations of people to these resources and to one another, specifically, the social division of labor into classes and the laws of property. Finally, in the area of social consciousness or ideology are those general ideas of the culture, from law and politics to art and everyday life, that further legitimate the mode of production (GI 421–22). In the engineering metaphor of base and superstructure, the forces and relations are the base, and consciousness is the superstructure that arises upon and reflects the base. Marx, Preface to *A Contribution to the Critique of Political Economy* [CCPE], trans. S. W. Ryazanskaya (New York: International Publishers, 1970), pp. 20–21, and *Capital,* vol. 1 [C,I], ed. Frederick Engels, trans. Moore and Aveling (New York: Modern Library, n.d.), p. 94n. Historical change occurs only when structural changes occur deep in the base. But this is inevitably and continually occurring either due to internal developments in the base or because of changes in other levels that then impinge on the base. When the forces of production change, the old relations of production become dysfunctional and obstructive, and the newly emerging social classes begin to chal-

lenge them, either explicitly or simply by their very existence (GI 423, 430–31, 453–54; CM 12–13). Also, a self-conscious vanguard of the old ruling class may perceive the changes and come over to the side of the insurgent class (CM 17). Marx and Engels, "The Communist Manifesto" [CM], in *Marx and Engels: Basic Writings on Politics and Philosophy,* ed. Lewis Feuer (Garden City, N.Y.: Doubleday Anchor Books, 1959), pp. 12–13, 17. This is a clear and powerful model of historical change, yet Marx seems to abandon it in his later work, specifically in his magnum opus, *Capital.* There the distinction between forces and relations of production is blurred, as is the distinction between relations of production and social consciousness. The independent and dependent variables are less clear, leading to a more structural theory. Étienne Balibar, "The Basic Concepts of Historical Materialism," in *Reading Capital,* ed. Louis Althusser and Balibar (New York: Pantheon Books, 1970), pt. 3, pp. 212–15, 235. Marx, GI 421; C,I 397. Louis Althusser, "The Object of *Capital,*" in *Reading Capital,* pt. 2, chs. 4, 5, and 9.

26. See also André Gorz, *Strategy for Labor,* trans. Martin Nicolaus and Victoria Ortiz (Boston: Beacon Press, 1969).

27. Theoretical opening: might not there be other kinds of sociopolitical activities that would establish this relation? It is even possible, and here I go out on a limb, that for the postcapitalist society Marx could envisage a passive, almost contemplative, relation of appropriation.

28. Marx considers the large city in "Oriental despotism" to be "merely a princely camp, superimposed on the real economic structure" of agriculture and manufacture in smaller, self-sustaining communities (PC 77–78, 70).

29. See also Nancy L. Schwartz, "Distinction between Public and Private Life: Marx on the *zōon politikon,*" *Political Theory* 7:2 (May 1979), p. 250.

30. Production, the aim of the property relation, assumes a broader meaning. It includes not only the making of material goods and cultural artifacts, but also the manufacture of a political good—citizenship itself.

> Among the ancients we discover no single enquiry as to which form of landed property, etc., is the most productive, which creates maximum wealth. Wealth does not appear as the end of production, although Cato may well investigate the most profitable cultivation of fields, or Brutus may even lend money at the most favorable rate of interest. The enquiry is always about what kind of property creates the best citizens. Wealth as an end in itself appears only among a few trading peoples . . .
>
> Thus the ancient conception [is one] in which man always appears (in however narrowly national, religious, or political a definition), as the aim of production . . . (PC 84)

What this broadening does to the specificity of Marx's concept of property and production—as covering discrete phenomena which can then be asserted to have definite roles in social causation—is another question.

31. Though there is an ambiguity in these Marx passages (PC 69, 73) as well as in related Weber ones (E&S 1311, 1313).

Chapter Five

1. Arendt Lijphart, *Democracies* (New Haven, Conn.: Yale University Press, 1984), ch. 9.

2. For a recent discussion illuminating the relation of American democracy to the preservation of local ties, see Joshua I. Miller, "To Preserve Democratic Custom: The Antifederalist Theory of Scale," in *Decentralization in American Politics: Theories of Local Autonomy* (Ph.D. diss., Princeton University, 1984).

3. Robert G. Dixon, Jr., *Democratic Representation: Reapportionment in Law and Politics* (New York: Oxford University Press, 1968), pp. 10–11.

4. Ibid., pp. 60–64, esp. chart 1, and chart 2, pp. 68–69.

5. Ibid., pp. 66–90.

6. *Brown v. Thomson*, 77 L.Ed. 2d 214 (1983).

7. Dixon, pp. 91–94; *Times* (London), Jan. 25, 1982, p. 8a; Dec. 14, 1982, p. 3f; Jan. 5, 1983, p. 18a; Mar. 2, 1983, p. 4; Mar. 3, 1983, p. 4.

8. Samuel H. Beer, *British Politics in the Collectivist Age* (New York: Alfred A. Knopf, 1966), chs. 1 and 3. Although on recent developments in the direction of romantic individualism, see Samuel Beer, *Britain against Itself* (New York: W. W. Norton & Co., 1982).

9. Gianfranco Poggi, *The Development of the Modern State* (Stanford, Calif.: Stanford University Press, 1978), ch. 2, esp. pp. 20–22, ch. 3, esp. pp. 42, 47.

10. "A statute of 1413 required that a representative be a resident of the borough that chose him, but the lawyers in the House of Commons quickly interpreted this to mean that he need not be a resident of the borough that chose him." Edmund S. Morgan, "Government by Fiction: The Idea of Representation," *Yale Review* 72:3 (April 1983), p. 331. See also Helen Cam, *Liberties and Communities in Medieval England* (Cambridge: Cambridge University Press, 1944), ch. 16, pp. 236–37.

11. David Nicholls, *Three Varieties of Pluralism* (London: Macmillan Press, 1974).

12. Hume and Montesquieu, on custom, geography, and a people's character, are exceptions to this generalization. Miller, pp. 6, 8–10, 17–18, 22–24.

13. *Brown v. Thomson*, at 225.

14. John Locke, *An Essay Concerning the True Original, Extent and End of Civil Government* (Second Treatise) in *Social Contract*, ed. Ernest Barker (New York: Oxford University Press, 1962).

15. Jeremy Bentham, *The Principles of Morals and Legislation* (New York: Hafner Publishing Co., 1948).

16. Edmund Burke, *Selected Writings*, ed. Walter J. Bate (New York: Modern Library, 1960).
17. Plato, *The Republic*, trans. F. M. Cornford (New York: Oxford University Press, 1970).
18. Ibid., bks. III, 412b–IV, 427c; IV, 445b–V, 466d.
19. Ibid., bks. II, 357a–376e; IV, 427c–434d, 441c–445b; IX, 588b–592.
20. Ibid., bk. IV, 434d–441c.
21. Allan Bloom, "Interpretive Essay" on *The Republic of Plato* (New York: Basic Books, 1968), p. 392. See also Herbert Marcuse, *Eros and Civilization* (New York: Vintage Books, 1962); and Wendy Brown, " 'What If Truth Were a Woman?' Plato's Subversion of Masculine Discourse" (Paper presented to Yankee Conference on Political Thought, March 1985), 34 pp. Also Plato, bks. V, 474b–475; VI, 491–92; VIII, 550c–569; IX, 571–89.
22. Plato, Ibid., bks. II, 376e–392c; III, 414–15.
23. Ibid., bk. VII, 518; Plato, *Meno*, in *Protagorus and Meno*, trans. W. K. C. Guthrie (Baltimore, Md.: Penguin Books, 1961).
24. Plato, *The Republic*, trans. Paul Shorey, Loeb Classical Library (London: William Heinemann, Ltd., 1978), bk. IX, 590d, p. 409.
25. W. J. Verdenius, "Plato's Doctrine of Artistic Imitation," in *Plato, II*, ed. Gregory Vlastos (Garden City, N.Y.: Doubleday Anchor Books, 1971), pp. 259–73.
26. Jean-Jacques Rousseau, *The Social Contract*, trans. Gerard Hopkins, in *Social Contract*, ed. Ernest Barker (New York: Oxford University Press, 1962).
27. Jean-Jacques Rousseau, "Discourse on the Origin and Foundations of Inequality" (*Second Discourse*), in the *First and Second Discourses*, trans. Roger D. and Judith R. Masters, ed. Roger D. Masters (New York: St. Martin's Press, 1964).
28. Rousseau, *Social Contract*, bk. I, ch. 3, p. 185.
29. Rousseau, *Second Discourse*, pp. 114, 95–96, 130–32.
30. Rousseau, *Social Contract*, bk. II, chs. 2, 4, pp. 191–99; ch. 6, pp. 201–3.
31. Ibid., bk. II, ch. 3, pp. 193–95; ch. 6, p. 204; bk. IV, ch. 1, pp. 269–71; ch. 2, p. 273.
32. Ibid., bk. III, ch. 15, p. 262.
33. Ibid., bk. II, ch. 11, p. 217.
34. See ch. 7, n. 1.
35. Rousseau, *Social Contract*, bk. II, ch. 1, pp. 190–91; bk. III, ch. 15, pp. 259–61.
36. Karl Marx, "On the Jewish Question," and "Critical Notes on 'The King of Prussia and Social Reform,' " in *Writings of the Young Marx on Philosophy and Society*, ed. Loyd Easton and Kurt Guddat (Garden City, N.Y.: Doubleday Anchor Books, 1967), pp. 235–40, 345–50. See also Frederick Engels,

Anti-Dühring, trans. E. Burns (New York: International Publishers, 1971), p. 281; and Shlomo Avineri, *The Social and Political Thought of Karl Marx* (Cambridge: Cambridge University Press, 1968), ch. 7.

37. Marx and Engels, "The German Ideology," in Easton and Guddat, eds., pp. 420–22.

38. Marx, "Economic and Philosophic Manuscript," in ibid., pp. 287–300.

39. Raya Dunayevskaya, *Marxism and Freedom* (London: Pluto Press, 1971); István Mészáros, *Marx's Theory of Alienation* (London: Merlin Press, 1970).

40. Karl Marx, *Grundrisse: Foundations of the Critique of Political Economy (Rough Draft),* trans. Martin Nicolaus (Harmondsworth: Penguin Books, 1973), p. 84.

41. Ch. 4 above, n. 25. See also Marx, *Capital,* vol. 1, trans. S. Moore and E. Aveling (New York: Modern Library, 1906), pt. 1, ch. 1, sec. 4; pt. 2, ch. 6; pt. 3, ch. 10; pt. 4, chs. 13–15.

42. In "The Civil War in France" Marx lauds the democracy of the Paris Commune, which included electing delegate representatives from geographic as well as functional units. But this article, despite its theoretical contributions, has to be seen also as Marx's attempt to generally celebrate an unprecedented uprising of the workers, one that had occurred without the First International's approval and before conditions for communism were ready. Marx, *The First International and After, Political Writings,* vol. 3, ed. David Fernbach (Harmondsworth: Penguin Books, 1974), pp. 209–10, 236, 251–52. Engels later commented that the Commune was in no way socialist, nor could it be.

43. Sheldon S. Wolin, *Politics and Vision* (London: George Allen & Unwin, 1961), ch. 2, sec. 4, pp. 51–55.

44. On the idea of a common interest in a unitary democracy, see Jane J. Mansbridge, *Beyond Adversary Democracy* (Chicago: University of Chicago Press, 1983), pt. 1, chs. 1–3, esp. pp. 26–28.

45. James MacGregor Burns, *Leadership* (New York: Harper & Row, 1978), pt. 3, pp. 139–254.

46. Wilson Carey McWilliams, *The Idea of Fraternity in America* (Berkeley: University of California Press, 1973), chs. 5 and 6, esp. pp. 125 and 137–38.

47. Plato, *Republic,* bk. VII, 514a–521b.

48. Ibid., bk. VII, 509d–511e, 521c–535a. See also Robert S. Brumbaugh, *Plato for the Modern Age* (Westport, Conn.: Greenwood Press, 1979), pp. 48–50, 92–103.

49. Norman Jacobson, "Invitation to a Public Execution: The Just Chastisement of Thrasymachus" (Paper delivered to Conference on Public Language, Rutgers University, New Brunswick, N.J., April 29, 1978), 18 pp.

50. Hans-Georg Gadamer, *Dialogue and Dialectic: Eight Hermeneutical Studies on Plato,* trans. P. Christopher Smith (New Haven, Conn.: Yale University Press, 1980), trans. intro. and ch. 1, esp. pp. 2, 5–6, 9, 19–20.

51. Ibid., p. 12; Leo Strauss, *The City and Man* (Chicago: University of Chicago Press, 1978), pp. 51–61.

52. Rousseau, *Social Contract*, bk. II, ch. 7, p. 207; although this particular phrasing is Masters' (in his 1968 book, not his 1978 translation), n. 53 below, p. 363. "Les sages qui veulent parler au vulgaire leur langage au lieu du sien n'en sauroient être entendus," Rousseau, *Du Contrat Social* (Paris: Editions Garnier Frères, 1962), p. 262.

53. Roger D. Masters, *The Political Philosophy of Rousseau* (Princeton, N.J.: Princeton University Press, 1968), pp. 362–63.

54. Rousseau, *Social Contract*, bk. IV, ch. 8.

55. Ibid., bk. I, ch. 7, p. 184.

56. Lucio Colletti, "Marxism: Science or Revolution?" in *From Rousseau to Lenin* (London: New Left Books, 1972), p. 236; and V. I. Lenin, *What Is To Be Done?* (New York: International Publishers, 1969), p. 78.

57. Marx and Frederick Engels, *The Communist Manifesto*, and Marx, "Address of the Central Committee to the Communist League," in *The Revolutions of 1848. Political Writings*, vol. 1, ed. David Fernbach (Harmondsworth: Penguin Books, 1973), pp. 77, 324–27.

58. Ibid., p. 324.

59. Marx, "Critique of the Gotha Program," in Fernbach, ed., vol. 3, p. 354.

60. V. I. Lenin, *What Is To Be Done?* (New York: International Publishers, 1969), pp. 78, 81, 86.

61. Ibid., pp. 66–67, 69, 70, 73, 77–79, 87 (italics his).

62. Christopher Reinier, "Politics as Art: The Civic Vision," in *The New Student Left*, rev. ed., ed. Mitchell Cohen and Dennis Hale (Boston: Beacon Press, 1967), p. 27.

63. Leo Strauss, *Natural Right and History* (Chicago: University of Chicago Press, 1965), pp. 291–94; Allan Bloom, "Jean-Jacques Rousseau," in *History of Political Philosophy*, ed. Leo Strauss and Joseph Cropsey, 2d ed., (Chicago: Rand McNally, 1972), pp. 550–52.

64. Gadamer, p. 128.

65. Karl Marx, "Toward the Critique of Hegel's Philosophy of Law: Introduction," in *Writings of the Young Marx*, pp. 262–64, 256–57, 259; Antonio Gramsci, *The Modern Prince and Other Writings*, trans. Louis Marks (New York: International Publishers, 1970), pp. 42–51, 66–67, 87.

66. Hegel's *Phenomenology of Spirit*, trans. A. V. Miller (New York: Oxford University Press, 1977), sec. B. IV. A, pars. 178–96, pp. 111–19.

67. Hannah Arendt, *The Human Condition* (Garden City, N.Y.: Doubleday Anchor Books, 1959), ch. 5, esp. pp. 155–66, 173–77, 184.

68. Saul Alinsky, *Reveille for Radicals* (New York: Vintage Books, 1969), ch. 5, esp. pp. 73–74.

69. Roger D. Masters, *The Political Philosophy of Rousseau* (Princeton, N.J.: Princeton University Press, 1968), pp. 357–58.

70. Hilail Gilden argues that there are two legislators rather than one. There is the original founder or "early legislator who first makes appeals to the sacred character of the common good possible and the later legislator who establishes a political order" (p. 86). Gilden notes, "The recognition that two legislators are needed rather than one and that the first must not make the work of the second impossible is tantamount to an admission that a sound political order cannot be brought into being at a single moment" (p. 74). He does not then draw the conclusion I do, the implication that the founding is a continual process. Gilden, *Rousseau's Social Contract* (Chicago: University of Chicago Press, 1983), pp. 73–74, 76–78, 86–89.

Chapter Six

1. This is akin to Aristotle's notion of citizenship or political friendship, whose purpose is association for the good life. The polis is a self-sufficient community in which there is a necessary interdependence of the parts so that virtue may be exercised. The virtues are dispositions to act and ways of acting that cannot be developed in isolation, and hence the good citizen depends upon the community for his very identity. There are, however, ambiguities in Aristotle's vision, since the good man could conceivably exist without the polis and because there is often political conflict over what standards should be used for admission to citizenship. Bernard Yack suggests that, for Aristotle, citizens come together out of self-interest and do not really feel fully bound to each other in present virtue, yet they all must act as if they had virtue in order to approximate it at all. "Community and Conflict in Aristotle's Political Philosophy," *Review of Politics* 47:1 (January 1985), pp. 105–6.

2. *Random House Dictionary of the English Language* (New York: Random House, 1971), p. 894.

3. *Webster's New Collegiate Dictionary* (Springfield, Mass.: G. & C. Merriam, 1958), p. 524.

4. Michael J. Sandel, *Liberalism and the Limits of Justice* (Cambridge: Cambridge University Press, 1982), p. 87.

5. Ending a marriage engenders shame and failure and thus might seem to be an exception to these statements. But although marriage is a civil contract it has strong aspects of its prior status as covenant, to be discussed below.

6. On the threefold distinction between instrumental, sentimental, and constitutive conceptions of community, see Sandel, pp. 148–50. For a similar distinction between relations of use and of experience (I-It relations) and those of loving knowledge (I-Thou relations), see Martin Buber, *I and Thou*, 2d ed., trans. Ronald Gregor Smith (New York: Charles Scribner's Sons, 1958). These distinctions seem to hearken back to Aristotle's three kinds of friendship, in

which the purpose is either the useful, the pleasant, or the good. *Nicomachean Ethics,* trans. Martin Ostwald (Indianapolis: Bobbs-Merrill, 1962), bk. 8, secs. 2–4, 1155b–1157b, pp. 217–23.

7. John H. Schaar, "The Case for Patriotism," in *American Review,* no. 17 (May 1973), ed. Theodore Solotaroff (New York: Bantam Books, 1973), pp. 59–99, esp. sec. 2, pp. 68–78.

8. H. Mark Roelofs, *The Tension of Citizenship: Private Man and Public Duty* (New York: Rinehart & Co., 1957), ch. 2, sec. B, pp. 60–80.

9. Michael A. Mosher, "Civic Identity in the Juridicial Society: On Hegelianism as Discipline for the Romantic Mind," *Political Theory* 11:1 (February 1983), p. 127.

10. St. Thomas Aquinas, *The Summa Theologica,* I–II, QQ. 90–97, in *The Political Ideas of St. Thomas Aquinas,* ed. Dino Bigongiari (New York: Hafner Press, 1953), pp. 3–85. See also Sandel, pp. 1–10, 165–68, 170–71, 173–74.

11. The modern state is an entity existing in an international system of other sovereign states. Each, in theory, has the right of self-determination, with the fullest power and authority available at the time to determine its internal affairs. To be sure, this sovereignty is not absolute; transnational processes from world trade to the logic of nuclear deterrence put severe limits on what a state can actually do. But these processes, except when embodied in international law, do not express the collective self-consciousness of an international polity and hence do not violate state sovereignty directly; they are unintended or partial processes that impinge on particular countries as impersonal necessity.

12. Charles A. Beard and John D. Lewis, "Representative Government in Evolution," *American Political Science Review* 26:2 (April 1932), pp. 230–31; Alfred de Grazia, *Public and Republic: Political Representation in America* (New York: Alfred A. Knopf, 1951), pp. 4, 14–15; Edmund S. Morgan, "Government by Fiction: The Idea of Representation," *Yale Review* 72:3 (April 1983), pp. 324–26.

13. Beard and Lewis, pp. 232–35; de Grazia, pp. 15–49; Morgan, p. 326.

14. Bernard Yack, "The Rationality of Hegel's Concept of Monarchy," *American Political Science Review* 74:3 (September 1980), pp. 713–14 ff. See also Lis Harris, *Holy Days* (New York: Summit Books, 1985), p. 253, for an account of the limits even the Lord encountered in His role as sovereign, bound by the structure of the system He created: "The Bible does not account for the creation of demons, but according to Talmudic tradition they made their debut on the first Sabbath eve, when God was putting the finishing touches on the world. As the day was waning, according to one source, He turned His attention to those beings 'who, though included in the plan of things as they were to be, might well be left for last. He had not progressed beyond the fashioning of their souls, however, when the hastening Sabbath overtook Him, and He was obliged to sanctify the first day of rest. So it is, that demons have no bodies, but are constituted wholly of spirit.'"

15. Gordon S. Wood, *The Creation of the American Republic 1776–1787* (New York: W. W. Norton & Co., 1969), ch. 9.

16. Samuel P. Huntington, "Political Modernization: America vs. Europe," ch. 2 in *Political Order in Changing Societies* (New Haven, Conn.: Yale University Press, 1968), pp. 96–98.

17. Bertrand de Jouvenel, *On Power*, trans. J. F. Huntington (1945; reprint, Boston: Beacon Press, 1962), chs. 2, 7, 13, 14; and *Sovereignty*, trans. J. F. Huntington (1957); reprint, Chicago: University of Chicago Press, 1963), chs. 10–12; Joshua I. Miller, "The Federalist Doctrine of Popular Sovereignty" (1985), 32 pp.

18. Aristotle, bks. II–IV, VI–VIII.

19. Alasdair MacIntyre, *After Virtue* (Notre Dame, Ind.: University of Notre Dame Press, 1981), pp. 190–209. Also Sandel, p. 179.

20. G. W. F. Hegel, *Philosophy of Right*, trans. T. M. Knox (New York: Oxford University Press, 1967), Intro., pars. 5–7, pp. 21–24; J. N. Findlay, *The Philosophy of Hegel: An Introduction and Re-examination* (orig.: *Hegel: A Re-Examination*) (New York: Collier Books, 1962), pp. 226–31; Yack, "The Rationality of Hegel's Concept of Monarchy," pp. 710b–711a.

21. John Charvet, *A Critique of Freedom and Equality* (Cambridge: Cambridge University Press, 1981), pp. 161 ff.

22. Ibid., pt. 3, esp. pp. 197–98.

23. Immanuel Kant, "Foundations of the Metaphysics of Morals," in *Immanuel Kant: Critique of Practical Reason and Other Writings in Moral Philosophy*, ed. Lewis White Beck (Chicago: University of Chicago Press, 1949), p. 63.

24. Hadley Arkes, *The Philosopher in the City* (Princeton, N.J.: Princeton University Press, 1981), pp. 47–48, 225, 335.

25. Karl Marx, "On the Jewish Question," in *Writings of the Young Marx on Philosophy and Society*, ed. Loyd Easton and Kurt Guddat (Garden City, N.Y.: Doubleday Anchor Books, 1967), pp. 223–27; Nancy L. Schwartz, "Distinction between Public and Private Life: Marx on the *zōon politikon*," *Political Theory* 7:2 (May 1979), pp. 247–48.

26. Hegel, pars. 7, 12, 152; pp. 23, 26, 109; and H. B. Acton, "Introduction" to Hegel, *Natural Law*, trans. T. M. Knox (Philadelphia: University of Pennsylvania Press, 1975), pp. 21–27.

27. Leonard Krieger, *The German Idea of Freedom* (Chicago: University of Chicago Press, 1957), pp. 101, 130.

28. Hegel, par. 148 and Remark; par. 149, pp. 106–7.

29. Charles Taylor, *Hegel and Modern Society* (Cambridge: Cambridge University Press, 1979), pp. 154–64.

30. Ibid., pp. 103, 114–17.

31. de Jouvenel, *On Power*, ch. 12, pp. 230–33.

32. Hegel, pars. 251–56, 308, 311; pp. 152–54, 200, 202; Krieger, p. 138, n. 175.

33. Roelofs, pp. 142–47.
34. Krieger, p. 127.
35. See also Bartolus of Sassoferrato on whether citizenship came from a ward or the commune as a whole, Ch. 7 below, n. 31.
36. Gerald Frug, "The City as a Legal Concept," *Harvard Law Review* 93:6 (April 1980), pp. 1057–1154, esp. pp. 1066, 1077, 1095, 1121.
37. Mosher, p. 126.

Chapter Seven

1. Sheldon S. Wolin, *Politics and Vision* (London: Allen and Unwin, 1961), pp. 5, 414–19.
2. Wolin, "Contract and Birthright," *Political Theory* 14:2 (May 1986), pp. 181–82.
3. Quentin Skinner, *Foundations of Modern Political Thought,* vol. 1, *The Renaissance* (Cambridge: Cambridge University Press, 1978), chs. 2 and 3, esp. pp. 27, 59–60. See also Hanna Fenichel Pitkin, *The Concept of Representation* (Berkeley: University of California Press, 1967), pp. 235–38.
4. On action, see Hannah Arendt, *The Human Condition* (Garden City, N.Y.: Doubleday Anchor Books, 1959). On affection, in the context of a higher love, see Wilson Carey McWilliams, *The Idea of Fraternity in America* (Berkeley: University of California Press, 1973).
5. Marvin B. Becker, *Florence in Transition,* vol. 1, *The Decline of the Commune* (Baltimore, Md.: Johns Hopkins Press, 1967), p. 32.
6. J. G. A. Pocock, *The Machiavellian Moment* (Princeton, N.J.: Princeton University Press, 1975), pp. 48–50, 62–65, 74–75.
7. Skinner, p. 45.
8. Gene Brucker, *Florentine Politics and Society (1343–1378)* (Princeton, N.J.: Princeton University Press, 1962), p. 134. Under the Priorate were the city's civil servants, and it could also constitute special commissions (*balìe*) to oversee particular matters such as war, finance, or electoral reform. A number of other groups advised and consulted with the Signoria, including an informal council of respected citizens (*Consulte e Pratiche*), the captains of the Guelph party, the consuls of the guilds, and the entire guild membership. There were two large legislative bodies, which served four month terms: the Council of the Commune, two hundred citizens, which could include those of magnate status as well as the people (*popolani*), and the Council of the *Popolo,* three hundred citizens, including the members of the *Tre Maggiori,* and from which the magnates were excluded. The approval of both these assemblies by two-thirds majorities was required to pass a law. There were three high judicial organs, which earlier had had greater executive power and which also reflected earlier military splits between the *magnati* and the *popolani:* the *Podestà,* the Captain of the *Popolo,* and the Executor of the Ordinances of Justice. In order to promote the

impartial administration of justice in this fractious city, these three posts were always filled by leading citizens of foreign cities, the *Podestà* and Captain by noblemen, the Executor by a commoner.

9. Pasquale Villari, *The First Two Centuries of Florentine History*, trans. Linda Villari (London: T. Fisher Unwin, 1905). A recent study stresses the declining role of the guilds, but in so doing still shows their importance: John Najemy, *Corporatism and Consensus in Florentine Electoral Politics, 1280–1400* (Chapel Hill: University of North Carolina Press, 1982), pp. 178–79.

10. I.e., residency, age, the paying of a tax or the posting of a bond, either monetary or personal, the political approval of the Guelph party, and the ultimate approval by the councils of the commune. Becker, *Florence in Transition*, vol. 2, *Studies in the Rise of the Territorial State* (Baltimore, Md.: Johns Hopkins Press, 1967), p. 97.

11. Villari, pp. 269–70.

12. John Najemy, "Guild Republicanism in Trecento Florence: The Successes and Ultimate Failure of Corporate Politics," *American Historical Review* 84:1 (1979), p. 58.

13. Brucker, pp. 29–35. Also Brucker, *Renaissance Florence* (New York: John Wiley and Sons, 1969), pp. 23–25; D. V. and F. W. Kent, *Neighbours and Neighbourhood in Renaissance Florence. The District of the Red Lion in the Fifteenth Century* (Locust Valley, N.Y.: J. J. Augustin Publisher, 1982), p. 8.

14. Dale Kent, "The Florentine *Reggimento* in the Fifteenth Century," *Renaissance Quarterly* 4 (1975), p. 613.

15. Niccolo Machiavelli, *History of Florence*, trans. M. Walter Dunne, ed. and intro. Felix Gilbert (New York: Harper & Brothers, 1960), p. 53.

16. David Herlihy and Christiane Klapisch-Zuber, *Les Toscans et leurs familles* (Paris: Presses de la foundation nationale des sciences politiques, 1978), p. 123; Samuel Kline Cohn, Jr., *The Laboring Classes in Renaissance Florence* (New York: Academic Press, 1980), pp. 25–26.

17. Cohn, p. 175.

18. "District" is being used to cover either the four quarters or the sixteen wards, whichever is relevant to the office.

19. The Scrutiny Council consisted of the Signoria and the colleges, the captains of the Guelph party, the six of the Merchant's Court, the proconsul of the guild of Judges and Notaries, all sitting *ex officio;* and one consul from each of the twenty-one guilds and eighty members chosen by the *Tre Maggiori*.

20. D. Kent, p. 633.

21. Nicolai Rubinstein, *The Government of Florence under the Medici (1434 to 1494)* (Oxford: Clarendon Press, 1966), p. 5; Brucker, *Florentine Politics*, pp. 212–13; Najemy, *Corporatism and Consensus*, p. 180.

22. Rubinstein, pp. 33–34.

23. Ibid., p. 36, n. 1.

24. Becker, vol. 2, p. 120. Other organs of government structured along ward

lines include some *balìe*, executive commissions of temporary duration. After the Black Death, for example, a *balìa* to reconstitute the government with the people who survived had three citizens from each of the sixteen wards, and one from each of the twenty-one guilds. Brucker, *Florentine Politics,* p. 121 and n. 66.

25. Rubinstein, p. 56 and n. 2.

26. D. V. and F. W. Kent, p. 19.

27. The list of nominees that went from gonfaloniers of the wards to the Scrutiny Council were usually in a certain order: those who were currently serving in high office, those who had previously been drawn, those whose ancestors had served, and then the others—and those at the top of the list were voted on first. D. Kent, p. 589 and n. 69, pp. 618–20; and D. V. and F. W. Kent, pp. 17–19.

28. Gene Brucker, *The Civic World of Early Renaissance Florence* (Princeton, N.J.: Princeton University Press, 1977), pp. 22, 312; Francis William Kent, *Household and Lineage in Renaissance Florence* (1977), pp. 171–75. The wards also held formal meetings, but not many citizens came, and they did not do the nominating. D. V. and F. W. Kent, pp. 75–76.

29. Villari, pp. 120, 191–92, 267–68, 289–93.

30. Najemy, "Guild Republicanism," p. 68.

31. Local patriotism could become so strong that the legal theorist Bartolus of Sassoferrato could inquire whether one could consider oneself a citizen of the ward one was born into and yet not be a citizen of the whole commune? He replied that one could not, for the commune itself was philosophically prior to its parts; one was not naturally a citizen of one's ward, for citizenship was not by nature, it was a civic creation, enacted by the city as a whole acting as its own prince. Practically, Bartolus's hypothetical case could arise when a man wanted to avoid paying communal taxes by moving to another ward. More generally, Bartolus was addressing the question of naturalizing citizens, of dealing with the new men who wanted to be admitted to citizenship. He argues that the basis of their citizenship was no different from that of the native-born citizens, who also received it by grant from the state. Julius Kirschner, "*Civitas Sibi Faciat Civem:* Bartolus of Sassoferrato's Doctrine on the Making of a Citizen," *Speculum* 48:4 (October 1973), pp. 695–96, 699, 705.

32. Becker, vol. 1, pp. 211, 224–25; vol. 2, p. 89.

33. Villari, p. 129. Villari thinks this requirement existed because moving would affect the proportional representation of citizens in each district. I doubt this; it sounds too numerically modern, Villari writing in the late nineteenth century. See also below, n. 43.

34. Becker, vol. 1, pp. 191–92; vol. 2, pp. 156–57.

35. Brucker, *Renaissance Florence,* pp. 143–46; Becker, vol. 1, p. 156.

36. Becker, vol. 1, pp. 85–86; vol. 2, pp. 193–94; Brucker, *Florentine Politics,* pp. 92–93.

37. Brucker, *Renaissance Florence*, p. 144; Brucker, *Florentine Politics*, pp. 82, 42–46; Herlihy, p. 26.
38. Becker, vol. 1, pp. 140–41.
39. Najemy, *Corporatism and Consensus*, pp. 176–77.
40. Although compare Najemy who, in his critique of civic humanism and defense of earlier guild corporatism, calls the civic humanist citizen passive, and says that the nominating and selection procedures became so complicated that most citizens could not understand them. Ibid., pp. 301, 303, 306–7, 312.
41. Hanna Fenichel Pitkin, *The Concept of Representation* (Berkeley: University of California Press, 1967), pp. 144, 237.
42. Najemy, *Corporatism and Consensus*, pp. 45–67, 136–37.
43. D. Kent, p. 615.
44. Pitkin, chs. 3–6, 10.
45. Brucker, *Florentine Politics*, pp. 170–72, 190–92, 208–10.
46. Pitkin, p. 207.
47. Heinz Eulau et al., "The Role of the Representative: Some Empirical Observations on the Theory of Edmund Burke," *American Political Science Review* 53:3 (1959), pp. 742–56; and Pitkin, chs. 7–9.
48. Brucker, *Renaissance Florence*, p. 235; Brucker, *The Civic World*, p. 310.
49. Pitkin, pp. 84, 69, 67.
50. Najemy, "Guild Republicanism," pp. 62–63.
51. D. Kent, p. 592; Brucker, *The Civic World*, pp. 21–30; F. W. Kent, p. 172; D. V. and F. W. Kent, p. 1.
52. W. H. Auden, "Horae Canonicae," in *Selected Poems*, ed. Edward Mendelson, new ed. (New York: Vintage Books, 1979), p. 232, in a poem about the city as the locus of shared guilt as well. Max Weber also cuts through much of the sentimentality about neighborhood as he describes the way neighbors are naturally jealous of their privacy, mindful of their enmities, and helpful only in times of economic distress, "by and large oriented toward maintaining the greatest possible *distance* in spite (or because) of the physical proximity, and some social action is likely only in cases of common danger." Weber, *Economy and Society*, ed. Guenther Roth and Claus Wittich (Berkeley: University of California Press, 1978), vol. 1, pt. 2, ch. 3, sec. 2, pp. 360–63.
53. They did not, however, go all the way to the position that no property was required. See Ch. 1, nn. 71–75 above.
54. Skinner, pp. 44, 73.
55. Becker, vol. 1, pp. 3–4 and ch. 1; vol. 2, ch. 4.
56. Skinner, pp. 181–82, on Machiavelli writing that "tumults deserve the highest praise." Machiavelli, *The Discourses*, ed. Bernard Crick, trans. Leslie J. Walker, S. J. (Harmondsworth: Penguin Books, 1970), bk. I, ch. 4, p. 115.
57. Brucker, *The Civic World*, pp. 283–302.

58. Becker, vol. 2, p. 86.
59. Brucker, *The Civic World,* p. 303.

Chapter Eight

1. See introductory paragraphs to Ch. 3 above. See also Edward Banfield and James Q. Wilson, *City Politics* (New York: Vintage Books, 1963), chs. 3–4, 7–13; Samuel P. Hays, "Political Parties and the Community-Society Continuum," in *The American Party Systems,* ed. William Chambers and Walter Dean Burnham, 2d ed. (New York: Oxford University Press, 1975), pp. 152–81.

2. Ch. 6 above, "Four Parts of Ethical Life." The kind of knowledge required, however, departed from the Kantian ideal of justice, since the reformers often assumed the running of a city to be akin to the running of a business, in which case the relevant knowledge was economics and administrative science; hence their innovation of the city manager.

3. Fred Greenstein, "The Changing Pattern of Urban Party Politics," *Annals* 353 (1964), pp. 1–13; David Morgan and John Pelissero, "Urban Policy: Does Political Structure Matter?" *American Political Science Review* 74:4 (1980), pp. 999–1006; Albert K. Karnig and Susan Welch, *Black Representation and Urban Policy* (Chicago: University of Chicago Press, 1980); Robert J. Mundt and Peggy Heilig, "District Representation: Demands and Effects in the Urban South," *Journal of Politics* 44 (November 1982), pp. 1035–48; Heilig and Mundt, *Your Voice at City Hall* (Albany: SUNY Press, 1984); Kenneth J. Meier and Robert E. England, "Black Representation and Educational Policy: Are They Related?" *American Political Science Review* 78:2 (June 1984), pp. 392–403.

4. Peter L. Berger and Richard John Neuhaus, "To Empower People: The Role of Mediating Structures in Social Policy" (Washington, D.C.: American Enterprise Institute for Public Policy Research, 1977).

5. Ibid., pp. 42–43, 2, 4.

6. David E. Price, "Community, 'Mediating Structures,' and Public Policy," *Soundings* 62:4 (1979), pp. 386–90.

7. Berger and Neuhaus, p. 35.

8. George Lukács, *History and Class Consciousness,* trans. Rodney Livingstone (London: Merlin Press, 1971), p. 299.

9. David R. Mayhew, *Placing Parties in American Politics* (Princeton, N.J.: Princeton University Press, 1986), pp. 4–5, 9, 13.

10. *Random House Dictionary of the English Language* (New York: Random House, 1971), pp. 314, 1389–90.

11. Graham Maddox, "A Note on the Meaning of Constitution," *American Political Science Review* 76:4 (December 1982), pp. 806–8.

12. *The Shorter Oxford English Dictionary,* 3d rev. ed. (Oxford: Clarendon Press, 1967), p. 378.

13. George Kateb, *Hannah Arendt. Politics, Conscience, Evil* (Totowa, N.J.: Rowman & Allanheld, 1983), pp. 130, 136–38.
14. Ibid., pp. 137, 142.
15. Ibid., p. 130.
16. Philip E. Converse and Roy Pierce, *Political Representation in France* (Cambridge, Mass.: Harvard University Press, 1986), pp. 418, 422–26, 488.
17. Kateb, p. 138.
18. Ibid., p. 119.
19. Thomas Jefferson, "Letter to Kercheval" (Sept. 5, 1816), *Writings,* vol. 10, ed. Paul Leicester Ford (New York: G. P. Putnam's Sons, 1899), p. 45.
20. Jefferson, "Letter to Kercheval" (July 12, 1816), p. 39.
21. Ibid., p. 41.
22. Avraham Brichta, "1977 Elections and the Future of Electoral Reform in Israel," in *Israel at the Polls,* ed. Howard Penniman (Washington: American Enterprise Institute, 1979), pp. 45–47.
23. Michael Walzer, *The Revolution of the Saints* (New York: Atheneum, 1970); Samuel P. Huntington, *Political Order in Changing Societies* (New Haven, Conn.: Yale University Press, 1968), ch. 7.
24. Hanna Fenichel Pitkin, *The Concept of Representation* (Berkeley: University of California Press, 1967), pp. 55–58.
25. David R. Mayhew, "Congressional Representation: Theory and Practice in Drawing the Districts," in *Reapportionment in the 1970's,* ed. Nelson W. Polsby (Berkeley: University of California Press, 1971), pp. 260–61.
26. V. O. Key, Jr., *Public Opinion and American Democracy* (New York: Alfred A. Knopf, 1965), pp. 32–35, 75, 168.
27. Mayhew, pp. 262–66, 274–85.
28. Theodore J. Lowi, "Party, Policy, and Constitution in America," in *The American Party Systems,* ed. Chambers and Burnham, esp. pp. 239, 255, 263–64, 268–72, 276.
29. John Plamenatz, *Democracy and Illusion* (London: Longman, 1973), pp. 200–3, 183–86, 189.
30. Ibid., p. 182.
31. Ibid., pp. 164–65, 172, 181.
32. Ibid., pp. 53, 80–81, 87, 98, 110, 114, 177–78, 199, 193–98.
33. *New York Times,* Aug. 22, 1984, I, 1:3; Sept. 15, 1984, I, 23:2; Nov. 4, 1984, I, 50:1.
34. Mayhew, pp. 260–61.
35. In addition to their stress on responsiveness and the will to represent, Converse and Pierce mention descriptive representation but claim that it derives from an unintentional or "accidental" source, resulting in "the representative *malgré lui.*" But this is not the case; it is intentional. If the representative has lived in the district and, "following his conscience," in fact mirrors his constitu-

ency, his self-conscious choice to follow his conscience involves the intention to depict (pp. 502, 607–15, 664).

36. G. W. F. Hegel, *Philosophy of Right,* trans. T. M. Knox (New York: Oxford University Press, 1967), Third Part: Ethical Life. (i) The Family, (ii) Civil Society.

37. Karnig and Welch, p. 8.

38. Arend Lijphart, "The Relative Salience of the Socio-Economic and Religious Issue Dimensions: Coalition Formations in Ten Western Democracies, 1919–1979," *European Journal of Political Research* 10 (1982), pp. 202, 205–6, 209.

39. Converse and Pierce, pp. 165, 177, 179–80, 775.

40. Thomas Brom, "San Francisco Gays Politick for Clout," *In These Times,* Chicago, Ill., 7:4 (December 8–14, 1982), pp. 2, 22. These clubs existed in a city without constituency-based elections. The gays allied with other traditional ethnic groups attempting to change San Francisco to ward-based elections.

41. Richard G. Niemi, Lynda W. Powell, Patricia L. Bicknell, "The Effects of Congruity between Community and District on Salience of U.S. House Candidates," *Legislative Studies Quarterly* 11:2 (May 1986), p. 188.

42. And on the nationalization of political issues see Donald E. Stokes, "Parties and the Nationalization of Electoral Forces," in Chambers and Burnham, eds., pp. 182–202.

43. In territorial representation the within-district variation in opinion can be greater than the between-district variation, yet the range of variation is quite restricted. To the extent that issues coincide with geography and demographics, such as urban-rural and race cleavages, then interdistrict variation is greater and conflict must be resolved at the national legislative level. For those issues that occur within most districts due to their heterogeneity, such as class, sex, and foreign policy, political conflict will be greater within the district than in the legislature. Converse and Pierce, pp. 515–20.

44. Isaiah Berlin, "Two Concepts of Liberty," in *Four Essays on Liberty* (New York: Oxford University Press, 1968); Hannah Arendt, "On Violence," in *Crises of the Republic* (New York: Harcourt Brace Jovanovich, 1972), p. 143.

45. I would stay with the word faction except that it has some bad connotations, especially since Madison's *Federalist* 10. I think Samuel Huntington is right that factions are weak parties.

46. Gerald M. Pomper, "Ethnic and Group Voting in Nonpartisan Municipal Elections," *Public Opinion Quarterly* 30 (Spring 1966), pp. 79–97.

47. Bertrand de Jouvenel, *The Pure Theory of Politics* (New Haven, Conn.: Yale University Press, 1963), chs. 3, 4.

48. Richard R. Fenno, Jr., *Home Style: House Members in Their Districts* (Boston: Little, Brown, 1978), p. 236.

49. On the importance of "the left-right super-issue" as a way for representatives to organize a range of national policy issues, although it does not play the same role for the constituents, see Converse and Pierce, pp. 233–39, 256–57, 611, 720.

50. Transmission belt theory might solve for the fit between the representative's vote and the views of his electoral supporters, rather than the views of the total district or entire electorate, much less their needs.

51. Jeremy Bentham, *Bentham's Political Thought,* ed. Bhikhu Parekh, (New York: Harper & Row, 1973), p. 217.

52. Edmund Burke, *Reflections on the Revolution in France* (and *The Rights of Man* by Thomas Paine) (New York: Doubleday Anchor, 1973); "Thoughts on the Present State of the Nation" (1770) and "Thoughts on the Cause of the Present Discontents" (1770), in *The Philosophy of Edmund Burke,* ed. Louis I. Bredvold and Ralph G. Ross (Ann Arbor: University of Michigan Press, 1960), pp. 133–38; Heinz Eulau, "Changing Views of Representation" (1967), in *Contemporary Political Science: Towards Empirical Theory,* ed. Ithiel de Sola Pool (New York: McGraw-Hill, 1967), pp. 74–75.

53. And territorial constituencies are more open to new issues surfacing than are functional or corporatist systems where interests are defined at the outset. Converse and Pierce, p. 525.

54. John Neville Figgis, *Churches in the Modern State,* 2d ed. (London: Longmans, Green and Co., 1914), pp. 39–40.

55. Ibid., pp. 65–67, 68, 88, 70–71.

56. G. D. H. Cole, "Guild Socialism," Fabian Society Lecture, King's Hall, Covent Garden, November 7, 1919. Supplement no. 6 to *The New Commonwealth* (London, November 21, 1919), p. 3. See also Carole Patemen, *Participation and Democratic Theory* (Cambridge: Cambridge University Press, 1970), pp. 35–43.

57. Jean-Jacques Rousseau, *The Social Contract,* bk. 2, ch. 4; Bertrand de Jouvenel, *Sovereignty* (Chicago: Phoenix Books, 1963), p. 93.

58. Edmund Burke, "Speech to the Electors of Bristol" (Oct. 14, 1774), in *Burke's Politics,* ed. Ross J. S. Hoffman and Paul Levack (New York: Alfred A. Knopf, 1949), pp. 114–17; Converse and Pierce, p. 523.

59. Charles A. Beard and John D. Lewis, "Representative Government in Evolution," *American Political Science Review* 26:2 (April 1932), p. 239.

60. Hannah Arendt, *The Human Condition* (Garden City, N.Y.: Doubleday Anchor Books, 1959), ch. 5, esp. secs. 25–26, pp. 163 ff.

61. Hanna Fenichel Pitkin and Sara M. Shumer, "On Participation," *Democracy* 2:4 (Fall 1982), p. 47. Also Pitkin, *The Concept of Representation,* p. 218, drawing on Sheldon Wolin, *Politics and Vision* (Boston: Little, Brown & Co., 1960), pp. 63–66.

62. Pitkin, *The Concept of Representation,* pp. 216–18.

63. Pitkin and Shumer, p. 50.

Index

Accountability, 21, 54, 117, 118, 130, 131–34
"Acting for," 54, 117, 118, 121, 130, 141–43
Action, 12, 29, 55–56, 86, 106
Adams, John, 6
Affection, 17, 20, 78, 79, 106, 138, 142, 145, 166nn. 1, 6, 169n. 4
Agent: district member as, 3, 19, 103; representative as, 28, 30. *See also* Delegate representation
Anti-Federalists, 17
Appetite. *See* Passions
Appropriation, 20, 71, 141, 145; in Florence, 109; property relations and, 66–70; structures of, 73, 78, 79, 81, 123
Arendt, Hannah, 7, 10, 11, 15, 56, 60, 139
Aristocracy, natural, 6, 46, 87
Aristotle, 7, 58, 105, 120, 121, 134
Assent. *See* Consent
Association, 7, 15, 20, 71, 139, 141, 145; in Florence, 110, 112, 119; legitimacy relations and, 60–66; structures of, 73, 78, 79, 81, 132. *See also* Citizenship; Parties, political
At-large districts, 6, 14, 22, 36, 39, 41, 43, 124, 129, 174n. 22
Augustine, Saint, 99
Authorization, 4, 21, 54, 117, 130, 131–34
Autonomy, 2, 54, 60; defined, 7, 9, 18, 97; political, 62, 65
Avery v. Midland County, 39

Bachrach, Peter, 34
Baker v. Carr, 39, 41, 51, 74
Banzhaf, John F., 45
Baratz, Morton S., 34
Becker, Marvin B., 121
Benevolence, 29
Bentham, Jeremy, 28, 32, 33, 35, 75, 141
Berger, Peter L., 125–26
Berlin, Isaiah, 139
Blackman, Justice Harry A., mentioned, 43
Blackstone, Sir William, 5
Boundaries: exclusionary, 41; external, 4–5; internal, 1, 6, 10, 22, 73, 74; and membership, 55–56; privileged, 50. *See also* Constituency; Districts
Brennan, Justice William J., Jr.: mentioned, 41, 42, 43, 52; quoted, 42, 47, 49, 50, 55
Brown v. Thomson, 74–75
Burger, Justice Warren E., mentioned, 43
Burke, Edmund, 27, 46, 49, 76, 134

Character, 12–13, 22, 115, 129, 139
Charvet, John, 95
Church, 99–100, 108, 109, 111–12. *See also* Religion
Citizen, 1, 2, 7, 57, 58; distinct from person, 2, 7, 10, 12, 57, 96, 107; equality, 40, 53; interaction, 10, 14, 30, 35
Citizenship, 7, 58; in communitarian

Index

Citizenship (*continued*)
  theory, 57, 60, 105; defined, 10, 18, 71, 105; and goal of political representation, 50, 89, 115; in liberal theory, 57, 105; political individuality as, 89, 98, 137–41; preconditions to, 58, 70–71, 144. *See also* Individuality, political
City: characteristics of, 61, 63–66, 68; classes and alliances in, 66–67; compared to nation, 73, 106–7; fraternal association of, 61, 65, 69; preconditions to, 58; and relation to individuals, 69; territory and kinship in, 63, 64, 69
City-state, 1–2, 58, 59, 69, 106–7
Civic humanism, 16, 18, 108, 109, 115, 120
Civic republicanism. *See* Civic humanism
Clark, Justice Tom C., mentioned, 50, 51
Class, 66–67, 100, 134–36
Coercion, 8, 78
Cohn, Samuel Kline, Jr., 111
Cole, G. D. H., 8
Communitarian theory, 20, 51, 76–77, 107
Compassion, 79
Consent, 2, 4, 76, 128
Constituency, 3, 19, 26, 50, 128–29, 137–41, 143–45
Constituents. *See* Constituency
Constituting, 127–28, 131–32
Constitution, 1, 6, 86, 94, 127, 128
Constitutive representation, 21, 129, 130, 143
Contemplative reason, 11, 77
Control, 7
Converse, Philip E., 136
Corporate political body, 27, 82, 116, 128
Corporations, 3, 75, 99
Corporatism: feudal, 108, 125; political, 76, 110, 116
Covenant, 91, 92, 129

Dahl, Robert A., 30
Delegate representation, 3, 24–26, 28–32, 44, 46, 49, 115, 118. *See also* Agent; Representative
Deputy. *See* Agent
Desires. *See* Passions
Dialectical cycle of differentiation, 95, 96, 100, 116, 121, 125–26, 128, 137–38
Dialogue, 86
Districts, 12, 20, 30, 39, 49, 51; and Anglo-American practice, 5–6, 73–75, 124, 129; equality and, 39, 43, 133; in Florence, 21, 109, 111, 112–16, 119, 120–21; and internal ties, 13, 51–52, 54, 101–3, 142; and local as compared to national interest, 28, 141–42; nonsovereign, 6, 89, 102; political meaning of, 53–54, 75, 101–3, 112–16, 120–21, 138; political theories and, 30–32, 35–36, 74–76, 82, 143-45; single-member, 10, 22, 39, 44, 123, 130. *See also* At-large districts; Boundaries; Constituency
Division of labor, 2, 66, 77–78
Domination, 2, 9
Douglas, Justice William O., mentioned, 41, 42, 52, 55
Downs, Anthony, 29–30, 32, 33, 34

Education, political, 8, 37, 40, 108
England, Robert, 19
Enlightenment, 17, 97, 125
Equality, political, 7, 40, 45, 52–53, 59, 139–40
Eros, 8, 78, 145
Ethnicity, 42–43, 45–49, 100, 135, 136
Euben, J. Peter, 59
Eulau, Heinz, 19, 23, 26
Experience, political, 16, 51–52, 71, 107–22, 144. *See also* History, political

Factions, 6, 108, 116, 118, 139, 175 n. 45
Family, 90, 98, 108, 109, 113, 114, 125, 126, 134–35
Federal. *See* State

INDEX

Fellowship. *See* Affection; Association
Fenno, Richard R., 138
Florence, early Renaissance, 21, 107–22, 123. *See also* Districts
Fortson v. Dorsey, 42, 47, 50
Founding, political: the founder in, 21, 82–85, 87; the process of, 85–87, 127, 128, 144–45
Frankfurter, Justice Felix: mentioned, 41, 50, 52; quoted, 51, 56
Freedom: abstract, 97; concrete, 96, 97, 98; negative, 139; political, 2, 7, 40, 89, 91, 138–39; positive, 2, 79, 139; and shaping of character as self-determination, 95, 102. *See also* Liberty
Freud, Sigmund, 8
Friendship. *See* Affection

Gaffney v. Cummings, 55
Gerrymanders, 47, 54. *See also* Districts
Gierke, Otto von, 3
Gomillion v. Lightfoot, 40, 55
Gray v. Sanders, 41, 48, 50
Greece, classical, 1, 23. *See also* Aristotle; City-state; Homer; Participation; Plato
Guild, 108, 109, 110, 118–19, 123

Hare, Thomas, 14
Harlan, Justice John Marshall: mentioned, 41, 42, 55; quoted, 48, 50
Harrington, James, 16, 17
Hegel, Georg Wilhelm Friedrich, 22, 67, 95, 96, 97, 100, 125, 126, 134
History, political, 52, 75, 121, 144. *See also* Experience, political
Hobbes, Thomas, 3, 6, 24, 28, 83, 127
Homer, 58

Ignorance, 29
Individual, 9, 20, 28. *See also* Person
Individualism, 27, 108, 125; formal, 21, 89, 98, 105, 130, 131–34
Individuality, 64, 65, 80, 89, 95, 96, 97, 125; political, 21, 89, 98, 100–102, 116, 120–21, 125, 128–29, 130, 137–41; social, 21, 89, 98, 100. *See also* Citizenship
Influence, 17, 20, 45, 55
Interest, 18, 24, 26, 32, 33, 118; common, 81, 145; functional, 48, 99, 119, 156n. 40; local, 28, 35, 46, 141, 145; national, 15, 28, 35, 46, 141

Jefferson, Thomas, 5, 129
Jewell, Malcolm, 26–27, 31
Justice, 12, 13, 59, 78, 79, 97

Kant, Immanuel, 97, 124
Karps, Paul, 19
Kateb, George, 128
Kent, Dale, 116
Key, V. O., Jr., 131
King. *See* Sovereign

Labor, 11, 33, 66, 68, 80, 120
Laslett, Peter, 15
Law: divine, 15, 71, 82; natural, 15, 92; positive, 2, 15, 79, 92–93
Legislature. *See* Representation
Legitimacy, 3, 61, 62
Lenin, Vladímir Ilyích, 32, 33–34, 35, 82, 84–85, 87, 144
Liberal political theory, 10, 20, 28–33, 35–37, 52–53, 74–76
Liberty, 15, 17, 90, 133; Christian, 17; private, 96, 99; republican, 118, 139. *See also* Freedom
Lijphart, Arend, 135
Locke, John, 11, 15, 16, 75
Lottery, 109, 115
Lowi, Theodore J., 132
Lucas v. Colorado General Assembly, 44

Machiavelli, Niccolò, 10, 12, 16, 18, 83, 103, 108, 111, 114, 117, 121
McWilliams, Wilson Carey, 10, 17, 57
Madison, James, 5–6, 8, 52
Maitland, Frederic William, 3
Majority rule, 15, 132, 139–40
Marshall, Justice Thurgood: mentioned, 42, 43, 50, 51, 52, 55; quoted, 47

Index

Marx, Karl, 11, 20, 60–61, 66–70, 70–72, 77, 80–81, 82, 84, 86, 87, 100, 125, 134, 143, 144
Mastery. *See* Domination
Mayhew, David, 53, 131
Medici: Cosimo de', 109, 115; family, 113, 119
Medieval: city, 59, 69–70; origins of representation, 2, 74–75
Meier, Kenneth, 19
Membership, 4, 22, 50, 89, 103; defined, 70, 90; establishment of, 77–81, 116; identity and, 86; natural, 90, 91, 92, 96; spiritual or covenanted, 91, 92, 94; voluntary, 90, 91, 99
Militia, civil, 108, 114
Mill, James, 32, 35, 75
Mill, John Stuart, 8, 13, 52
Minority: groups, 42–43, 45–49, 51, 53, 132, 136–37; rights, 133, 139
Mobile v. Bolden, 39, 43, 44, 47, 51, 52, 56
Monarch. *See* Sovereign
Multimember districts and elections. *See* At-large districts
Myth, 71, 78

Nation. *See* State
Neighborhood, 54, 108, 109, 113–16, 119–20, 125, 129–41
Neuhaus, Richard John, 125–26
Niemi, Richard G., 138

"One person, one vote," 20, 39, 45, 133, 171n. 33

Paideia, 58, 121
Participation, 2, 7, 8, 12, 59–60, 78–79, 81, 116, 144
Particularity, 95, 96, 100, 116, 125, 128, 137
Parties, political, 29, 36, 47, 52, 126, 130, 132, 140, 157n. 63
Passions, 8, 28–29, 33, 78, 79, 108, 116, 169n. 4
Pateman, Carol, 8
Person, 2, 3; and citizen, 2, 9, 10, 53. *See also* Individual

Pierce, Roy, 136
Pitkin, Hanna Fenichel, 3, 7, 10, 21, 22, 24, 26–27, 116, 117, 131
Plato, 8, 58, 77–78, 80, 81, 82–83, 85, 86, 87, 144
Plurality rule, 132
Pocock, J. G. A., 10, 16, 108
Pole, J. R., 27
Political sphere, as compared to social, 9, 10, 53, 105, 119–21, 137–43
Politico, 25
Politics, transformative role of, 37, 80, 122
Powell, Justice Lewis F., Jr., mentioned, 43
Power, 23–24, 30, 34; as collective ability to act, 55, 56, 71–72, 139, 145; as control, 20, 24, 30
Price, David E., 126
Progressives, 39, 52, 123
Property, 33, 68, 70, 120, 144
Proportional representation (PR), 14, 31, 44, 48, 157n. 64, 171n. 33, 174n. 22
Public and private spheres, 9, 11, 16, 97, 106, 107, 121–22, 123, 144
Purpose, shared, 71, 138, 143

Reason, 8, 15, 78, 81, 92, 126, 143–44
Recognition, 12, 86, 129
Redenius, Charles, 50
Rehnquist, Justice William H.: mentioned, 43; quoted, 52, 55
Religion, 2, 16, 17, 91, 92, 99, 136. *See also* Church
Representation, 1, 3, 27, 31, 72, 129, 145; as constitutive, 3, 89, 129; historical practices of, 2, 3, 74–75, 93–94, 112–13; illegitimate, 79, 80, 81; legislative, 5, 23, 33, 73, 143; Pitkin's categories for, 21, 54, 96, 117; as symbolic, 4, 23, 118–20, 120–21, 134–37, 137–40. *See also* Representative
Representative: as agent or delegate, 3, 4, 30, 57, 94; as constitutive founder, 71, 85–87, 128; linkage of, 32, 33, 105, 131, 132; local ties of, 3, 14, 31, 144; national connection of, 3, 4, 93,

180

121, 142; roles of, 24–26, 37; as trustee, 25, 27, 33, 46, 49, 93, 121, 141–43. *See also* Representation
Responsibility, 27, 74, 133
Responsiveness, 19, 25, 26, 31, 40
Reynolds v. Sims, 39, 41, 48, 50
Rights, 15, 20, 40–56, 133, 139
Rogowski, Ronald, 45, 49
Rome, classical, 2, 24, 127
Rome v. U.S., 39, 43, 49, 52, 55
Rotation, 18, 21, 109
Rousseau, Jean-Jacques, 8, 77, 79–80, 81, 82, 83–84, 85, 86, 87, 118, 144
Rubinstein, Nicolai, 112

Schapiro, Leonard, 34
Self-consciousness, 12, 91, 95, 102
Self-determination, 95, 139
Self-rule, 8, 65, 97
Shapley, Lloyd, 45
Shubik, Martin, 45
Single-member districts and elections. *See* Districts
Skinner, Quentin, 106
Slaves, 79, 86, 107, 136
Social compact. *See* Social contract
Social contract, 3, 15, 79, 135
Sovereign, 4, 23, 79, 92–94. *See also* Sovereignty; State
Sovereignty, 5, 9, 18, 75, 91–94, 101; historical, 2, 3; opposition to, 5, 75. *See also* Sovereign; State
Speech, 11, 15–16, 18, 83–85, 86
"Standing for": descriptive, 117, 118–20, 130, 134–37; and representing by reflection, 54; symbolic, 117, 118, 120–21, 130, 137–41
State: federal and, 40, 74, 76; nation-, 73, 76, 106–7; as political whole, 21, 111, 141–43; and society, 79, 80, 98, 109, 126; sovereign and, 33, 92–94. *See also* Sovereign; Sovereignty
Stevens, Justice John Paul, mentioned, 43
Stevens, Wallace, vii
Stewart, Justice Potter: mentioned, 43, 48, 50, 51, 55; quoted, 44, 51, 56

Still, Jonathan, 45
Stokes, Donald E., 31
Stories, 144
Supreme Court, 20, 39–56, 124–25
Symbolism, 3, 19, 137–41

Teleology, political, 37, 89, 122, 133, 141, 143
Tocqueville, Alexis de, 14–15
Transmission belt theory, 20, 28–36, 44–49, 76, 131, 141
Trustee representation, 24–26, 32–36, 46, 48. *See also* Representative

United Jewish Organizations v. Carey, 42, 47, 48, 137
Universality, 95, 96, 100, 116, 121, 126, 128, 137–38
Utilitarianism, 13, 15, 28

Virtù, 16, 108
Virtual representation, 27, 46, 48, 118, 142
Virtue, 7, 15, 108
Vote-dilution, 40, 42, 46
Voting, weighted, 133, 140
Voting Rights Act, 42, 43, 49, 125, 136

Wards. *See* Districts
Warren, Justice Earl, quoted, 41, 50
Weber, Max, 20, 60–66, 70–72, 143, 144
Whitcomb v. Chavis, 39, 42, 45, 50, 52, 140
White, Justice Byron R.: mentioned, 43, 48, 50, 51, 140; quoted, 42, 45, 48–49, 52, 55, 156n. 40, 157n. 63
White v. Regester, 39, 42, 45, 47, 49, 52, 140
Whittaker, Justice Charles E., mentioned, 56
Whole, national or political. *See* State
Will: general, 79, 125, 126, 131, 157n. 69; personal, 3, 16, 79, 118
Wolin, Sheldon S., 10, 106
Work. *See* Labor